ABANDONED ON BATAAN

ONE MAN'S STORY OF SURVIVAL

To: Graybill Harman
One who helped bring
me home.

Oliver Allen
Mildred Allen

Oliver Allen has shared in dramatic, first-person fashion a powerful narrative of courage and faith amidst years of brutality, disease and hunger ... I recommend this adventurous book to anyone interested in history and the human spirit's will to rise above suffering.

—Dr. Michael D. Dent, Senior Pastor
Marvin United Methodist Church, Tyler, Texas

ABANDONED ON BATAAN

ONE MAN'S STORY OF SURVIVAL

OLIVER 'RED' ALLEN
AS TOLD TO MILDRED ALLEN

CRIMSONHORSE
ENTERTAINMENT & PUBLISHING CO.

Published by
SAN: 2 5 4 - 4 5 1 2
Crimson Horse Entertainment & Publishing Company Co.
103C Parkway
Boerne, Texas 78006
www.crimsonhorse.com
See also www.abandonedonbataan.com

Printed in the United States of America

Library of Congress Cataloging-in-Publication Data

Allen, Oliver Craig, 1921-
Abandoned on Bataan: One Man's Story of Survival / Oliver Craig
Allen, Mildred Faye Allen. -- 1st ed.
    p.cm.
ISBN 0-9713184-1-7 (pbk. : alk. paper)
1. Allen, Oliver Craig, 1921- 2. World War, 1939-1945--Personal
narratives, American. 3. World War, 1939-1945--Prisoners and prisons,
Japanese. 4. World War, 1939-1945--Concentration camps--Philippines.
5. Bataan, Battle of, Philippines, 1942. 6. World War, 1939-1945--Atrocities.
I. Allen, Mildred Faye, 1927- II. Title.
D811.A559 A3 2002
940.54' 7252--dc21

                                                    2002007845

TABLE OF CONTENTS

Preface   i
How World War II Began   vi

The Beginning

  1 • I Want to Fly   2
  2 • Texas Buddies   12
  3 • Across the Pacific   22
  4 • At War—Clark Field is Bombed   29
  5 • Down to Bataan   40
  6 • The Front Line   44
  7 • No Escape   54
  8 • Prisoner of War in the Philippines—The March   64
  9 • Camp O'Donnell   79
10 • Bridge Over the River Penaranda   87
11 • Camp Cabanatuan   96
12 • Prisoner of War in Manchuria
     Mukden and MKK   108
13 • Tragedy   115
14 • Food and Kitchen Stories   120
15 • Ways to Be Free   130
16 • The Sick and the Dead   138
17 • Daily Life   144

The Beginning of the End

18 • Bombing of Mukden   154
19 • Free at Last   160
20 • Tables Turned   169
21 • Seeing Manchuria as a Tourist   172
22 • Going Home   176
23 • Back to the U.S.A.   188

Consequences

24 • Aftereffects   202
25 • I Return   210

Conclusion – Unit 731   219

Footnotes   ii

Appendix A – Service Record of Oliver Allen
Appendix B - Map of the Philippines and Manchuria
Appendix C – Outline of Events courtesy of the *Battling Bastards of Bataan*

PREFACE

In the play *1776* the dying soldier sings a mournful dirge that ends with these words, "Is anybody there? Does anybody care?" This has also been the cry of the men who, at the beginning of World War II, were abandoned to their fate by a nation which poured arms into the European campaign, leaving our men in the Philippines to fend for themselves. Their battle cry tells the story:

> *"We're the battling bastards of Bataan,*
> *No mama, no papa, no Uncle Sam,*
> *No aunts, no uncles, no nephews, no nieces,*
> *No pills, no planes, no artillery pieces.*
> *...And nobody gives a damn!"*

Manuel Quezon, then-President of the Philippines,[1] said, "America writhes in anguish at the fate of a distant cousin, Europe, while a daughter, the Philippines, is being raped in the back room."[2]

The Japanese did not observe the Geneva Convention regarding prisoners of war.[3] Often the prisoners were lectured, "As a guest of the Emperor, you will . . ." Or sometimes, "As a slave of the Emperor . . ." Perhaps 'slave' was the more appropriate word.

To be an unwilling "guest" of the Emperor of Japan was a terrible thing. The Japanese proudly claimed descent from the gods, and until 1945 their emperor was revered as a god. To die for the emperor, their god, was heroic. Kamikaze Japanese pilots often committed suicide rather than surrender. To surrender, they believed, was cowardly and beneath the dignity of their race. So American and British and other prisoners of war were less than human, something to be scorned and tortured. The Japanese people were told they were crusaders in a holy war. The people believed this, and the military acted upon it.

This book describes several specific means of 'hell' inflicted upon the prisoners of war.[4] The Death March alone extinguished the lives of thousands of men. The steamy jungles of the Philippines took more. The frigid hell of Manchuria, one could reason, should have snuffed out any feeble flames that remained. Those who survived all this, these men, came home needing help in adjusting, but often failed to find it. America was tired of war, and wanted to put it and all thoughts of it behind her, so many of the former prisoners of war failed to find the understanding and assistance they needed. It was like going through Hell, and then having to prove that's where you got scorched. Then Unit 731, with its germ warfare experiments on prisoners, rears its ugly head, and we find that those responsible for such experiments were given immunity in exchange for information. "But that was a long time ago," you say. Yes, sadly, it has been a long time. Do you wonder why they ask, "Does anybody care?"

"Can you forgive the Japanese for what they have done?" you may wonder. Yes, because we must. To forgive isn't easy; it takes prayer and introspection. And time. Forgetting is impossible. But then, perhaps we shouldn't forget. Perhaps the world should re-member, and in remembering prevent it from happening again. But we must forgive and ask God to help us love them as His children.

This is the story of a hero—not a military leader who planned great campaigns, not a spy who uncovered dastardly plots, not a soldier who went into battle with guns blazing, but a hero, nonethe-less—Private Oliver ("Red") Allen, a gentle, naive, inexperienced country youth who often let others take advantage of him, and who survived one of the worst tortures ever inflicted by one group of humans upon another. Many times he came near death, but by sheer willpower, and indeed, some miracles, he survived.

It was after Oliver retired that I suggested he should tell his experiences, for it is certainly part of the history of the world. He spent several months alone in the afternoons with our old tape recorder before him, talking to those in the future who will listen. When I retired I took it upon myself to transfer his words to paper, editing, putting events in chronological order, avoiding repetitions as much as possible, doing whatever was needed to stay true to his words. This was the easy part; the hard part was listening to the words on tape telling so calmly the terrible things he and others had to endure for nearly four years. I am inspired by his determination to live, and awed by the obvious miracles that abetted it. I must admit there were times when tears blurred the words I was putting on paper, and there were several occasions when I had to put it all away for awhile.

Oliver occasionally reads accounts of other prisoners that are different from his own. This is to be expected. When a person is sick, hungry, thirsty, exhausted and in constant peril, it is impossible for him to be fully aware of what is happening to others. Each man tells his story as it happened to him, not necessarily as it happened to others. Some of the men refuse to talk about it. They cannot tolerate being forced to speak of it. Some men, like Oliver Allen, can talk about it. But can they tell it so that you can feel their pain, hear the whacks of the sabers, the gunshots, the groans and cries of the wounded men? Can they make you actually smell the odor of sweat, filth, the stench of dysentery and vomit? Can they make you feel the anger and darkness of despair? No. But if they could do all these things, you could not tolerate it. You would scream, "Tell me no more!"

So, because they, too, can tolerate it no more, they approach it as they would a steep precipice, knowing that one more step forward would lead to destruction. So they take a step. Backward. Only then can they tell somewhat dispassionately of the things they would prefer to forget, but cannot.

Together we added a chapter, telling briefly some of the things that have happened to Oliver during the years since he came home. Then we wrote a last chapter upon his return home from his trip to the Philippine Islands in April 2002, the sixtieth year since the fall of Bataan. It was a well-deserved trip, dramatic and satisfying, a welcoming to a returning hero!

—∿— Mildred Allen

Special thanks to: Jeffrey C. Hunt, Curator of Collections, Admiral Nimitz State Historical Site/National Museum of the Pacific War, Fredericksburg, Texas, for his assistance with WWII documentation; Major Richard Gordon (USA (Ret.), Burnt Hills, N.Y.) for a short timeline and history from the website of the Battling Bastards of Bataan (http://home.pacbell.net/fbaldie/Battling_Bastards_of_Bataan); *Barbara Hendricks for her expertise in editing; and Lorraine Shirkus for her patience and inspired contributions in graphic design.*

HOW WORLD WAR II BEGAN

The war with Germany almost certainly had its roots in World War I in 1918. With the aggressive spirit still alive in the German population, the indignity of losing the war still rankled. Upon the surrender, the Treaty of Versailles turned Europe into a patchwork of new countries, shrinking many old ones. Not only did Germany lose territory, the Treaty put many of its people under foreign rule. Germany was allowed neither a navy nor an air force, only a skeleton of an army and a limited merchant fleet. The manufacture of heavy armaments was forbidden, as well as conscription.[1]

When Adolf Hitler became Chancellor of the Third Reich in 1933, Germany was in bad shape. Disarmed and nearly bankrupt, with great unemployment and political dissension, it was fertile ground for the 'vagabond from the gutters of Vienna.' Yet in less than eight years Hitler had transformed it into the mightiest state in Europe. He maneuvered the Reichstag into turning over its constitutional power to him, supposedly on a temporary basis. This was called the Enabling Act, and made it possible for Hitler to rule by show of legality. The legislature figuratively committed suicide and signaled the end of parliamentary democracy in the Third Reich.[2]

Hitler soon banned all opposition parties and enforced his rule by means of concentration camps and systemized terror. He regimented Germany and began nazifying its institutions one by one. He destroyed the power of labor unions, bound farmers to the land as serfs, forced businessmen into the ranks of wage-earners. He seized control of churches and schools and muzzled the press, making it a Nazi propaganda tool.

He literally erased all individual freedom and put in its place a regimentation unequaled even for Germany. Yet he received incredulous public adulation. Why? Mostly because six million wage earners had been out of a job and now had one with the assurance of keeping it. Also, in his crimes against humanity Hitler unleashed a power of inestimable size which had been pent up in the German people.[3]

To really try to understand Hitler's psyche, one should read *Mein Kampf,* in which he explains his hopes and visions and methods of realizing them. This detailed blueprint of his thoughts was deeply influenced by Machiavelli's *The Prince.*[4]

Hitler's tactics were to talk peace while secretly preparing for war, careful to avoid preventive measures by the Versailles powers. The army was to triple its 100,000 number to 300,000 by October 1, 1934. Propaganda Minister Joseph Goebbels was ordered to never let the words 'General Staff' appear in the press, since Versailles forbade its existence.[5]

Versailles prohibited submarines, but Germany was constructing them secretly in Finland, the Netherlands and Spain. Herman Goering, Minister of Aviation, put manufacturers to work designing airplanes and training military pilots under the camouflage of 'League for Air Sports.' By the end of 1934 rearmament had become so large it could no longer be concealed. By then the 'peacetime' army had grown to half a million men.[6] That was the end of military restrictions of the Treaty of Versailles—unless France and Great Britain took action. As Hitler had anticipated, they protested but did not act.

That was the beginning. Hitler went through Europe, seizing

country after country. Benito Mussolini, imitating Hitler, began his own conquests. The League of Nations was proving itself unable to halt the determined aggressors.

Hitler gave orders to march into the Rhineland. Some of his generals were afraid of defeat as France was much better prepared militarily. But France did not fight. Hitler appeared before the German people. One journalist quoted Hitler,

" 'Men of the German Reichstag!' Hitler said in a deep resonant voice, 'In this historic hour, when, in the Reich's western provinces, German troops are, at this very moment, marching into their future peacetime garrisons, we all unite in two sacred vows ... 'He could go no further. It was news to this parliamentarian mob that German soldiers were already on the move into the Rhineland. All the militarism in their German blood surged to their heads. They sprang, yelling and crying, to their feet, their hands raised in slavish salute. The new messiah played his new role superbly. His head lowered, as if in humbleness, he waited patiently for silence. Then, his voice choking with emotion, he uttered two vows: 'First, swear to yield to no force whatever in restoration of the honor of our people. Secondly, we pledge that we have no territorial demands to make in Europe! Germany will never break the peace!' It was a long time before the cheering stopped."[7]

The French did not make the slightest move to stop the Germans. It could have, and would have almost certainly, been the end of Hitler. For France, it was the beginning of the end.

Austria was given an ultimatum to turn over the Austrian Government to the Nazis within one week. At a meeting with Austrian Chancellor Schuschnigg, Hitler lost control of himself. The Chancellor, feeling threatened, signed the agreement. Austria embarked on the path of appeasement. But it was Austria's death warrant, and there was no interference from Britain, France or America.

The sides were lining up. Hitler and Mussolini made their "Pact of Steel,"[8] but Mussolini reneged on the event of the allies taking action. Now add Czechoslovakia, and the occupation of Albania. The German-Soviet Pact was signed in time for Germany to invade Poland. Some of Hitler's generals disagreed, but with no unity between them, the Fuehrer prevailed. France and Britain conferred, and Prime Minister Chamberlain went to Germany to meet with Hitler. The result: "Peace in our time." The British were elated. This was the Munich Agreement. Completion of Sudetenland was achieved by October 19, 1938.[9]

The German people were now beginning to oppose war—aggressive war. That was no problem for Hitler; he would simply give the people a propagandist reason for starting the war, "whether it was plausible or not." So the war on Poland was begun by German soldiers simulating a Polish attack on Germany.[10]

Holland, Belgium, Denmark, Norway, France and eventually its ally, Russia, became targets.

Finally, on September 3, 1939, Great Britain and France declared war on Germany.

JAPAN—ANCIENT AND ISOLATED

Japan—ancient and isolated. What brought about her reckless quest for power? Could it have been, ironically, Commodore Matthew Perry who dropped the anchors of his four warships in Tokyo (then Yedo) Bay in 1853? He had been sent by President Fillmore to negotiate a treaty with Japan, who was then isolated from the rest of the world by choice. The treaty was for peace, amity and commerce. This visit exposed the Japanese people to Western ideas, production techniques and military systems. By 88 years later Japan was no longer a feudal state, but one with an army and navy as well-equipped as any power in Europe.[11]

In 1894 the militaristic leaders launched an attack on China, giving the Nippon possession of Formosa (Taiwan) and the Pescadores. The Sino-Japanese War lasted several years. In 1904-05 the Russo-Japanese War was fought over rival claims in Korea and Manchuria. Russia was defeated, and Japan annexed Korea in 1910.[12]

Japan entered World War I in 1914 on the side of the Allies, and was a member of the League of Nations. Anti-Western feelings within Japan began when the Japanese government agreed to keep her navy smaller than those of the United States and Great Britain, with a 5-5-3 ratio. Two years later the United States passed an immigration act barring Japanese (and other) nationalities.

In 1931 Japan overran Manchuria, turning it into a puppet state they called Manchukuo. When the League of Nations condemned Japan for doing this, Japan resigned its membership. Clashes with the Chinese became warfare in 1937, and Peiping (now Beijing), Shanghai, Nanking, Hankow, Canton and Tungshan (now Suzhou) were captured. By then, the master plan was for Japan to dominate Southeast Asia and western islands in the Pacific.

After the fall of France in 1940, Japanese troops moved into Northern Indochina (with the permission of Vichy France). All this was aimed at obtaining rich resources in these areas.

For two years the United States had used diplomatic efforts to stop Japan. President Roosevelt could have declared that a state of war existed and invoked the Neutrality Acts, preventing exports to Japan of scrap iron, aviation gas and other munitions, which she was building up to use against the U.S.[13] But an embargo, according to the Neutrality Act, must be applied impartially. This would have hurt China's cause far more than it would have hurt Japan.

All efforts to stop hostilities between Japan and China failed. Japan replied that the "China Incident" was her affair and hers alone.

American churches, hospitals, universities and schools throughout China had flag markings on their roofs, but the Japanese bombed them anyway. American missionaries and their families were killed. Even the sinking of the *USS Panay* and the shooting of the survivors failed to rouse America from its dream of peace.[14] Of course, the Japanese promptly apologized and expressed their readiness to make reparation. It was a face-saving ploy. Though the United States knew the sinking was deliberate, they accepted the "mistake" theory.[15]

The outrages against Americans in China continued. The Secretary of State announced that the United States "strongly opposed the sale of airplanes and aeronautical equipment" to any nation who practiced the bombing of civilians.[16]

Japan could cope with the loss of aeronautics but not with oil and iron ore. Why did the United States allow exports of oil and scrap iron to continue? Legally, any such restriction would violate the existing trade treaty. The American ambassador warned that if Japan were deprived of oil, it would move south and take what she wanted from Sumatra, and that no sanction should be applied unless the United States was prepared for war.

Several clashes occurred on the border between Manchuria and Siberia involving Japan and the Soviet Union, in which Japan was badly beaten by the Russians. They were willing to provoke war with the United States, because they were contemptuous of its power to fight a war across the Pacific, but they feared Russia.

In April 1939, Hitler wanted an unconditional pact between Germany, Italy and Japan. There was controversy, pro and con, in Japanese leadership.

On January 6, 1940, when Admiral James Richards became Commander in Chief of the American Fleet, he arrived in the Philippines to find that a large part of the fleet had been sent to Hawaii. On April 2, the remaining U.S. fleet departed the West Coast for Hawaii, where it conducted maneuvers. The admiral was advised that he would be based in Pearl Harbor until further notice.[17]

On September 7, 1940, Japan formally joined the Axis. They wished to frighten the United States with a threat of a two-ocean war. On February 1, 1941, Admiral Richardson was relieved of command. The fleet was renamed the Pacific Fleet and remained at Pearl Harbor.[18]

The United States was becoming uneasy over her moral position. She was protesting aggression in the Far East while selling the material means to Japan. She was even allowing Japan to bid against the United States Armed Forces in the home market for steel, oil and other strategic items. The National Defense Act was the answer. It allowed keeping strategic materials at home. On July 26, 1941, President Roosevelt issued an executive order to freeze Japanese assets in the United States. A freeze also occurred in Great Britain. This made the war with Japan inevitable. Japan had imported 88 per cent of all oil products consumed in Japan, and 80 per cent of that total came from the United States.[19] The American people were tired of placating Japan. They did not understand that this would cause war. On July 26, 1941, President Roosevelt signed an order nationalizing the Armed Forces of the Philippine Commonwealth, and appointed Douglas MacArthur as Commanding General.[20]

WHY COULD THE SNEAK ATTACK SUCCEED?

It had begun actively in September, 1941, when Japanese senior naval officers met at the Naval College in Tokyo to discuss strategy on an attack on Hawaii. On October 5, pilots were briefed on the plan. On November 25 (U.S. time), a task force sailed from the Kurile Islands. Under radio silence, they had instructions to sink any vessels they encountered.

On November 30, Japanese diplomats and consular agents were signaled by coded message to destroy all papers. The next day the order came to attack Pearl Harbor. On December 2, the ships refueled at sea and set their course toward Pearl Harbor. On December 3, they reached their rendezvous point, 1,460 miles northwest of Pearl Harbor. On December 7, shortly after 7 a.m., two American soldiers were watching their mobile radar set on the northern slope of Oahu. The signal began to blip wildly, showing what seemed to be a swarm of aircraft coming in from a distance of 137 miles. They informed an officer on the phone. He told them to ignore it, assuming they were B-17s expected from the mainland.

Earlier, in October 1941, Prince Fumimaro Konoye, who had struggled for moderation, resigned as premier and was succeeded by Hideki Tojo, who was called "Razor Brain."[21] On November 14, 1941, Tojo's envoy arrived in San Francisco and traveled to Washington. It is possible that neither he nor the ambassador, Admiral Kickhisaburo, knew they were decoys in the game. The Japanese demands ("minimum demands") included an end to American financial and economic embargoes; cessation of military and economic aid to China; a hands-off policy in China; recognition of Manchukuo and full access to the Netherlands East Indies for Japan. The envoys requested Secretary of State Cordell Hull take the demands to President Franklin Roosevelt without delay.[22]

The response of November 26, 1941, was a note of strongly worded counter demands by Washington: withdrawal of Japanese forces from China and Indochina; a joint guarantee of the territorial integrity of China; Japanese recognition of the Chinese Nationalistic Government of Chiang Kai-Shek; a non-aggression pact among Pacific powers; future adherence of Japan to rules of law and order in her relation with other countries; and the Japanese withdrawal from her association with the Axis powers. In effect, a complete about-face.

In the meantime, the United States Army and Navy cryptanalytic division, called "Magic," had broken the Japanese radio code. But one important communication was missed by the Americans: on November 5, 1941, the Combined Fleet Top Secret Operational Order Number 1 was issued: the order to invade Pearl Harbor.[23]

On December 6, 1941, Japanese forces from troop ships and

planes poured into Indochina. At the same time "Magic" intercepted Tokyo's answer to Secretary Hull's counter demands. It was, of course, a rejection. The same day President Roosevelt sent a personal appeal to Emperor Hirohito to give more thought to restoring amity and preventing further death and destruction in the world.

The next day, December 7, 1941, with no reply coming from Tokyo, the emissaries asked for a meeting with Cordell Hull. He agreed to meet them at 1:45 p.m. They arrived at 2:05, twenty minutes late. Hull kept them waiting another fifteen minutes in an outer office. At this moment Hull received the news of the attack on Pearl Harbor. The envoys entered the office and handed him the Japanese reply to the formula for peace in the Pacific. Hull read the message and turned to the Japanese and gave them an unforgettable blasting. "I must say that in all my conversations with you during the last nine months I have never uttered one word of untruth. This is borne out absolutely by the record. In all my fifty years of public service, I have never seen a document more crowded with infamous falsehoods and distortions—infamous distortions on a scale so huge that I never imagined that any government on this planet was capable of uttering them." Without a word, the Japanese left.[24]

Only a few hours after the attack on Pearl Harbor, the Japanese issued a declaration of war: "We, by the grace of Heaven, Emperor of Japan, seated on the throne of a line unbroken for ages eternal, enjoin upon you, our loyal and brave subjects: We hereby declare war on the United States of America and the British Empire."[25]

Upon hearing this, Hitler was ecstatic. They had proved that they deserved the title "honorary Aryans" which he had bestowed upon them.

GREAT BRITAIN

The British were not forgotten by the Japanese. In Singapore at 1:15 a.m. on December 8, 1941, (December 7, U.S. time) Japanese landed at Kota Bharu, 400 miles east of Malaya. Precisely three hours later, at 4:15, bombs began falling on the city. By breakfast the news came over the radio about Pearl Harbor. Incredibly, the news of the Singapore raid was taken lightly, as well as the Japanese being in Kota Bharu.[26] It was announced: "Our defenses are strong and our weapons efficient." But it wasn't so. Inter-service rivalry had plagued the British in Singapore since 1925, with almost no cooperation between the services. Getting naval help from England, they figured, would take six months. The Royal Air Force (RAF) had 158 operational aircraft, most of them obsolete.[27] On December 10, the voice from the radio brought the news that *HMS Prince of Wales* and *Repulse* had been sunk; these were ships Churchill had ordered sent to Singapore. The British were at a decided disadvantage in Malaya because of the impenetrable jungle; the Japanese simply mingled with the natives, and sometimes even bicycled through the rubber plantations and the roads that joined them. Also, the British had only 50 planes compared to 530 for the Japanese. Singapore remained indifferent and poorly defended and surrendered within two months.[28]

WHAT WERE THE PEOPLE OF AMERICA DOING?

What were Americans doing when World War II began in 1939? They were coping with a decade of the Great Depression. The United States was overwhelmingly isolationist. The war had not hit them personally, and they were determined to stay out of it. Fears for her own safety were growing as Nazi aggressions and Japan's drive in Asia spread. Sympathies were caught by the fate of these victimized people. As the world situation worsened, it caused pressure for action; yet non-involvement sentiment was too strong to allow what most people called meddling.

Depression years were lightened by the singing of *Happy Days Are Here Again* rather than *Brother, Can You Spare A Dime?*, by listening to hucksters on their soap boxes promising cures for the world. To escape the worry of joblessness or welfare work, people enjoyed song and dance diversion; jitterbug, big name bands, sports and movies reached their heights of glory.[29]

Prohibition was lifted in 1933 and people began drinking again. The radio was a means of entertainment and of information. People kept their ears tuned to the news from Europe, not wishing to miss a bit of it. Theater had many unforgettable hits: *Arsenic and Old Lace, Life With Father,* and others. Movies of that era were *Gone With the Wind* and *The Grapes of Wrath.* Charlie Chaplin took on the Fuehrer on the screen in *The Great Dictator.* In 1938, Orson Welles caused sincere jitters in his *The War of the Worlds.* Oh, how naive America was in those days![30]

When Great Britain entered the war in 1939, national support was shown in Bundles for Britain, when one and a half million Americans volunteered their services. Only after France fell to the Nazis in June, 1940, did a majority favor meaningful aid to the Allies. Most people were willing to risk extending aid to the Allies short of war. One historian wrote: "The relentless march of satanic evil from triumph to triumph offends the Puritan conscience of America. The strength of isolationism was being slowly eroded . . ."

Congress repealed the provision of the Neutrality Act of 1939 that prohibited the sale of every type of armament. The Administration's priority was to rearm the United States as quickly as possible. The President's request for huge defense budgets was met. This "arsenal of democracy" was geared to full production before Japan hit Hawaii. This abundance of jobs ended the Depression.

The U.S. Navy was patrolling the approaches of the Atlantic, under orders to destroy German or Italian men-of-war intruding into the patrolled area.

When Germany invaded Soviet Russia on June 22, 1941, Russia was hailed as an ally. Some of the Lend-Lease armament was sent to the Soviets. On August 9, 1941, Churchill and Roosevelt met to form the Atlantic Charter aimed at "the final destruction of Nazi tyranny."[31] This was pushing America to the brink of war. No debate followed, for the Japanese bombs fell on Pearl Harbor on December 7, 1941, and about four hours later on Clark Field in the Philippine Islands.

THE BEGINNING

I WANT TO FLY

The war had already begun in Europe and Asia and had been in progress several years before I became involved in it. From the early thirties, news of foreign events had been before us, in the newspapers and on the radio, talk that we would get involved, talk that we wouldn't. Debate as to whether we should or should not intervene ran more to the negative.

"That's their problem. Let them handle it."

"Why should we stick our necks out for them? What have they ever done for us?"

"Get our boys killed for something that's none of our business? No way!"

We knew of, but felt detached from, Japan's early invasion of Manchuria. We listened with a little more interest as Germany went into Austria, and as Hitler's political maneuver in the Munich Conference robbed Czechoslovakia of Sudetenland. We grew nervous as we questioned the wisdom of Chamberlain's deal with Germany.

Then as Japan took province after province in its invasion of China, there was talk of a Japanese threat that might affect us, also. We shook our heads and frowned, and perhaps prayed a little, but who could believe that a tiny island of strange, slant-eyed people with their curious ways and pagan religion could be a threat to us?

I was living in the small rural community of Springhill in northeast Texas, where I was born and had lived for eighteen years. This place of small hills and flowing springs, where the Caddo Indians had camped, is located about twenty miles northeast of Paris, Texas, a town of twenty thousand, county seat of Lamar County whose northern boundary, Red River, is the dividing line between Texas and Oklahoma. I'd attended my last two years of high school in Paris, going in on a bus which ran from the east, from Kanawha in Red River County. The winding road paralleled the winding Red River.

School in Paris was different from our small rural school. We were placed in full classrooms which did not need more students. Some of the bussed students dropped out of school, but I didn't. I knew that an education was my escape from the grueling sawmill work and from the nasty, greasy garage my father ran. My light frame needed something different, as did my mind.

Cousins Pauline Fodge and M. L. England also continued in school. We had started first grade together and were very competitive. Between M. L. and me there was a special rivalry, as we were always best friends and, at times, worst enemies. We were born two weeks apart. M. L., being the older and larger in size, often made it hard for me to keep up with him.

In the autumn of 1939, I entered Paris Junior College on the old campus, the "concrete campus." It was on Monday, September 4, that I was in the president's office with other future freshmen, when college president, Dr. J. R. McLemore, said, "I've got the radio on; let's see if we can get some news about what's happening over there." He turned his chair to face the radio, turned up the volume, and we grew silent, listening. Then a voice spoke, saying that Prime Minister Neville Chamberlain had announced that as of Sunday, September 3, 1939, a state of war existed between Great Britain and Germany. Later in the day we learned that France, too, had declared war on Germany.

In September, 1940 the Selective Service Act was passed, and we began to think seriously that this could indeed affect us. Some of the young men had joined the National Guard, and when it was mobilized in the fall of 1940, many of them left college to go into active duty. So in my second year at PJC, when we had moved to a new campus, I became interested in flying. The college was offering a federally-granted Civil Aeronautics course that taught navigation and meteorology. I took the course.

My first taste of flying had come in 1936, when Dad, Mama, my younger brother Clif and I went to Dallas, driving over in our 1933 Plymouth, to spend a day with friends King and Inus Harris. King's young brother Bruce was there, and after lunch we three boys caught a streetcar and rode out to Love Field, the major Dallas airport at that time, to watch the planes come and go. For Clif and me, traveling meant riding our bikes over dirt roads, with an occasional trip to Paris or the small town of Blossom with Granddad England to buy groceries and other goods for his Springhill country store. A trip to Dallas was a special treat.

A pilot of a small plane which could hold two passengers was taking up riders for one dollar each. We stood around and watched enviously as pilot and passengers rose into the air, then would circle and disappear. We gazed wistfully skyward, dreaming that we were up there with them.

The sun was getting low in the west, and we had started to leave, when I got enough nerve to approach the pilot who was quitting for the day, as it was late and the fares had stopped coming. After some consultation he agreed to take the three of us up for the money we had in our pockets, which amounted to two dollars. I'll never forget it; that was the day I fell in love with the sky and decided I was going to be a pilot.

So when global events began to look as though they might affect us after all, I didn't have to think twice about what I wanted to do. I knew I was going to fly. There were thirty of us in the aeronautics class, and only ten of us could actually get to fly, so there was stiff competition. An old airfield west of Paris was the place where the students got their training, using two Piper Cub aircraft. At the end of the semester I ranked number twelve, and wouldn't be one of the fortunate ten who would get to fly.

When the second semester started one of the previous ten had dropped out; number eleven had taken his place, and I became number one on the next list. Number one! Now all I had to do was pass my physical exam. There wasn't any doubt in my mind that I'd pass. After all, I was used to hard work; I'd been helping Dad and Uncle Willie Fodge at the sawmill for two summers. You couldn't get work much harder than that. But what I hadn't reckoned with was that this hard work had pulled my weight down. Added to that was the anxiety I'd felt over trying to be one of the top ten so I could make flight training. Then, too, pride would play a part in my downfall. At the old campus most of us who were bussed in from the country had brought our lunches with us. It was no embarrassment to brown bag it then. Now it was. Almost everyone was buying his lunch in the cafeteria, but I couldn't afford to, so I didn't eat.

The day I took the physical examination and was told that my weight was too low was the darkest day of my life—up until then. The doctor said, "Go home and eat a bunch of bananas, kid, and come back. It's only a matter of a few pounds." But when I asked for permission to take the physical exam over, the college refused to allow it. My whole dream was gone, vanished, a bubble that burst because of less than five pounds of weight.

I was so disappointed as a result of this, I decided to do something drastic. I went into the Green Dragon, a hangout for college students, and asked for a package of cigarettes. "What kind?" the clerk asked. I tried to think of the brand Dad used, but couldn't. "Old Golds," I said, seeing that brand on an advertisement tacked to the wall. I had to bum a match. Then I lit a cigarette, took a couple of puffs, determined to smoke myself to death. A couple more puffs almost accomplished the feat. I was so sick I didn't care whether I lived or died. I took the remainder of the pack home and gave it to Dad.

In the weeks that followed, I moped and grieved, then began to think of alternatives. I knew that when I finished junior college, I'd probably be drafted into the army as no money was available for me to continue in school. There were no grants or loans as there are now. Besides, Clif would be ready to start college, and what little the family could afford would be spent on him. After all, it was only fair that he have his turn.

It was in the early spring of 1941 that one of our local school board members approached me with the idea of teaching school the next year, after I'd finished junior college. It wasn't uncommon for a person to get one or two years of college and begin teaching. Well, I'd failed to become a pilot. If I could teach for a while it would give me a job, and also give me time to see whether there was going to be a war before I committed myself further. Perhaps I could go on to college later. When the school board met and decided I was too young, too inexperienced and too immature to handle a classroom, I was dealt another severe blow. This was during the depression years; people who had teaching jobs weren't giving them up easily, so there were no other vacancies. Besides, there were family men out of work; if any kind of job became available, these men were hired in preference to single men.

It was then I decided to join the Army Air Corps. There didn't seem to be any alternative. My folks didn't approve of this decision as I was under age and Dad refused to sign a permission slip allowing me to enlist. He'd been in World War I and had seen action in France, in the Argonne, and knew first-hand that war is hell. My mother signed after I nagged and complained and wore her down. And I did something I've regretted, the first of many regrets in this matter. Dad went on a fishing trip, and by the time he returned, I'd joined the Air Corps and was gone.

I had been told by the recruiting officer that if I joined the Army Air Corps I could apply for pilot training. I joined the Army believing I'd finally get a chance to fly, but this never happened. Before I was in the service four months I was sent overseas. When I got another chance to take pilot training, after I'd reached the Philippines, Dad was happy to sign for me, so I could return home to take the training. I left for the Army after I'd finished my courses at college, after the tests, but before the graduation ceremony. The night of my college graduation was my first night at boot camp in California.

After saying good-bye to Mama and Clif, I caught a ride with a neighbor for the twenty miles into Paris. He let me out in town, and I walked to the recruiting office where the officer gave me a ticket to Dallas. As I walked toward the train station I met Uncle Marvin England, Mama's brother. "Oh, son, I sure hate to see you go."

"It's too late now, Uncle Marvin, I've already got my ticket." I continued on the dozen or so blocks to the red-roofed train station where I boarded a motorized one-car train that stopped at every town along the way. It took on and let off passengers at every stop, along with freight, most of which was farm produce—vegetables, chickens and eggs. It took four hours to go the one hundred miles from Paris to Dallas. I boarded the train with five dollars in my pocket. Five dollars, to take me half way around the world, and five years to bring me home again. It was the twenty-fifth of May, 1941.

There was another Paris boy, by the name of Oswald Hobbs, who was on the train, going to March Field, California, for training as I was. Hobbs had no money for a meal, so neither of us ate lunch or supper on the 25th. The next morning we were sworn in. I remember the Major saying, "Now this is your last chance to back out. Think about it. Once you take the oath, you're in." Many times later I was to wish I'd given the matter more thought. We were given a train ticket and three dollars and seventy-five cents traveling money. Three dollars and seventy-five cents is not a lot of money. Hobbs spent his three-seventy five before he left Dallas. Fortunately, he had a sister in Dallas, and she and her husband took us to their home where they fed and entertained us until it was time for us to board the train.

THE JOURNEY BEGINS

The train left Dallas, going toward the open flatness of west Texas. We'd begun our journey into the unknown, into the shadowy haze of a nightmare from which we'd not soon awake. Meal time came on the train, and since Hobbs had no money, when we went to the dining car to eat it was my treat. The meals were seventy-five cents each! I was dumbfounded. Men were working for a dollar a day and feeding their families. After I'd spent a dollar and a half for one meal, I knew we couldn't do that again. We fasted until a stop somewhere in Arizona where a man boarded the train selling dates for twenty-five cents a box. We lived on dates the rest of the journey.

The trip across the Southwest was a new experience for me. I was sleeping in a Pullman car at night; in the daytime I was seeing sights I'd only read about. We traveled slowly, stopping often to take on and let off passengers. When we got to El Paso, Texas, about mid-afternoon of May 27, we were told we'd be there about an hour. So Hobbs and I decided we'd take a stroll, stretch our legs, look at the sights and maybe find something cheap to eat. We'd walked only a short distance along the depot area when we saw the blackest cloud I'd ever seen, with giant fingers of lightning flashing all around; it was a wicked cloud that filled the sky. We hurried back to the train for shelter, expecting wind, rain, hail and heaven knows what else.

Within a few minutes porters and passengers were closing windows and securing doors. The storm hit, and sand was pouring into every opening. The "cloud" was sand, being blown in from the desert. Despite our best efforts, grit began to cover the surfaces, and the smell of soil filled our nostrils. We were relieved when the train started up again, taking us slowly out of the first real sand storm I'd ever witnessed.

We arrived in Colton, California, on May 28th, about four in the afternoon. Colton is roughly half way between Riverside and San Bernardino. A driver in a command car picked us up at the station and took us to March Field. As we entered the gates, I saw row upon row of beautiful stone buildings with red tile roofs, built in the Spanish style.

"What are those?" I asked the driver.

"Barracks."

"Which ones do we get to stay in?" I was feeling a lot better than I'd felt so far on this trip. It couldn't be so bad here if they provided big beautiful barracks to live in.

"You don't get any of those yet. You have to go through boot camp first."

"Boot camp! Nobody said anything about boot camp!" They'd said a lot of things but I was sure they'd never mentioned boot camp! I'd come here to learn to fly, not march up and down on a parade ground and fire a noisy rifle!

"Do you mean you haven't been told you have to go through basic training?" He snorted and gave a nasty little laugh that indicated he didn't believe anyone could really be that stupid. I looked wistfully back at the receding barracks as he drove us to Tent City where we'd be housed for basic training. The area was large enough to take care of six platoons, with forty men to a platoon, and six men to a tent. The tents were set up in neat straight rows, each one precisely in line with all the others. There was a mess tent, a shower house and a latrine, with neat paths of white stone leading to each.

My tent was on one end of Tent City, and the latrine was on the other. My parents were staunch believers that the way to keep the human system functioning properly was to keep all parts well oiled and moving. My dad accomplished this with frequent doses of castor oil, pouring liberal spoonfuls down Clif and me at the slightest indication of a slow-down. So when I got to camp and realized that my gears were grinding a little bit slower than usual, I unwisely took

9

a dose of laxative, not thinking that having eaten so little since I left home, plus lack of exercise, might reasonably be the cause of the problem.

About eleven o'clock that night I started down between the tents, running as fast as my urgency would let me. But some smart aleck had stretched his tent ropes across the gravel path. I tripped, fell headlong on the white stones and cannot put into print what happened next. My only consolation was that I don't believe I could have reached my destination anyhow. After a long shower and a change of clothes, I returned to my cot, vowing never to take another laxative as long as I lived, a vow I've faithfully kept, except when I was in the hospital and had no control over the situation.

Hobbs and I were still together and both needed toilet articles. He didn't have any money and my funds were meager. I bought two toothbrushes, a tube of toothpaste and shaving soap and a razor for Hobbs. (I had no use for a shaving kit.) We put these articles into a cigar box and shared them. When we got our first paychecks, Hobbs bought a complete new set of toiletries. He gave me the new ones and he took the old ones. We stayed together until I shipped out, and then we were separated.

My nine weeks of basic training consisted mainly of drilling: about face, column right, column left. We learned to clean, assemble and disassemble our rifles and forty-fives, which included putting them together blindfolded. We did lots of "kitchen police" (KP), some charge of quarters and a lot of marching to base headquarters to take aptitude tests. Whatever we did, we knew we were there to "keep 'em flying!"

There was little to do in the way of recreation after a day of drilling. We all looked forward to going to the Post Exchange on Saturday night. Those who had money made a call home. It helped some of the new recruits, away from home for the first time. I didn't call home. I didn't have the money, and there were no telephones in Springhill Community, Lamar County, Texas.

For many soldiers—those who had no friends in California, no money to spend, no transportation to leave the base for a day and get away from it all—life was dull. It was less so for me, perhaps, as about the only recreation we had back home was volleyball when the weather was good, and an occasional "play party," which was just a get-together for the young people in the community, where we played such games as *Spin the Bottle* and did some occasional smooching. The big thing for me was the Saturday movies in Paris.

My mother had been a relief case worker. Since she couldn't drive, and Dad was usually busy at the grist mill or at his garage, I started driving her into town in our Model T when I was twelve years old. While she was making her report, Clif and I would go to a movie. We called them "picture shows." We always went to the Lamar Theater, where we could count on seeing a good western every Saturday with such stars as Tom Mix, Buck Jones, Ken Maynard, Bob Steele or Gene Autry, to name a few. There was usually a serial, a cliffhanger that showed a fifteen-minute episode. I remember distinctly *Flash Gordon* and *The Black Ace*.

So, on a Saturday night at March Field, I was quite content to go to a movie, though I was often disappointed because they showed so few westerns and too many Clark Gable films. The ticket to the theater cost a nickel. Then afterward, for the price of ten cents, I'd treat myself to ice cream and a coke. So for fifteen cents I could have a night out, then go back to my tent, satisfied.

We had to stand guard as part of our duties. I remember standing guard on one particular night; the moon was full and rising in the east. I thought, "Old Moon, if I could walk a straight line toward you right now, I could walk plumb home to Springhill." I guess the thing that helped me most to keep going was the thought of finishing basic training and moving into one of those beautiful stone barracks.

CHAPTER 2

TEXAS BUDDIES

After we completed our training at March Field, we were assigned to squadrons. Mine was the 32nd Air Base Group, 43rd Materiel. (The 44th was there, too.) We were leaving Tent City for good, we thought; stone barracks, here we come! We gathered up our personal belongings and started walking toward the stone barracks. Every step took us closer to them. But strangely, the sergeant in charge led us past them.

"Hey!" we yelled.

The sergeant just turned and shook his head and pointed to a sign that was posted by the side of the street. It informed us that the red-roofed Spanish-style barracks were filled to capacity with men who had arrived before us, who had done their basic training and had not yet been given other assignments.

No one can know how great my disappointment was as I moved my mattress and other belongings from one tent to another at the far end of the runway. This was like moving from the pot to the fire; every time a plane took off in the morning, the draft of its propellers would blow dirt all over us. There was no way we could keep things clean in Tent City. I'd see grit and sand cover my bunk and remember the dark cloud of El Paso.

I moved my cot into a tent to join four other cots that were already there. There was not a soul around when I moved in, but under each cot stood a pair of cowboy boots. Yep, I thought, we're all Texans in this tent. I was right; these four men who had finished their basic training just ahead of me were all Texans. There was Clifton Cochran from Powderly, which is all of ten miles from Spring-hill; one fellow by the name of Stanley Fisher was from Abilene; and John Milton was from the Temple area. The fourth was George Alexander from Lubbock. He called me "Booger Red."

There was another fellow that buddied with us by the name of Ray Thompson. He'd been in the army a while, was a corporal and had quarters in the stone barracks. He'd been in chemical warfare division and had gone off to school. It was his understanding he was to be made chemical warfare sergeant when he returned. Instead he was assigned to the supply room. When he complained to the First Sergeant, the sergeant said, "I'll get you out of it."

The sergeant was true to his word. There was a notice on the bulletin board the next day that *Private* Ray Thompson was to report for reassignment. We six were to stay together, loosely, through most of our ordeal.

At this time there wasn't a great deal of duty to perform around camp. I'd been there about a week and wishing for something interesting to happen, when the call came for us to "fall out." We were told to get our full dress uniforms and meet in front of the barracks. I thought we were really going somewhere; at least something was going to happen at last. I ran to my tent, all the way past eight hangars, to the end of the hangar line, jerked on my new dress khakis and brand new shoes and ran all the way back. The truck was pulling out and had to stop and wait for me. I jumped aboard, excited; I didn't want to miss anything. We might really be going somewhere.

We went somewhere, right enough—about fifteen or twenty miles up into the San Bernardino Mountains. The truck finally stopped in front of an abandoned Civilian Conservation Corps (CCC) Camp Building. The CCC was a program begun by the government

13

during the depression to provide jobs for unemployed young men so they could be of help to their families. This was later ended after the United States was at war. We were given a blanket apiece for the night, for the air was nippy when the sun went down. Early the next morning the sergeant rolled us out and took our blankets, and we boarded the truck again and went down a few miles. There we joined a long line of civilians, rangers and soldiers waiting for a breakfast of bacon and eggs, toast, jelly and coffee. When we'd finished eating we were given a sack lunch and a canteen of water. By the time we left the truck and started hiking, we knew quite well where we were going. A forest fire had been raging in the San Bernardino hills for several days and had caused extensive damage. We hiked to the fire line, and the ranger ordered us to begin cutting a fire lane between the burned and unburned areas. We chopped and raked all day, and it was hot, hot, hot. Our new dress khakis had black markings all over them, and our shoes were scuffed and skinned. We got black soot all over us, on our hands and faces, in our hair. Our water in the canteens barely lasted till we got to the top of the mountain. We worked up there all morning, finished our little lunches without water and, by the end of the day, were in terrible shape.

Our sergeant told the ranger in charge that he was taking his men out and down the mountain. The ranger countered, "You don't have the authority. These men are under me."

"We'll see."

"I'll see that you are court-martialed for this."

"Try it. My men are leaving these hills."

We were ready to collapse from lack of water, but began our trek out. One of the men had fallen and injured his back earlier in the day. Four others had made a make-shift stretcher and were trying to get him down the mountain. They had gone three or four hours ahead of us, and we overtook them when we were nearly out of the hills. There was a clear, pure-looking stream coming down out of the mountain in the place where the truck was waiting. Everyone of us went into that stream, trying to wash the black ash from our faces and hands. Oh, that water was good. It may not have been fit to drink, but we didn't ask. We couldn't resist it.

The sergeant was never reprimanded, as far as I know. That was the end of our fire fighting. And I never volunteered for any more alerts. My shoes were ruined, would never polish out. I sent my shirt and pants to the laundry; they came back with black streaks on them. I solved that by trading them in for new ones. I also got a pair of used coveralls that had belonged to a sergeant. They were faded, and where the sergeant stripes had been, the material held the color. From a distance or at a glance, one might think the stripes were still there. I wore these faded coveralls till they were ragged, and the men were always saying, "Hey, Sarge." Me, a buck private, being treated like a sergeant! I liked it.

THE FIRING RANGE

After we returned from fighting the fire I was assigned to six weeks of guard duty. It was while I was on this duty that we got further instructions in weaponry on the firing range located on a dry lake in the Mojave Desert area, about fifty miles north of March Field.

While in this guard camp we were drilled by an old sergeant. I say "old" because he had been in World War I, had all kinds of decorations and citations and had a permanent rank of Tech Sergeant. The brass, so I heard, had done everything they could think of to break him. They'd tried advancing him to Master Sergeant and to Sergeant Major and even giving him a commission, so they would be in a position to take away his rank. He wouldn't take the advances; he kept what he had been awarded. He was entrenched and wouldn't budge. Because of this he had the upper hand; he could get away with almost anything.

He had a habit, during Saturday morning inspection, of turning everybody's bunk upside down and tossing every bit of their clothes out of their lockers onto the barracks floor. So a scared country kid was easy prey to this bully. He thought he had my number. Well, he did! When we'd drill, he was always yelling, "Red!" in a loud voice, loud enough for everyone to hear.

He seemed to get quite a kick out of embarrassing new recruits, and I was his favorite enjoyment. "Listen up, you blockheads," he'd bellow. "Shave. You gotta shave every day. The army don't want no beards. I wanta see those faces smooth. Smooth, you hear me, *smooooth.* All except Red here. He's gotta shave once a week whether he needs it or not." Then he'd throw back his head and laugh and slap his leg with glee while I burned with embarrassment. It was humiliating to be twenty years old and not have a hint of a beard.

This sergeant was in charge of our weapons practice. Again, he was giving me a hard time. We were drilling and stacking rifles. I was "on stack" and was supposed to pass the rifles to the men. Some kid jerked his rifle out before I could pass it and they all fell. My punishment was to double time around the truck shed, about half a mile, running full port.

Now that we were on rifle range at the dry lakes, we were firing, lying on our bellies. I was lying with my heels sticking up. Infuriated, he jumped on my heels with both his feet, and I could have screamed with pain as I felt the bones crunch, but I wouldn't give him the satisfaction. As this happened I pulled the bolt on my rifle. The strap was too tight, and I dragged a fingernail along the side of my face, scratching it. Blood began streaming down my cheek.

He then told us to lay down our rifles and stand up and pick up our pistols. He said, "Just pick out a rock and start firing." I was hitting rocks every time, but not necessarily the ones I aimed at, as there were rocks all over the place. Then he gave the order to fire five times as fast as possible. I stood there with the perspiration dripping from me (the heat of the summer was fierce), sand and grit from the dry lake bed mixed with the blood and sweat. I fired five rapid shots.

The pistol kicked, and with each successive shot it jumped higher and higher. By the time the fifth shot was fired, my pistol was aimed upward almost straight over my head.

The sergeant was still right behind me, just inches away from me. He bellowed, "Red!" at the top of his voice, and I turned to face him, automatically lowering my pistol as I did, and stood with my gun pointing directly into his stomach. Dark-skinned by nature and from frequent exposure to the sun, he now turned deathly pale. I'm sure when he saw the blood flowing and the sweat and the dirt, and no telling what kind of look on my face, he figured I'd flipped my lid.

He was telling me to move my gun, stuttering and sputtering, not yelling as usual, and I didn't understand what he was saying. I suppose I was in a bit of a daze. When I realized what was happening, I stood there, gun still pointed, for a good fifteen seconds, pretending I didn't understand. I had my sweet revenge!

However, all this had taken its toll, and on the way back to camp that afternoon I was sick. Sick enough to ...well, to need the back of the truck to myself. The old Tech Sergeant moved the other men to the front of the truck and stood in the back with me and held my head.

From then on, when he came through with his usual Saturday morning rampage, beds were overturned, clothes were flung to the floor, but never mine. He never touched my things again, nor cracked jokes at my expense.

The highlight of my guard duty at March Field was when I was assigned to guard the B-19. I say *the* B-19, because I believe it was the only one ever made. This huge bomber was the forerunner of the B-29. I was in boot camp when it came into March Field, making its very first landing. It bounced hard, and to my understanding, broke through the runway. I wasn't close to it then, but I know the repair crew worked several days on the runway.

This plane didn't have dual wheels as bigger planes usually do, but single landing gear wheels—huge wheels—about eight feet high.

The B-19 was meant to be a long-range bomber. The engineers worked on it, and pilots tested it while it was at March Field. Sometimes it was my duty to go out to the highway that ran near the airfield and stop traffic while the huge plane took off. Once it got into the air, traffic could flow again. They were so unsure of the plane, they were afraid it would crash on takeoff. Then every day when it came back in, some sheet metal would have to be replaced, as the rivets had ripped out. This four-engine mammoth was magnificent to behold, but impractical to fly.

After coming off the firing range and having finished guard duty, I was assigned to the hangar line, working as a mechanic. The crew I joined was working on a PT-18 Trainer, a two seater bi-plane with an open cockpit that was used at this time to train pilots. They had taken the plane apart and were putting it back together when I joined the crew. I watched the others assemble the wings, and decided I could put the tail section on. After all, I'd been helping Dad take cars apart and put them back together since I was five years old.

Before I started, the sergeant in charge sent me to the supply room for a pair of tensiometers. To my great relief, Milton was working there, so I got him off to one side and said, "Say, Milton, do you have such a thing as a tensiometer?" I figured Milton was as green as I was, and he wouldn't laugh too much if I'd been made a fool of. For I'd figured tensiometers were in the same category as left-handed monkey wrenches and sky hooks. I was relieved when he said, "Sure. Do you need one?"

The sergeant showed me how to use the instrument and left me to do my job. I put the tail section together, no sweat. I'd assembled the entire tail section, put on all the guy wires, and put it to the tension they'd told me. When I finished, the crew chief said, "Private, did you put the right hand threads up and the left hand ones down?" (Or vice versa, I've forgotten which.) I replied I didn't know anything about that.

So then he instructed me on the proper way, and I checked and every one of them was wrong. Not part of them, but every one. I had to take the tail section completely off, every nut, every bolt, every guy wire, and then turn everything around. The rest of the crew had the wings on and were waiting for me when I finally got the tail section reassembled. I had thought when I started, "Oh, boy, I'm going to make some real pointers here; I'm going to put that tail together and show them what I can do." I showed them, all right.

I stayed on the hangar line about a week, until a runner came around picking out all the yard birds, all the unimportant expendables. We were sent out on detached service in the High Sierras near Bishop, California. We stayed there two weeks as a supply outfit for a pursuit squadron that was there on maneuvers. It was more like a vacation than anything I had ever had in the army.

THE END OF A DREAM

After we got back to March Field from this detached service, I returned to the hangar line and worked there about two more weeks. A sergeant came into the hangar and began calling out names, saying, "All of you men have been relieved of duties. Report to the Post Theater (PT)." There was quite a bunch of us who went to the PT and sat there wondering what was up. A Major came out and said, "You men are to pick up your gear. Leave your bunks, get all your personal items and report to Tent City." Well, I thought, another move and still no Spanish-style stone barracks.

We stayed in Tent City two or three weeks—I don't remember exactly—not knowing what was happening. One day we would be issued woolen olive drab uniforms, then the next day they'd take up the woolen uniforms and issue sand tans. Then a couple of days later the sand tan uniforms would go and it would be OD time again. This went on for the entire time we were there.

I had taken a round of regular inoculation shots the first week

I was in basic training. They'd lined us up and marched us to the hospital for shots. Nine weeks later when I was assigned to the squadron, they could find no records for the first shots, so I took them again. Now we moved back into Tent City, and what was the first thing they did to us? They lined us up and took us to the hospital for another round of shots. We protested, "We've had those @#$%!* shots twice already!" Sorry, no record. So we get them for the third time, because we're shipping out.

Shipping out! And I still hadn't gotten a chance to do what I started out to do. We'd taken aptitude tests during basic training. When the major who was administering the tests had interviewed me, he said, "I've been doing this for about four months, giving and checking these tests, and you've got the highest score of any I've checked so far. Private Allen, you should have your chance to go to just about any school you choose."

Boy, did I feel good! I had a chance to go to school. At last something was going my way. When I went by the First Sergeant's office to put in my application, to fill out the necessary forms, I went in and told him I wanted to see about going to school. "Get out of here!" he yelled. "Get OUT! I'll let you know when it's time to go to school!" I kept trying to tell him what I was there for, but he wouldn't let me explain.

When I had finished my six weeks' guard duty, he asked me what I wanted to do, and I told him I wanted to go to school. "Let's see where you stand." He thumbed through the papers and looked up puzzled. "Your name's not on the list."

"I know it's not."

"How do you expect to go to school if you don't put your name on the list?"

"I came in here six weeks ago and you ran me out."

He laughed and said he'd put my name on the list. A lot of good that did. As far as I know it's still not on the list. I never did get to go to school. A lot of the guys did. If I'd held my ground with the sergeant I'd have gone to school instead of being shipped out. I'd have had the opportunity to fly a plane, and to be the pilot I dreamed of being.

CHAPTER 3

ACROSS THE PACIFIC

After weeks of waiting, the second stage of my journey began the last week in September, 1941. There were fifty of us in the group who would travel from March Field to San Francisco to Angel Island. From there we would travel to Hawaii, to Guam, and finally into Manila Bay in the Philippines, where we left the ship for our destination, Clark Field.

The journey began in two old army GI (government issue) trucks called six-by-sixes, with the tarp over the back and seats that hung down from the sides. We loaded out early in the morning, left March Field, rode all day and made it into an air base at Bakersfield, California, where we spent the night in transient quarters and were fed in the mess hall. After breakfast the next morning, we showered, gathered our few belongings together, and boarded the trucks for the final leg of the trip to San Francisco.

We arrived in San Francisco about mid-afternoon of the second day. That was quite a sight for me! I'd never seen the ocean before, never seen huge ships lying in berth at a pier, never seen the white triangular sails row on row in the marinas, nor the sun reflecting a million times off the water till it nearly blinded me. And I'd never seen such steep hills. I couldn't understand why anybody would build houses in such a place. I thought we had hills at home, but these were *hills!*

The old truck pulled down into the lowest gear, and someone yelled, "Everybody out ... we gotta push!" We laughed a little nervously, for pushing did seem a distinct possibility. Then we got to the top of a hill and started down and I could feel myself plummet as my stomach rose into my throat, and I prayed silently that the brakes on the truck weren't as worn as the truck seemed to be. I was relieved when we finally got to the docks and unloaded. There was a little diesel-driven inter-island boat waiting for us—just one—bobbing up and down in the water like a cork. There were no seats; we either sat on the bottom of the boat or stood along the rail.

My first experience on the ocean wasn't quite the experience it should have been. We went aboard the boat, and even before we left the dock I was seasick. Not green-to-the-gills sick, but sick enough to be miserable. I was aware when we went past Alcatraz, but was too sick to give it more than a passing glance. We went beyond Alcatraz to Angel Island, an old army base built during World War I, with barracks and other facilities obviously old and well-used. It was now used as a place of embarkation. One thing was certain, there would be no AWOLs (absent without official leave) here, for the only way on or off the island was the little boat which had brought us here, and as soon as the last of us was on the rocky soil of Angel Island, it put back into the Bay, headed for port in San Francisco.

About all we did here was sleep and eat; there was nowhere to go, no entertainment. The place was crowded with men waiting to be shipped out. The mess hall couldn't accommodate everyone at once, so they served three breakfasts, three dinners and three suppers. The kitchen never closed. The staff was cooking and serving around the clock.

In supper line one night a soldier looking pained and puffing heavily, got in line behind me. He said, "This is wearing me out."

"What do you mean? " I asked.

"I just get up from one meal and they call for the next one. It's taking all my time."

"Do you mean you're getting in line every time they sound mess call? You don't have to do that; that's nine meals a day!"

"I know," he said, "but the food's so good I can't turn it down."

I hope he got enough to last a while, because in a few short weeks food of any kind would become a mighty scarce commodity.

Many of the men got KP duty at this place, and they thought it was going to kill them. They went on duty at six o'clock in the morning and didn't get off duty till the same time the next morning. It was a solid twenty-four hour job and, with serving one meal almost right after the other, there was never time to "take five."

Our group was unassigned and didn't know which group we'd eventually be with. Consequently there was no list with our names on it, so we didn't get KP while we were there.

Just before we left Angel Island, our March Field group joined the 7th Materiel Squadron of the 19th Bomb Group, which had come in from Albuquerque, New Mexico, just before we did. The pilots and crews of the bomber group had already flown with the B-17s to the Philippine Islands. We would join them there shortly.

After spending a few days—three or four, which seemed like an eternity—on Angel Island, the 19th Bomb Group was assembled. The bobbing little boat reappeared and, after several trips, managed to get us across the bay, into San Francisco harbor and aboard our ship, the *Holbrook*. It was one of the President Line. We had a sister ship with us, but I don't remember the name. The government had taken them over to transport troops and supplies. They no longer looked like luxury liners, but more like cargo ships.

From the moment we pulled out under the Golden Gate Bridge that October 4, 1941, I began to be seasick. When we went to mess the first evening I ate my supper. It was good; I enjoyed it. By the time I got to my bunk we hit choppy water. The ship began to rock, and *mal de mer* came upon me. I was determined to keep my food down, so I lay on my bunk, flat on my back, not daring to turn right or left. Our bunks were way down in the hold; no air could get down there, it seemed. I stayed on my bunk from then till the day before we got to Hawaii.

We were still together, the six of us—Milton, Fisher, Thompson, Cochran, Alexander and myself. They tried to see after me, bringing me fruit juices and oranges from the chow line. Sometimes one of them would go to the ship's store and buy lemon drops. Now and then I'd be able to eat a lemon drop. This went on for the first five days.

I finally decided I felt well enough to go up for a meal. I got off my bunk and walked up the stairs. Okay so far. Up to the deck. Oh, boy, the breeze was so cool, the first breath of fresh air I'd had in days. I felt extremely well. As I entered the galley door I got a whiff of the steamy kitchen odor. It was so strong it almost pushed me back. I just couldn't make it, so back to the bunk I went. I tried again the next day and finally managed to eat a meal. From then on I got my share of the food.

Excitement ran high as we steamed into port in Honolulu; we'd been issued four-hour passes. San Francisco, and now Honolulu! I was seeing the world. We didn't want to waste a minute of the four-hour passes, so we all tried to be first in the showers—salt water showers with soap made to use with salt water. I felt worse when I came out than when I went in, but I trust that I smelled better. I put on my dress best and stood on deck trying not to appear too anxious, gazing out on the bluest water I'd ever seen, seeing ships of all sizes, busy tugs moving about, and listening to the band on the dock, and watching the hula dancers gyrating their welcome. And not far from where we docked we could see the Aloha Tower. I was beginning to enjoy being in the Army Air Corps.

Then just before letting down the gangplank, they ordered us to fall in and demanded the passes back! No, they couldn't do that to us! To get this close and not let us go ashore; it was unfair, it was cruel! When the gangplank went down, only those who were assigned to Pearl Harbor left the ship. When we woke the next morning, we were already at sea; we'd pulled out sometime that night while we slept.

"Say," I asked around, "have you seen old Smithwell?"

"Smithwell?"

"I think that's his name. He borrowed my cap. I want it back." I'd bought a new garrison cap, an OD (olive drab), when I was at March Field during one of those periods when we were being issued OD uniforms. About two hours before we were to go ashore this fellow had asked to borrow my cap. He didn't have one, so I let him use it.

"You'll never see that cap again, Red, if he was assigned to Pearl."

"You mean he went ashore in my cap, knowing he couldn't give it back?"

"Grow up, kid. You're out in the world now. You gotta start watching out for yourself."

The next land we saw was Guam. I'd gotten over my seasickness by then and was enjoying myself because I'd still not been assigned any duties. While it seemed I'd never get off this ship, I was having a pretty easy time of it.

This came to an end the day we rested at Guam; I was assigned KP duty. I'd have been bitter about it if I'd been missing an onshore pass. But no one except the officers and nurses left the ship. We were anchored offshore, and they had to leave the ship by going down a swinging ladder and hopping into waiting ship-to-shore boats.

I watched them return to ship late that night. I figured everyone of them was drunk, because we had to lift them aboard from the launches; they couldn't climb the ladder. It would have been easier if we could have just dumped them all in the ocean, then thrown out a big net and pulled them all in like so many fish. I didn't begrudge them their leave just because I didn't get one. They could get time off and they took advantage of it. I'd have done the same thing if I'd been in their shoes.

When we left Honolulu we had been joined at a distance by a naval escort; it had closed in and there were now three ships steaming toward Manila Bay. We pulled out of port at Guam sometime that night after I'd gotten off KP duty and hit the bunk, exhausted. I enjoyed the journey from Guam to Manila. I watched the flying fishes; they would soar right through a wave. Sometimes the ship would go through a school of them, and there would be dozens flying at one time, a sight I'd never seen before. "On the road to Mandalay, where the flying fishes play," I sang to myself so no one else could hear.

We didn't see many other ships on the high seas, but we realized the situation must be getting serious, with two transports full of military men and equipment, with the naval escort we'd picked up when we left Hawaii. We heard rumors that Japanese were pretty thick in the area, lots of ships and subs.

The diesel turbine engines were going full force, puffing out clouds of smoke from the smokestacks as we moved toward the Philippine Islands. It was a sight to see as we entered Manila Bay. Patrol Torpedo (PT) boats came out to greet us, circling the three elephantine vessels, as Air Corps planes flew above us—quite an impressive welcoming committee.

We pulled into Manila Bay, Philippine Islands, on the 24th day of October, 1941. We went ashore, and there we got on trucks and were taken to Clark Field, Pampanga Province, P. I. We had quarters there, more or less permanent. For the first time since I'd joined the army, except for the few days at Angel Island, I didn't have to live in a tent. Even if it was bamboo, it was as good as anyone had—bamboo, with no windows, just square holes covered with bamboo shutters which we kept open most of the time. About the only time they were closed was during a heavy rain storm.

We got paid on the first day of November. The thirty-six dollars overseas pay nearly doubled the twenty-one dollars I'd been getting. Furthermore, they paid us in Philippine pesos, and I got seventy-two.

I didn't know what to do with all that money. I sent ten dollars home to Mama to pay on the tuition I owed at Paris Junior College.

During the first week we were at Clark Field, our dining hall hadn't been set up, and we had to go visit our neighbors. The other kitchens hadn't been allowed rations for us, so we were eating whatever was left. I kept thinking they were serving an awful lot of prune juice and wondered why they didn't serve prunes occasionally. They did; it was just that the prunes were all gone before we got there. I thought, too, that the Philippine Islands had the smallest bananas I'd ever seen. I found out later that the Islands grow lots of good bananas. It was just that someone always beat us to the big ones. Sometimes we'd get a little toast, sometimes some oatmeal. It was mighty, mighty skimpy eating. Pretty soon our dining hall was set up, and we began to eat at our own place. Rations got considerably better.

On the 24th day of November—we'd been in the Philippines one month—we were packing and crating and getting ready to move out. Our group, the 19th Bomb Group, was going to the island of Mindanao, the largest in the Philippine group, south of Luzon. We were going to a place called Del Monte Air Base; the 19th would operate out of there.

About fifty men in our squadron, the 7th Materiel, had already gone on advanced detail to Mindanao to make arrangements for the 19th Bomb Group. We were scheduled to leave Clark Field for Del Monte on December 10th. We had things at Clark Field packed and loaded, and two days before we were to leave, all hell broke loose. Our world as we knew it came to an end. Our Age of Innocence was over.

The Japanese Imperial Air Force hit Pearl Harbor a little before eight a.m., and four hours later they hit us. That was the end of our move to Mindanao; after the bombing was over, there was no place to go except into the hills.

CHAPTER 4

AT WAR—CLARK FIELD IS BOMBED

On the morning of December 8, around 7:30 or 8:00—I'd just finished breakfast—we were alerted. Shrill sirens sounded and we hurriedly assembled on the parade grounds where Major Davis told us he'd just received news that Pearl Harbor had been bombed by the Japanese. This announcement was followed by instant activity: orders were issued, people were running right and left, planes were taking off.

Earlier in the day, word went around that Colonel Eubank had sent out reconnaissance planes, and they had reported seeing sixty Japanese troop transports off the shore of the northern tip of Luzon. After the news of the bombing of Pearl Harbor, Col. Eubank asked for permission to destroy these ships, but was refused.

After learning they were not to take action against the Japanese, the B-17s returned to Clark Field where pilots and crews were ordered to stand by their planes. Everyone else was to go about his ordinary duties and await further orders.

I had been building desks in the day room. These desks were to be put in one end of the day room for the soldiers so they could write letters and read the library books that were there. I went on about my business in the day room for a while. Then as more news came in and the seriousness of the situation became more evident, men began to check out their weapons and head for the bunkers. They had observation stations, machine gun posts, artillery positions—places to which they were assigned. I had no post; the small group from March Field was, for all practical purposes, still unassigned. Although we were attached to the 7th Materiel Squadron of the 19th Bomb Group, we had no duties of importance. We didn't fly the planes nor man the machine guns or the anti-aircraft guns. We didn't even do KP. I'd never been issued a rifle, and I often wondered what the heck I was doing there.

About midmorning the sirens sounded again. I ran out of the day room and met the Commanding Officer (CO) coming out of his office next door. "Major Davis, what do I do, sir?"

"Where are you assigned, private?"

"I don't have any assignment, sir."

"Then find a hole and get in it." I did just that.

Very shortly the siren stopped; the air raid warning was over. This had been a test run. After that there were no thoughts of desks in any day rooms, or of any other non-vital jobs. All of us "reserves" went back to our barracks and stayed there till the first call for mess sounded at eleven o'clock. Since the dining area couldn't accommodate all the men at once, there'd be another feeding at twelve. The men in the hangar line would eat at the twelve o'clock sitting, so they were still on duty.

We had our meal at eleven, returned to the barracks and were sitting on the edges of our bunks, talking seriously, trying to appear casual and nonchalant while deep inside we were scared. Talking as though this wasn't anything we couldn't handle, we listened intently to a radio broadcast from Manila.

"See, I told you we should have gone!" I said suddenly.

"What are you talking about?"

"*Gone With the Wind.* I told you we should have gone to see it yesterday. I bet they don't even show it tonight."

"Oh, for Pete's sake, Allen, how can you think of a picture show at a time like this!"

On Sunday, December 7, Philippine time, the post theater was showing *Gone With the Wind* (a novel by Margaret Mitchell which premiered as a blockbuster film on Dec. 15, 1939), and we wanted to see it before we left for Mindanao. The show ran for about four hours, so we didn't have a great deal of choice as to the time when we could see it. For me Sunday afternoon was the best time, as I had no particular duties then and had time on my hands. So I'd suggested that we six—Alexander, Thompson, Fisher, Milton, Cochran and myself—all go to see *GWTW.*

One or two of them had objected. "This is Sunday. Sunday's no time to go to a picture show." Even though my Granddad Allen and a couple of great grandfathers had been ministers and my Granddad England had played the organ at church, my parents hadn't reared me to have such strict religious convictions. "If we don't go on Sunday, when are we going to have time to see it?" I countered.

So we'd batted this back and forth for a time, and had decided to go on Monday night, not knowing that by show time Monday the post theater and several reels of *Gone With the Wind* would no longer exist.

We sat quietly now, concentrating on the news broadcast. Then Alexander spoke: "No convertible, either." We all looked up, startled, then someone said softly, "No. No convertible." We thought that over for a while. We'd talked about it, the six of us, going in together and buying a sporty used convertible that we could use when we got weekend passes. No, if we were getting into a war, we wouldn't be getting a convertible.

There we sat, thinking partly of our ruined plans and partly about what the radio was telling us, while Don Bell—I believe that was his name—a news commentator from Manila, was telling about the attack on Pearl Harbor. Suddenly he interrupted himself to say that he'd just received a bulletin that Clark Field was being bombed.

We looked at each other in amazement. Clark Field being

bombed! How could that be? We were there, and it certainly wasn't ... The sirens sounded again, and we ran out of the barracks and looked up at the sky.

"Hey, look at the navy planes!" someone shouted.

"Navy planes, my eye! They're Japanese bombers!" Heavy bombers, flying in V formation; I could see three or four flights just then. They were flying high, but not so high that we couldn't see the bombs falling. In fact, I saw some of the bombs when they were just released from the bomb bays. For a moment I stood, fascinated by the thought that the bombs looked like raindrops falling, glistening in the sun as they dropped to earth. Then I yelled, "Oh, my gosh, they're bombs!"

There was a small trench just outside our barracks, so I headed for it, and a young soldier by the name of Applegate jumped in beside me. By the time we got to the bottom of the hole, bombs started hitting the ground. The ground was vibrating, shaking, no let up, just explosions and screams and more explosions.

Somebody yelled, "We've got a fire!" We stuck our heads up enough to see that the chemical warfare tent, not more than forty feet from us, was burning. The tent which sheltered warfare chemicals was placed smack dab in the center of the barracks area. Not in some remote area safely out of the way, but right in the center of the place where we slept and ate.

When I saw the tent in flames, I left the shelter of our small trench and ran for the long row of zigzag trenches we'd dug on the outside of the barracks area. I ran the seventy-five yards, dodging flying dirt and shrapnel, and following close on my heels was Applegate. There we rode out the attack. The first attack lasted about ten minutes, but seemed an eternity. When the raid let up for a moment, Applegate said, "I'll never do that again!"

"Do...what?"

"Change foxholes in the middle of a bombing raid."

"You'd rather get burned up?" I rebutted. I guess in war there are very few safe alternatives.

We really didn't have time to catch our breath or relax or to get out of the trenches, for right on the heels of the heavy bombers which had flown in from Formosa, came the light aircraft, dropping their light bombs and strafing. These smaller aircraft came from three Japanese carriers anchored off the east shore of Luzon. For forty-five minutes this merciless pounding went on—the noise, the screams of the shells, the rat-a-tat of the strafing guns, the cries of the men when they were hit. Smoke was so thick in places we couldn't breathe. I used my gas mask for protection.

When the pilots of these small planes found a man vulnerable, they'd make a target of him. One fellow told of a horrifying "game" he and a pilot played. The man was caught in the open and ran for the only thing that resembled a shelter, a mounded ditch. When the plane came shooting at him from one direction, the soldier would hug the bank on the safe side. Then the plane would bank, make a turn, and come back at him from the opposite side, and he'd jump over the mound and hug the other side of the ditch. This went on a few times till the pilot got tired of the chase and came down the length of the ridge, spraying it with machine gun fire. The soldier said all he could do was pray. He was saved when the pilot left to join his formation as it headed back to the aircraft carriers.

The anti-aircraft guns were manned during the attack, but were virtually ineffective. The heavy bombers flew too high, and the small planes flew in very low, under the range of the guns. Some of the men had rifles and valiantly fired at the swooping airplanes which swarmed all over the place, like hornets. We were helpless against them. We "reserves" were especially vulnerable. We had no rifles, no grenades, not so much as a stick to shake in their faces.

When the raid was over and we came out of our foxholes, we looked around us at total destruction of our military equipment. The planes were melted on the runway, the hangars were hanging in shreds, trucks containing aviation fuel which had been lined up for a mile were all burned, melted to the ground.

Now permission came to attack the Japanese. We'd had four hours. Four hours in which our bombers and fighters could have damaged the Japanese army so they could not have done to us what they did at Pearl Harbor. Four hours in which we might possibly have put a stop to the whole thing. Four hours that might have changed history.

Thirty-five men from the 7th Group died during the first attack. We were especially hurt by the loss of our commanding officer, Major Davis. We'd met him first at Angel Island when our small group from March Field had been attached to the 7th. He came into our barracks where we six, the six good friends, were housed.

"Where are you boys from?"

"We're from Texas, sir."

"All of you?"

"Well ...Thompson, he's from Arizona."

He asked each one of us which town we were from, how we were getting along, chatted a bit, then grinned. "Well, I can see no reason why we can't get along. I'm from Texas, too. Beaumont."

Then he went on through the barracks to greet the other new men under his command, leaving us feeling that we'd get along. So his death was a special blow.

Hospital ships took all our injured to Australia after the first bombing raid. After that there were no ships that came in, hospital or any kind, to carry anyone out. We were again on an island with no way to get off.

Since we'd lost our commander, Major Davis, the adjutant, Captain Jack Kelly, took over. He was as shaken as the rest of us, but he rallied the noncoms and told them to group together, eight or ten men each, and find a place outside of camp to spend the night. We spent most of the first night digging foxholes at our new camp.

During the night we could hear more bombing. We thought it was Nichols Field near Manila which was fifty miles away, but we weren't sure. We weren't sure how far you can hear bombs exploding.

The sun rose the next day, as the sun has risen since the beginning, but I am sure it had never before shone down on such devastation. We had no planes to fly, nowhere to go, nothing to eat. We waited a while to see if the Japanese were coming back with the dawn, but things were quiet, so we went back to the base. Personnel there were busy cleaning up, so I asked what I could do. I was handed a shovel and ordered to the hangar line to help dig out men who were buried in the trenches.

We'd been instructed to squat in the trenches, with our heads below the level of the ground, but to keep as upright as possible. But it's only natural, when you're being bombed and shot at, to hug the bottom. That's what these men had done, and had been covered with dirt as bombs exploded near them.

I started digging, and with every shovelful I was afraid I was going to hit somebody, that I would uncover a face that I recognized. The soil there is fine and shifty, and for every shovelful I dipped out, it seemed that two rolled in its place.

Before long the air raid siren sounded again. I dropped my shovel and headed for my foxhole in the hills. I ran that mile and a half in record time. Planes had been spotted, but they didn't hit us this time. As soon as the "all clear" sounded, I went back to the base, hoping to find something to do other than wield that shovel at the hangar line.

Most of the men had come back from the hills to see what needed to be done. The first thing to do, of course, was to clean up the mess, try to bring order out of chaos and take stock of remaining supplies. Captain Kelly, our new Commanding Officer, told me to take a jeep and move a pile of debris from the far end of the runway, to clear the way for incoming flights. Eager to be of some real service, I jumped into a jeep and wheeled it around and headed in the direction he indicated. In about two minutes I was back.

"Captain Kelly, sir."

"Yes?"

"That trash you told me to move..."

"Yes?"

"I can't do it, sir."

"Why not, private?"

"It's a B-17, all melted down."

The mess hall and some of the barracks were still standing. It seemed the most important job of the moment was getting the mess hall functioning again. The Filipinos who had been doing KP duty had headed for the hills when we did, and they had not returned. It's likely they went to their villages, gathered up their families and went deep into the jungle to hide from the Japanese. The only kitchen personnel left were the cooks. That's when I went to work in the kitchen.

Some of the others pitched in, and we began picking up and putting away, scrubbing and mopping, getting things in working order. We were, at that time, the only functioning kitchen on the base, and the incoming pilots came to our mess hall to eat.

Oh, how I longed to be in their shoes; they were doing what I had tried to do, what I thought I should be doing right now. Well, I decided, if I can't be great, I can be near greatness. So when 2nd Lt. William Dyess and the four other pursuit pilots in his squadron came in to eat, I tried to be the one to see to their needs. I wanted to do my part to "keep 'em flying."

Lt. Dyess had just got his wings and had made a name for himself by being able to fly his P-40 out during the first raid. He was elevated to the rank of Lt. Colonel before Bataan fell. I used to watch him leave the mess hall, with that confident walk, in that leather jacket adorned with wings, and think, "There, but for the lack of five pounds, goes Oliver Allen."

HUNGER BEGINS

After we got the dining hall in working order, we cleaned up the barracks, ridding them of debris, smoke and dirt that had settled everywhere. Most of us returned to the barracks to sleep after this. Even though things were pretty quiet for a week, we were nervous, expectant, often hearing things that weren't there. One night I'd gone to my bunk after a hard day in the kitchen and fell asleep immediately. I'd just begun to have a good snooze when a young private shook me, and kept shaking me until I was awake.

"Allen," he whispered urgently, hovering over me, "Allen, listen! Listen! There are Japs out there. They're in the theater!" (This was a new theater building that had just been built and hadn't been opened for us. It was not damaged in the first attack.) I jumped up, ready to run to the hills again, when someone across the room growled, "Oh, hell, go to sleep. There ain't no damn Japs out there." I settled back and lay still, listening, sweating, until fatigue overcame me and I slept soundly until morning.

The kitchen functioned for about a week. I was helping cut up beef one morning when the siren sounded the air raid alarm. We dropped everything and ran to the V trenches near the mess hall. Planes were dropping their bombs outside the field, "mopping up," bombing whatever they had missed in their first raid.

The all clear sounded, and we vacated the trenches and went back to the kitchen to continue our butchering. We were still at work on the beef when the siren sounded again. Again we ran for the trenches. This time it was a false alarm. This happened several times until at last it wasn't a "dry run." It was a wet one—raining bombs and shells all over the place, dropped by heavy bombers, twin engine jobs, that came in too low for our anti-aircraft guns to put up an effective defense. We watched in terrified dismay as our mess hall and some of the barracks were blown away. I managed a quick irreverent thought that we wouldn't be having steak for supper tonight.

We were crouching in the trenches, dodging flying debris and praying the bombs would miss us. We'd been told—by somebody—that if you're watching a bomb that's falling directly down on you, it will miss if it has enough distance to follow the curvature of the earth. This was not true in this case, as the planes were flying very low. I looked straight up to see the bomb bays open and the bombs aimed directly at me. A bomb hit in the trench so near me it blew dirt that covered my entire right side, up to my ear. I felt a burning in my arm and nearly fainted. I thought I'd lost an arm. It had been talked around the barracks that if you lose a limb, at first you don't have a great pain, just a small burning sensation. I was afraid to pull my arm from the dirt, afraid I'd pull out a stump. I pushed dirt aside and felt around until I located my hand. When I realized my hand had feeling in it, I figured I could bear whatever I saw. I uncovered it to find the pain came from a small burn caused when a piece of flying shrapnel hit the bend of my elbow.

After that we loaded all our kitchen ranges that were salvageable onto an old Pambusco open bus that had been confiscated and stripped until there was nothing left but the floor and the roof. We drove this down to a river, about four miles from the base, and parked by the river bank where there were trees that would help hide it from an overhead attack. From there we fed the men.

There was no operation on the air field now, after the last bombing. The P-40s were flying out of somewhere else. For all practical purposes Clark Field was inoperable. Everything of importance had been destroyed. Some of the men would go there occasionally to see if there was anything that could be salvaged, but they usually came back empty-handed.

One group went on a foraging trip to Manila, and came back with coffee. A truck loaded with two-pound cans of Folgers coffee had been bombed, and cans of coffee had gone in every direction. They gathered them up and brought them to our kitchen. We hauled it down to Bataan and we were still drinking coffee when the war ended.

We did not, at that time, have any contact with Japanese land forces. They were on the island, having landed soon after the initial attack on Clark Field, but they weren't pressing us at first. There were Rangers, part of a Filipino Scout Group, who were trying to hold them in the northern part of Luzon. The 192nd Tank Division and the 31st Infantry were there, trying to form a line of defense. I don't think they ever got a line formed, for the Japanese kept pushing on down and were very near Clark Field at the time we were pulling out and heading south.

I was heading south and leaving one of my most precious possessions, my high school diploma. That, along with whatever I had that was not absolutely necessary to survival, was buried in my foot locker, six feet deep in the soil of Clark Field. We buried these things in a place that is now covered by a concrete runway.

Not only was I leaving behind my diploma, but also my dream. I'd brought my diploma with me on the advice of the recruiting officer. He'd said I'd need it if I got the opportunity to go to school to train to be a pilot. And it had finally happened. Yes, it had! Not long after I came to Clark Field, there was a notice on the bulletin board saying that anyone with at least two years of college that was interested in cadet training could apply. Interested! I could hardly believe my eyes. I wasn't going to let anything or anybody stand in my way this time. I certainly didn't have to worry about being underweight. I now weighed one hundred fifty-four pounds.

I hurried as fast as I could to First Sergeant Dalton Russell for the application papers. Everything I needed from home: parental permission, recommendations, college transcript, birth certificate, all were on their way overseas when the war started. They were later returned to my parents by the Post Office. My dream ... so close. If the Japanese had waited two weeks, a month at most, I would have been back in the United States getting my long-awaited pilot training.

CHAPTER 5

DOWN TO BATAAN

It was on the 24th of December, 1941, when we got orders to move to Bataan. The Japanese were pushing us. As far as I know, no line had been formed. There was some action from the Philippine Cavalry and American tanks. An American Infantry Division had tried to hold the north part of the island, but was overwhelmed and fell back. The Philippine Cavalry and Artillery were using horse drawn weapons in fighting the Japanese. In some cases, the best they could do was to blow up bridges to slow the advance of the overpowering Japanese army.

During the two weeks we stayed on the outskirts of Clark Field our standard of living was reduced to a primitive existence. Instead of bunks, we slept in holes in the ground, or on the ground with all sorts of crawling and slithering creatures. I washed the pots and pans in the river, scrubbing them with sand in lieu of soap. It never occurred to us at that time that help would not be forthcoming. It was just a matter of time, we thought, until good old Uncle Sam would send reinforcements. I doubt that many of us knew then what the word "expendable" meant.

From Clark Field we moved south to Cabcaben on the Bataan Peninsula, within sight of Corregidor. We traveled by any means of transportation we could find. I rode in the cook truck, a converted

Filipino open bus that now carried a stove and cooking supplies. Unlike our buses, the Filipino buses were open, containing hard seats and an overhead cover. We had taken out all the seats and left just a platform for the stove. I rode wherever I could hang on.

There was a solid line of vehicles on the move—trucks, cars, buses, tanks, bicycles, even people on foot. Every means of transportation you could find on the island was seen in this caravan. There were, to the best of my knowledge, about twenty thousand Americans and perhaps forty to fifty thousand Filipinos, soldiers and civilians, all strung out on that one road that ran down the side of the island, partly paved, partly graveled, but all hard surface.

The Japanese were pounding us as we scurried before them, sending in their planes and hitting whatever was on the road, which was the only entrance to Bataan. I still don't understand why they didn't wipe us out then and there. They could have. They did a lot of damage; there were casualties, but they let us go on to Bataan. It is my opinion they let us go to get us out of the way. Without this motley mess of humanity to bother with, they could take the rest of the island, then work their way down to Bataan, which is exactly what they did.

We'd move along until an air raid, then everybody would stop, leave the vehicles and run away from the road, away from the bombs and strafing. It got so bad that every time a person thought he heard a plane he'd yell "air raid," and everyone ran. Often it was a false alarm. We were on the road a day and part of a night, and I guess I ran away from the bus at least twenty-five times. It finally got so ridiculous I thought I'd be better off walking than getting out of the bus and running at every sound. It seemed I was on the ground more than I was on the bus.

I changed my mind, however, when, after one scare, I thought the bus was going to leave me. We were being strafed and I jumped off the bus and pushed my way through a heavy thicket. When it was over and the all clear sounded, I couldn't get back through the thicket to reach the road. Everybody was loading into the vehicles and the engines were starting, and I was still in the thicket with no way out. I knew they were leaving me, and I started to panic. Then I found a small opening—I guess the one I made going in—and got back to the road in time to chase down the cook bus before it left me behind completely.

We arrived in Cabcaben on Christmas Day, 1941. I'll never forget my Christmas dinner. I shared a can of pork and beans, C-ration meat and beans, with another soldier. We ate our half can of beans and talked about turkey and dressing and all the trimmings. Later I was to see worse Christmases and look back with longing to a half can of pork and beans.

When we got to Cabcaben where our 7th Group were, we set up our kitchen, still in the bus, and operated from there. The first night after we'd gone into the hills of Bataan to set up the kitchen, I bunked down on top of the cook bus, feeling I was safer there than in the tall grass with all the "varmints." As I look back I can see that by this time we were already beginning to feel the hunger that would eventually devastate us.

During the night, sometime in the wee hours of the morning, I heard the cook making pancakes. At least I heard what I thought was the sound of the hand mixer hitting the sides of the huge corrugated can we used to mix batter. Oh boy! Pancakes for breakfast, a real treat. I lay there, half asleep, thinking about pancakes and butter and syrup like Mama made, when I came suddenly awake. That was definitely not the cook mixing batter. It was machine gun fire in the hills. The Japanese were closer than we thought. I quickly took my bed roll off the exposed top of the bus and got down into the comparative safety of the grass. Needless to say, we did not have pancakes for breakfast that morning.

Rifles and ammunition were brought in, and we were finally issued rifles. Some of the Air Corps men had never fired a rifle before, and they received some training.

Cabcaben is right on Manila Bay; we could walk a hundred yards and be on the beach. I could see the island of Corregidor from there; some late afternoons I'd go out alone and take off my shoes and let the waves ripple against my feet. I'd sit alone and look at the sky and watch the sun set and the stars that came out gradually one by one as the sky darkened. It was peaceful at home where Mama was, where Dad and Clif and Granddad and Granny England were. I wondered if they knew how horrible war really was.

CHAPTER 6

THE FRONT LINE

I was still working with the kitchen, scrubbing pots and pans. The officers' mess was arranged in a bamboo thicket where a table had been set up. Colonel Laughinghouse asked that I be assigned the duty of officers' mess, which meant that I brought the officers' food each meal, twice a day, set it up, served it and cleaned up afterward. This was fine with me; someone else would do pots and pans.

Then on New Year's Eve, 1941, we were ordered to take a change of underwear and a change of socks, as we were leaving and would be gone a day or two. We loaded onto trucks to be taken to the front line to fill a gap where the Japanese were filtering through. Our couple of days turned into months. We were on the front line and stayed there through January, February, March and part of April, 1942. We never returned to Cabcaben until the fighting was over for us.

After we got to the front line the kitchen force dropped behind. The situation was a confused one. Our men were trying to establish a line, but were having a hard time of it. I was trying to get food to the different groups by driving a Dodge panel truck up into the hills on a road that had just been bulldozed by the Corps of Engineers. It was rough going and dangerous, and I didn't know each time I was stopped whether the guard stopping me would be American or Japanese.

I remember one trip I made into the hills on this road. I knew where the men were supposed to be, but they weren't there. I drove around searching, but I couldn't find any of the men I was to feed. After what seemed an eternity, I was stopped by a sentry, fortunately an American, who agreed to take the food and see that it was distributed to the men. Then I returned to the kitchen, as the supply sergeant needed the truck to go to Mariveles for food supplies. Our rations were running very low, but a few things were still coming in from Corregidor.

The food I left with the sentry never reached the men on the line, as they were pulling back and had already begun to come in to the kitchen area by the time I got back there. We kept a stock of corned beef hash for an emergency. We felt, on seeing how tired and hungry these men were, this could be considered an emergency. I still remember how good that corned beef tasted.

Headquarters pulled all the men in, and we then went to the front line at Orion, another little town located on the beach. Here we turned into the edge of the hills off Manila Bay to establish a new line. The kitchen was set up about fourteen miles behind the troops. I didn't go with the kitchen; in fact, I never saw where the kitchen set up, as I stayed on the line to attend to the officer' mess. In addition to my other duties, I was "dog-robbing," getting five dollars per officer per month.

This involved setting up their tables, seeing that their food was served, seeing that their *quan* (whatever they had scavenged) was available to them, then cleaning up after them. Their food, as well as that for the men, was brought in by someone from the kitchen in the old panel truck that I'd driven into the hills.

This was a pretty good thing for me at first, as I could partake of the *quan* of each officer. One had managed to find several cases of shredded wheat; one had found some canned milk; and another brought in sugar. While they were rather close about sharing with each other, they were generous in sharing with me. I fared well as far as breakfast was concerned, for a while.

Quan didn't stop with food, however. One officer brought into camp a new Plymouth convertible. Instead of a six-shooter on each hip he had a machine gun mounted behind each door, and everywhere he went he had a couple of soldiers in the back seat, each manning a gun.

As I said, "dog-robbing" was in addition to my other duties. My regular duties included seeing to the water supply. I hauled it in a truck that was assigned to me, a 1940 Chevrolet which was stripped to the chassis. We had built a bed on it and a wooden seat for the driver. I hauled water in ten-gallon cans, similar to milk cans. I purified it, using a chlorine solution, then put it in a 'lister" bag. This was a big cloth or canvas bag which hung from a tree. The bag had spigots all around so the men could fill their canteens. I had to see that it was kept full.

Our water supply came from an artesian well, but a hand pump had been put on it to make the water flow easier. I became acquainted with some of the men from other units as I'd see them at the well each day. There was one old soldier I'd see, hauling water for his outfit as I was for mine. He was easy to remember as he'd let his beard grow down to this chest. His name was Williams; we called him "Pop." About two years after the war I was at a ball game in a small town near home, and someone approached me and said, "Hi there, Red!" I knew there was something familiar about this man, especially the voice, but the face meant nothing. He introduced himself, and there he was, old "Pop," without his beard, looking younger than I did!

The well where we got our water was near a building in the town of Orion where all the villagers would normally come to get water and visit with their neighbors. But now no one came to the well but soldiers. The Filipinos had left their village and fled into the hills for safety.

Even going to the well was a risky business because of the bombings. Some Filipino soldiers were at the well getting water when an observation plane dropped a bomb, just one—whoosh—and killed about a dozen of them. Instead of falling to the ground they had crouched behind trees, and the flying shrapnel hit them rather than moving through the air over them.

During a bombing raid a piece of shrapnel cut the rope of the lister bag, and it fell to the ground, spilling water everywhere. I picked it up, cleaned it and refilled it, to find that, luckily, there wasn't a hole in it anywhere. The same bombing raid sent shrapnel through the radiator of my Chevrolet truck in which I hauled water. Ray Thompson was a good mechanic, so he cut all the flues that had been hit and soldered them off. The truck would run again, but after running a few miles it got hot and boiled over because so much of the circulation had been shut off. It would last long enough for me to go to the well; it would cool while I filled the cans, then I could drive back to camp before it boiled over.

After this happened, we dug a "foxhole" for our truck. We used an old caterpillar tractor we'd come across somewhere and dug a ditch where we could bury the front so the radiator would be protected from shrapnel.

I was on my way to the well for water, on foot, while the truck radiator was being repaired by Thompson. Jap planes came over, dropping bombs, and the only hole I could find large enough to get into was a bomb crater. I reasoned that a bomb wouldn't be likely to hit exactly where another one had hit, so I jumped into the crater. The planes with their bombs didn't even come near me, but I was so exposed I felt like a sitting duck.

I had a rifle now, and carried it with me to the well and everywhere I went, but never had any occasion to fire it. In fact, there was very little firing at the enemy at this time, very little close contact. Except for sporadic bombing, we were left alone. A patrol might occasionally meet a Jap patrol and fire a round or two, but at this particular place and time, it was pretty quiet.

In addition to my working for the officers and seeing to the water supply for drinking, I also had to see to the supply of water needed for washing up the mess kits. I used three fifty-gallon drums. In one I kept a soapy solution for washing up mess kits; in the second was rinse water; and in the third was scalding water. The water was changed after every meal.

With a couple of helpers I cared for about two hundred seventy-five men at first. When we left Orion we had only about one hundred fifty, as many of the men were sick, most in the hospital suffering from malaria and dysentery. The two diseases were of epidemic proportions by this time.

There were two hospital units near Cabcaben in the timbered area. They consisted of bunks set up under the trees with mosquito netting for the patients' protection. The doctors and nurses had some medicines, such as quinine and sulfa drugs, but these were in short supply. These medical people worked hard to help the men with the few supplies available. One of the hospitals was bombed; it was a tragic situation. There were no big ships coming in now to take the wounded out. Some inter-island boats would come and go, but we had to be careful about hailing one. They usually turned out to be Japanese.

Most of our meager supplies came from Corregidor by boat, then by truck to the kitchen. Then the food was brought to the line from the kitchen in the hills. We were serving two meals a day, or trying to. Supplies were so short, we were always out searching for food. We'd have flapjacks when flour was available, which was rare now. Generally, for the morning meal we had *lugau*, which was our word for watery rice.

If we were lucky, we might have meat for the night meal. We butchered quite a few horses, sometimes a carabao, which is a Philippine water buffalo. With these we made a stew with whatever vegetables we could find. Sometimes we had abalone, but I didn't care much for that. I've read other accounts of these events, where the writer said they butchered monkeys and dogs and such. We never did that, even though we weren't getting much to eat before we were captured. About the only difference between what we got before we fell, and what we eventually got later, was that we had a little more of it before capture, and it was better seasoned.

At that time I had twelve officers to see to, in addition to the drinking water and washing up canteens, which entailed keeping fires going at all times. Frequently, as men came in after several days on the front line, having not had a change of clothes, we'd empty a vat and refill it so the men could do some laundry.

Amid a time of many dramas, one drama unfolded here that was both comic and tragic. A soldier by the name of Hillman came in wearing coveralls so stiff they could stand. Having been on patrol in a small abandoned village, he had found a box of powdered bleach. I'd filled the vat with water for him and had the water hot. Hillman said, "Red, do you know anything about this stuff?" indicating the bleach.

"No, not really. It's used to bleach clothes."

"How much do I use?"

I shrugged. I didn't know. Hillman stripped to his shorts, put his only pair of coveralls in the pot, emptied about half the box into the vat, mulled it over a few seconds, then dumped the rest of the bleach into the pot.

He returned to patrol, wearing only his shorts. When he came back later in the day, he got the punching stick and reached into the vat for his clothes. A surprised look came to his face.

"Hey, some son-of-a-bitch stole my clothes!"

"No, I reckon not. There hasn't been anyone here but me since you left."

We emptied the vat to find nothing but a few shiny buttons. The bleach had disintegrated his coveralls. We had a runner who went back and forth to the front line, and we instructed him to try to find Hillman some clothes, as he had nothing to wear except his undershorts. When the runner returned he had a pair of dirty castoff coveralls. So again Hillman put his coveralls in to boil, this time sans bleach.

While they were steaming in the pot, Japanese planes came over, dropping delayed-action heavy bombs right on top of us. I ran for my foxhole. The only shelter handy was Col. Laughinghouse's dugout. The dugout had been timbered over, then big boulders were placed on top and mounded over with sandbags and dirt. The men who were doing laundry ran for the dugout. They were Hillman, Thomason, Wilmouth, Knight and Sgt. "Skinny" Ervin. Sgt. Ervin was last, and there was no room for him, so he had to get into the trench next to the dugout.

A delayed-action bomb made a direct hit on the dugout. Sgt. Ervin, lying in the trench, didn't get a scratch, as everything blew up and away from him. The men in the shelter were in bad shape. Hillman was killed; the poor fellow never got to use his clean overalls. Thomason was dead, also. Knight had powder burns on his face and was blinded temporarily. Wilmouth got dirt in his eyes and had to go to the hospital unit, but was back on the line in a couple of days.

It puzzled us at first, their dropping a delayed-action bomb in our eating-laundry area. We finally reasoned that it must have been because of our smoke, perhaps a little occasional puff, rising from the trees. The Japanese may have thought we had artillery there. Thus the delayed bomb. If they'd just wanted to destroy personnel, they'd have dropped a bomb that would have detonated on contact and blown up on the surface.

The bombing raid was still going on, bombers coming in three and four to a flight, when I pulled these men from the dugout. Col. Laughinghouse scolded me for letting the men use the dugout, then in the next breath told me he'd recommend me for a citation for pulling them out. But this wasn't the time to stop and give medals, and so much happened later that no one could be expected to remember this one incident. The old colonel is dead now; so is Sergeant Ervin. In fact, nearly everyone in this incident of sixty years ago is gone.

That happened in February, 1942. Sometime before February

13, a submarine found its way in. It brought us mail and was to take out some of the wounded. There were three letters that came in for the entire squadron, and I got two of them. The submarine was to take some letters out. We were given a piece of paper and told to write a letter home, not more than twenty-five words, and to fold it and put the address on the back of the paper. They warned us, however, not to date the letters or give any other information that might be helpful if it fell into enemy hands. I didn't date mine, but did say that "Tomorrow is St. Valentine's Day." It got home to Texas, and the folks knew that on February 13, 1942, I was alive.

HUNGER AND SICKNESS

When we first got to the front, we weren't losing many men to illness because most of them were still in fair health. But in time, hunger and disease began to take its toll. We stayed on the front line nearly four months. During this time we stayed in damp, cramped foxholes and were constantly bitten by mosquitoes in the swamps. The men began to fall out from malaria. Then dysentery took over and spread as conditions were primitive and unsanitary. The men were losing strength from getting so little rest and from having almost no decent food to eat.

I was more fortunate than most. I "inherited" a mosquito net and cot and mattress from a young sergeant who had laughed at us when we ran for foxholes, preferring to stay above ground during a bombing raid. I used coffee grounds to dye the white net as it was better camouflaged that way. During the day I used it to cover the officers' mess and at night I spread it over my cot. During a foraging trip to an abandoned barrio I found some white sheets. Consequently I was sleeping on a mattress covered with white sheets, under a protective net while most of the men were being eaten alive by mosquitoes. I believe this kept me healthy enough to survive the march, while a lot of them died because they started the march already sick and weak.

In spite of white sheets and mosquito net, life got harder. As the men got sick their duties fell to the ones who were still able to go on. In addition to my officers, the water supply, the washing up of mess kits and providing hot water for laundry, I now had to stand guard over the water supply. I was working hard all day and staying awake every other night to guard our precious water. It seemed now that the men on the front were having it easier than I was.

One young soldier who helped me was named Edwin A. Petry. He was our runner. It was he who'd found the overalls for Hillman. Earlier, at Clark Field, one of Petry's friends had been wounded the day of the first attack and had left on the hospital ship. The friend had left behind a new Harley-Davidson motorcycle and had given it to Petry. As a result he was our runner, going back and forth between lines as messenger. One of his duties was to help me with the building of fires. We had our two little foxholes near our camp, but when the rainy season came we sought better shelter. In a Filipino village we found an abandoned hut, one probably used by a whole family, but just right for two GIs trying to get in out of the rain. We sawed the legs off just above the ground, and with one of us on each side, carried it to our camp. We made no effort to secure it to the ground, just set it on a level spot and made it our home. Very close to foxholes, of course.

There wasn't much time for leisure there under the mango and cashew trees. When we weren't on assigned duty, we were out searching for food. We never got any mangoes, as it was not the season for the ripe fruit, but we ate cashews. The nut grows from the end of a fruit that looks like a pear. The fruit is delicious, but watch out for the nut! Never attempt to eat it raw, as it contains a strong acid. After our duties were finished for the day, if the night were free from bombs and machine gun fire, we'd put the nuts in a pan and parch them over the fire. After they're parched, or roasted, they can be broken open and eaten. My, they were delicious! We also popped rice, much as we do popcorn, and poured sugar cane juice over them to make rice balls.

Our unit, the 7th Materiel Squadron, covered about half a mile of the front line. The 27th was on one side of us, and the 17th on the other. There was an infantry unit, the 31st, held in reserve. The Philippine troops were beyond us, but were leaving their line, coming through our lines in droves, so the American forces were constantly having to plug Filipino lines. The infantry would rush in, and after things were secure, they'd go "on reserve" again. But they were actually busy all the time, as the lines were constantly broken, shifting and needing reinforcements.

There was a landing field at Cabcaben that Col. Dyess and his squadron were using. They would circle the front line in their P-40s and do some light bombing and strafing, then return to the field and work on the planes to get them in shape to fly again.

No one came to help us. There was one battalion, we learned later, that had left Guam and was on its way to the Philippine Islands when Clark Field was bombed. But they rerouted themselves, heading for Australia. They landed on a southern island for refueling and were captured by the Japanese. This battalion was taken to Burma and worked on a Burma railroad during the war. It was known as the Lost Battalion.

CHAPTER 7

NO ESCAPE

Orders came for us to get our things together and be ready to pull out from the main line of defense on Bataan, the Orion Line. Col. Laughinghouse and Major Parker and some of the other officers had, by this time, been sent to Corregidor to strengthen defenses there.

On the morning of April 7, 1942, we were issued extra bandoliers of ammunition and started hiking to the reserve line after we'd put our bedrolls on the truck. This was the Chevrolet truck I'd used to haul water, that had been damaged by shrapnel and repaired to some extent by Ray Thompson. Many of us had personal belongings, bedrolls, things like that. By the time we'd tossed our things onto the truck it was pretty well loaded. These would be taken on ahead, while we followed on foot.

I was with Captain Kelly, the commanding officer, when we reached the reserve line, five miles back. He put me in a dugout, a machine gun pit, at a bend in the road—me and my rifle—and told me to watch the road in both directions. He told me not to dare leave my position before he relieved me, on threat of court-martial. I could never understand why he thought he had to say that. I figured a soldier knew he was to obey an order, and the consequences of disobedience.

So I stayed there, my first real experience as a soldier at war. I don't remember all the things I thought about, probably wishing for the millionth time I'd listened to Dad and stayed at home. Every movement and every sound sent a shiver of fear up my spine. I expected every moment to be confronted with a squad of Japanese soldiers, followed by certain death.

The Japanese did come, but not by the road. They came through the brush. I could hear their rifle fire all around, mixed with that of the Americans. The sound of the Japanese rifle was a little different from ours. Soon the outnumbered Americans began retreating. We were pulling back, a few at a time, one or two or three soldiers together. Mortar shells were falling all around. Japanese soldiers with knee mortars were closing in on us. They would set a gun on a knee, drop a shell into the barrel and fire. These mortar shells were much like hand-thrown grenades.

I wanted desperately to be away from there. Where was Captain Kelly? Had he been wounded? Was he dead? Had he retreated past me without my knowledge? Did anyone else know I was there? There I sat, the last American, being bombarded by mortars like a sitting duck, with my rifle, defending the rear of the retreating troops.

Where WAS Captain Kelly? I prayed. And got angry. And felt foolish for staying when others had left. I had huddled down, trying to make myself as small as possible, when a runner appeared and called in a frantic whisper, "The Captain says get yourself out of there!" He didn't say it twice. Captain Kelly was angry with me and told me in no uncertain terms how stupid I'd been to stay when the others had left. I was learning.

Our intentions were to drop back and relocate with some of our group that were fifteen or twenty miles farther south on the Bataan peninsula. We walked all afternoon, into the night, and got into a little town. I think it was Lamao. This was the headquarters of Major General Edward P. King, Jr. When we got there, tired and hungry, we were told to go one mile south of town and bunk down for the night, and the next morning we'd form a line.

Good. A night's sleep, perhaps some food, and we'd feel better. But it wasn't to be. As soon as we got there a runner came and told us that Gen. King said conditions had changed; we were to come back into town and form a line there. Any foot soldier knows very well the conversation that took place as we stumbled along in the dark, returning to town. Hungrier and dirtier and more tired and disgusted than ever, we got back to Lamao. The runner found us again and told us things had changed again; we'd put the line south of town, to return to the original plan. We turned around and started south. We didn't cuss the general any more. We'd already done a good job of that, and we were too tired to bother.

I was with Capt. Kelly during this walk. A truck pulled through our small parade and had to slow down to a crawl because nobody was breaking his neck making way for it. As it passed us, Capt. Kelly grabbed it and told me to do the same. I obeyed. The men on the truck yelled at us to get off; the truck was loaded. But Capt. Kelly said, "Don't touch me or I'll have you court-martialed." Consequently we got to ride part of the last mile.

From there we went up the side of a hill in the area where we were to regroup in the morning. Capt. Kelly said, "I'm going to sleep, and I'm issuing an order: don't wake me." He fell asleep immediately, and I did very soon thereafter. I was wakened in the middle of the night by bombs falling a few miles away. Capt. Kelly slept through it without so much as turning over. The sun came up the next morning, and he was still asleep. Finally I couldn't stand it any longer, and about nine o'clock I slid down the hill and joined my outfit, hoping to find some food.

"Where the hell is Kelly?" a major demanded.

"Still asleep, Sir."

"Asleep? Damn it, go wake him. We gotta get started. We got orders to form our line right here, and we need him. Tell him to get his butt down here right now."

I crawled back up the hill; he was still asleep. I cleared my throat and dropped a few items and banged some things against a rock until he woke up. He sat up and looked around. "What time is it?"

"It's getting on toward noon, Sir."

"Lord have mercy! Have I been asleep that long?"

"Yes, Sir. You slept through a bombing raid last night. I've been down the hill, and they're wanting you down there."

"All right. Fine. They'll just have to wait till I get there."

"Yes, Sir." I grinned to myself. Nobody could get the best of Capt. Kelly.

After the officers were together and had their orders, we got our group together and started hiking. We knew about where our position was to be, and as we went along we passed a small stream which was fed by a spring of clear water coming through the rocks down the side of the mountain. We walked along the stream, then up the hillside till it leveled off. That's where we were to take our positions, on this level portion of the hill. Capt. Kelly placed us at our stations, and we settled in.

Then we discovered our canteens were empty, and we didn't want to be caught this night, not knowing what faced us, without water. Since I'd been the "keeper of the water" back in camp, I figured I was the logical one to fetch water. I gathered as many canteens as I could carry strung on a long stick and headed back down to find the spring we'd passed coming up. The canteens rattled together, much as a cowbell on a cow ambling her way home for milking.

"Stop that blasted noise!" one sergeant yelled at me as I clattered past his group where they were dug in. "Want every damn Jap on the island to know we're here?"

I slowed down, trying to balance the stick over my shoulder so the canteens would sway more rhythmically and not bump against one another.

"Hey, quieten down, you idiot!" as I passed another platoon.

"Be quiet. You want the Japs to hear you?" All along the route as I back-tracked to the spring, I was cursed. I reached the main stream and was trying to locate the small spring of water coming out of the rocks, when I met a couple of soldiers coming across the stream, moving hurriedly in the direction I'd just come from.

"Where do you think you're going, Private?" the sergeant asked.

"For water. There's a spring around here somewhere, if I can find it."

"Go back the way you came. Pronto. The Japanese are right over the next hill, coming this way."

I looked at the water in the main stream and decided it looked clear and would be all right to drink. I filled the canteens, capped them off, strung them on my pole and headed back to my squad as fast as I could go. Being full, the canteens didn't rattle and sway so much, but they were a heck of a lot heavier.

I'd not gone far when I reached a squad, and the sergeant yelled at me that we were under attack and to find cover! No sooner had he said it than the bombs began to fall. I dived for the only thing I saw, a bush which wasn't big enough to hide me, so I wrapped myself around it. This time, in addition to personnel bombs, they dropped incendiaries. The place was ablaze. The grass was crackling and the bamboo popping. When the planes left I removed myself from my bush and made my way to the spot where I'd left my buddies when I'd gone to get water. I found them there, some of them dead, some wounded and crying for help. We rigged up a stretcher by fixing a blanket between two bamboo poles and took the wounded to where a first aid station had been set up. We worked there as long as there were wounded men that needed us. After seeing the wounded were cared for, I tried to find the people to give canteens to. I never gave them back, for everyone that I had canteens for had either been wounded or killed.

I'd given my rifle to Sgt. Hamilton to hold till I got back with the water. Now I could find neither the sergeant nor the weapon. Leaning against a tree was an Enfield rifle. We'd been using Springfields, but this fired the same kind of bullet. The clips were slightly different, but we could use Springfield clips in Enfield guns. Since no one was claiming the gun, and I couldn't find mine, I took it. It felt much better, being armed again.

NO HELP IS COMING

I joined Capt. Kelly and the others of our group in a trench behind the line. We were there about ten minutes when a runner came, saying the Japanese had flanked both sides of our line and were coming down the main highway. We were hopelessly outnumbered and there was no chance of reorganizing. He brought orders from Gen. King. We were to break into little groups and take to the hills. From here on we were on our own.

No help had come. No help was expected. We were no longer an army. We were ragged, hungry, tired, sick, wounded. We were individual men fighting against an Oriental horde.

There were ten of us in our group: Capt. Kelly, Lt. Glynn Rice, myself and seven others. (I'd lost my five good friends somewhere in the shuffle. I'd never see Milton or Fisher again.) But I learned we had a destination; we weren't going to wander around in the jungle, waiting to be done in. Capt. Kelly had a boat stashed in Cabcaben, with six fifty-gallon drums of diesel fuel. The boat would carry a dozen men off the island. We'd travel at night and hide in the daytime. We'd go south until we could find our way to Australia. Now that we had purpose, we had hope.

We began our walk. We stayed in close file and didn't talk much to each other. When it got dark and we couldn't see each other, we caught the belt of the person in front of us, walking for miles that way, going through gullies, up one side, then down and up another. We stepped in holes and fell and had to scramble around to get in line. We walked through brush and got tangled up in it. Mosquitoes swarmed us, getting in our eyes and noses, biting any place that was exposed. Occasionally we'd flash a quick light on Capt. Kelly's compass. When we finally decided we were walking in circles, we found a giant tree whose top roots were raised out of the ground like a bunch of protective arms, and we lay down and slept, keeping one man on guard.

I lay awake just long enough to remember the old tree back home, the one in the sandstone, rising above the spring where Clif and I and our cousins, M.L., Louise and Charles England, used to play across from Granddad England's store ... It had been so long ... I'd almost forgot ... Louise had died ... Aunt Myrtle had a new baby ... I went to sleep.

Sometime later the man on guard woke me and threatened to shoot me if I didn't stop yelling. I was having a nightmare. We changed guards then, and I sat for an hour, then called someone else. I settled back into the roots of the tree to sleep again.

Then we were all wakened, as the guard heard a noise. A patrol of soldiers was coming through, almost close enough for us to touch them. We kept quiet. We could have fired on them, but as we couldn't tell whether they were Filipinos or Japanese, we thought it best to leave well enough alone.

No sooner had we settled down from that disturbance than we could hear boom, boom, boom, one after another.

"Hey, what's that?" We all came up at once.

"The ammo! They're blowing it."

"You mean the Japanese ..."

"Use your head. The Japs don't have it. They wouldn't destroy it; they'd use it."

"Then what are we going to use?"

"Use to do what?"

We listened while explosion followed explosion. No sooner had the last echoes of the blasts died away when the ground began to shake. I don't know whether the exploding ammunition could cause such earth tremors or not. Whatever the cause, we had an earthquake that night following the destruction of the ammunition dumps.

As soon as it was light the next morning, we started on our way south, down toward Cabcaben and the boat. If we missed the boat, if it was gone or if we couldn't get to it, we'd go on to Mariveles and try from there. We walked a short while, still single file, with Capt. Kelly in the lead and me bringing up the rear, and came to an opening in the jungle where there was a banana grove. There were bamboo huts in the opening, and we headed there. We hadn't eaten in three days, and we might be able to find food.

We'd gone about half way down when we heard a sound like I'd never heard before. It sounded inhuman, like some animal noise that started low in the throat and rose to a pitch that would bust eardrums. I'd never imagined anything could be so terrible. We stopped in our tracks, horrified at what we'd heard. Two Filipino soldiers were hurrying up the trail meeting us, wide-eyed and pale-faced.

"What's going on?" we asked.

"Our companion, Joe." Their "companion," a lone Filipino soldier, had fallen into Japanese hands.

"How many?" we asked, indicating Japanese soldiers. They shook their heads in anguish, "Many, Joe, many," and hurried past us up the hill. We stood there stunned by the screaming, weighing the words of the soldiers. Capt. Kelly turned and looked at us. One Filipino soldier, seeing our hesitation, called back, "Many, Joe, many."

Many. No, we weren't able to encounter many Japanese soldiers, so we hurried back up the hill after the Filipino soldiers. We reached the top of the hill and went down the other side. The two Filipino soldiers had disappeared from view, but we could still hear the screams of the captive Filipino. Over and over and over. We tried to stop our ears to it, but couldn't shut it out. It was nearly noon before the screams stopped.

We'd walked a long way by then. That was when we met an old

friend. The Chevrolet truck, the one cut down to haul water, the one I'd driven to the well so many times, whose radiator had been punctured by shrapnel, the one we'd dug a special foxhole for, the one which had been loaded with our few possessions. There it was, by the side of the road, abandoned. Another casualty of war. Our belongings were still piled up on the bed, but we couldn't stop to get them. We couldn't take time to hunt through the many things piled on the bed. Nor could we take the chance; it would have exposed us to the enemy. We walked on past it, but I couldn't help turning and looking at it one more time.

The ten of us were struggling now, tired, hungry. We passed through an artillery emplacement where the guns had been blown up, destroyed. I'm not sure whether this was done by the Japanese, or by the Americans to keep them from getting into the hands of the enemy. These men had been living in tents, and they must have left in a hurry, as some of their possessions were still there, toilet articles and such, scattered about. Some of our group started gathering up soaps and shaving creams and other necessities of civilized living. But I gathered up all the razor blades I could find. I, who had never shaved, ignored all the other things I could have used, and had two pockets full of razor blades when we left the place.

Just outside the destroyed gunnery emplacement, we entered into a small banana grove. There we happened upon a case of meat and beans. It was C ration, but steak and potatoes couldn't have been better. There were ten of us and fifteen cans. So each of us took a can for future use, and the other five cans we opened and shared, two men to a can. It was the only food we'd had in three days, and would be the last for ... But I'm getting ahead of myself.

CAPTURE

After hiking the rest of the day, over hills, through brush, following Capt. Kelly's directions, we came to Cabcaben. We'd soon have our boat and be off this blasted island. We dropped off the hill that had been bulldozed to make a road, the one I'd traveled to deliver food to the troops. At four p.m. on the afternoon of April 9, 1942, we went down the steep embankment and came out on the main road. We were walking single file still, and I was at the end of the line.

As the first men got to the bottom of the hill, the ones in the lead, Capt. Kelly, Lt. Rice, the seven, one by one, raised their hands over their heads. I knew immediately what was happening. The Japs hadn't seen me and I hadn't seen them, and I had perhaps ten seconds to decide my fate. Turn and run? I still could. Run where? The Japanese were in front of us, to each side of us, and I knew they were behind us as the screams of the tortured Filipino still rang in my ears. If I'd been jungle wise, if I'd known where the boat was and if I'd had a lot of luck, I might have escaped. I believed then that my chances of staying alive were better if I stayed with my group. If I were captured alone, my fate would almost certainly be that of the Filipino soldier. So I, too, raised my hands and joined my companions in becoming a prisoner of war.

CHAPTER 8

PRISONER OF WAR IN THE PHILIPPINES—THE MARCH

The nightmare began. The Bataan Death March. Death and suffering. Suffering that brought death. Prolonged death. Sudden death. Suffering that made some wish for death.

The March began for me on the morning of April 10, 1942. On the afternoon before, ten of us had walked right into the hands of the Japanese. It was almost impossible not to walk into their hands; Japanese soldiers were everywhere on the island of Luzon.

We'd walked down the hill with our hands over our heads and saw an appalling sight—Americans, hundreds of them already taken prisoner, sitting on the side of the road across from Cabcaben Field. We learned later that thousands of Filipinos, too, had been taken prisoner wherever the Japanese found them.

We were ordered to unload ourselves. I tossed my hand grenades and ammunition onto an ever-growing pile, a pile already nearly as big as a house. We were told to unload our rifles before adding them to the pile. It was then I knew why the Enfield rifle had been abandoned. The bolt wouldn't work; I'd been carrying a useless weapon all this time.

My razor blades went into the pile, as did the can of meat and beans. I guess that hurt the worst; I was terribly hungry. I learned an important lesson: if I got my hands on any food, not to save it. Eat it before it was taken away from me.

The ten of us joined the long line of prisoners; we, too, sat on the ground by the side of the road. We were tired and hungry; some of us were sick or wounded; and all of us were dazed and scared. There was nothing in all our lives that had prepared us for this.

As we were the latest prisoners taken and I was the last in line, I was on the end of a long line of prisoners. There was a Jap guard right behind me; I was almost sitting on his toes. I crossed my legs and felt something hard, a rock, perhaps, under my legs. I reached to remove the stone, but there was nothing there. I ran my hand into a pocket and pulled out a hand grenade. I'd forgotten about the one hand grenade I had in my leg pocket and had failed to add it to the pile when we were disarmed.

I sat there, holding it in my hand, looking at it. Then I turned and handed it to the guard behind me. The guard took the object I held in my open hand and stared at it as I'd done a few seconds before. He took off in a run toward the headquarters tent. The Good Lord must have been watching over me better than I thought, for at that very instant artillery batteries from Corregidor began to shell us, hitting right where we were. For a few minutes there was pandemonium. Everybody ran, Americans and Japanese. As I dashed past the HQ tent amid all the shelling they were still looking at that grenade.

I ran about two miles up the road before I stopped. I wanted to put as much distance between me and the grenade as possible. I'd been sitting there before this happened, figuring I was as tired as a body could be and couldn't move another step. I found I was wrong.

When I joined Capt. Kelly later, I found that he'd been on one of the very few trucks to haul anybody off Bataan. "Why didn't you stay with me?" he scolded. "You could have ridden."

"Stay with you? Well, I'd not have made the march, that's for sure. The Jap guard I gave the grenade to would have shot me."

While I was sitting there on the side of the road, dazed, with my heart beating so fast I could hardly breathe, a Japanese soldier stopped and spoke. "You American? We are Japanese. We won the war in Singapore. We have won it here. We are going to Hawaii and then to San Francisco." He grinned at me as I stared at him wordlessly. Behind me a deep voice growled, "San Francisco? Like hell you are!"

I moved myself as far away from the road as I could because the horrors were already beginning. Japanese soldiers were coming in droves from the north, walking down the road, and they began to spit on us, then to throw stones at us. As their bravado grew, they began to step off the road and jab us with the butts of their rifles. I moved back so I could get away from the spitting and the jabs, and they'd have to have a good arm to hit me with the stones. The Japanese may be Westernized to a great extent now, but in 1942 they were as Oriental as Genghis Khan.

I'm not sure I ever knew exactly how many of us there were at the place where we began the march. Several hundred at least, perhaps as many as two thousand. My running away up the road put me in a good spot. I was close to the front of the line. I wasn't aware then, of course, how fortunate I was to be in that position.

We spent the night by the side of the road after the shelling from Corregidor and slept some even though there was constant noise and activity on the highway. Besides a constant stream of foot soldiers, there were tanks and artillery coming from the northern part of Luzon where they had landed and, with little effort, fought their way down. It was evident that the Japanese were amassing an enormous army in the Philippines.

Early on the morning of April 10, the first group of guards arrived who were to start taking us off Bataan. We lined up on the right side of the highway, four men to a row, and started walking. We'd gone perhaps three miles when we began to meet Japanese infantry, hordes of them, who had probably spent the night by the roadside a few miles north of us, had their bowls of rice and were on their way south.

These infantrymen began to come into our ranks, pick out a prisoner, search him and take whatever they wanted. Their favorite form of torment seemed to be to take our canteens, pour the water on the pavement, put the empty canteens down and smash them with the butts of their rifles, then pick up the ruined canteens and hand them back to us, with grins of delight on their faces. They would take helmets away from the men, especially the tropical helmets that shaded us from the fierce sun, and either throw them away or tear them to shreds with a bayonet. These were stiff, light weight hats, made of fiber and molded in the shape of helmets.

They never bothered my helmet as I had a steel helmet, and I figured they thought a steel helmet was torture enough in the tropical sun. I kept this helmet to hide my red hair as much as to shade my freckled face. I wanted to attract their attention as little as possible. My helmet became a valued possession, as I later used it as a wash basin, *quan* can, or whatever. They didn't get my canteen either, because I carried it in my coverall leg pocket, the same pocket that had recently held a hand grenade, and it was out of sight.

The Japanese were looking for souvenirs, not only American objects they could keep for themselves, but to see if the Americans had anything Japanese, especially money. Some of our men had found some and kept it as souvenirs. When these foot soldiers found this money, they pulled the owners out of line, and we never saw them again.

If they were found with anything made in Japan, men were beaten, not with fists, but with rifle butts, usually in the face. An item as innocent as a pocket comb, bought in the United States or in a military exchange, but stamped "Made in Japan" could cost a man his life. Word passed quickly for us to rid ourselves of anything Japanese. The words "Made in Japan" became anathema for us.

As soon as I saw what was happening, I maneuvered myself to the far right, where I wasn't so easy to reach. The first time I was ordered to empty my pockets, I took my Bible out of my coverall pocket and handed it to the soldier. He refused to take it. Instead he put his hands together and bowed his head in reverence. I nodded in agreement, and he left me alone.

After that, when I was jerked about and ordered to empty my pockets, I would hand them my Bible first. The reaction was always the same. I managed to keep some pictures I'd put inside the little Bible, and my billfold which had nothing in it, and also my canteen hidden in my leg pocket. The Bible was my link to God; the pictures of the family were my link to home; the canteen was necessary to my survival.

Our line had not been moving fast to begin with, and these robberies were making us slower and causing stragglers. We really tried to keep our ranks closed because we felt we were less exposed, less vulnerable that way. There was definitely safety in numbers. One soldier alone anywhere was in a dangerous position.

In spite of being hungry and thirsty, sick and weak and indescribably weary, the worst thing at this time was these troops coming into our lines and bothering us. After I moved to the right I wasn't bothered so much. When we'd meet a new squad of infantrymen they would move in and start harassing us, but I kept moving, not stopping or hesitating long enough to give them a good chance to collar me. Consequently, I was stopped no more than a half dozen times the first day. I had very little water in my canteen, but I didn't dare take a drink when there were soldiers near for fear of losing my canteen.

THIRST

My good sense faltered and my luck almost ran out about midmorning of the first day when we came to a public well. These wells are common in the Philippines; they are mostly artesian wells where the water flows all the time. The wells we encountered had hand pumps to give them more pressure and concrete curbs around them.

Being close to the front, I was among the first of my group to get to the well. I was trying to fill my empty canteen, but the thirsty men behind me began to push and shove to get to the well, much like thirsty cattle stampeding at the smell of water. Soon I had been shoved to the ground; I was down and couldn't get up. About the time I'd work myself into a position to rise to my feet, someone would step on me, or kick me, or push me back down. The longer it lasted the worse it got, as more and more men were piling on top of each other. I was getting trampled to death. Finally, by fighting and struggling, realizing my life depended on it, I grabbed hold of some of them on top of me and pulled myself up and got out of the melee and back on the road. I vowed I'd never let that happen again. From then on I'd get in quickly, get what I could and be out before the crowd hit. What was a little more water worth to someone who'd been trampled to death getting it? I'd get a little water each time, not much, but enough to survive.

After the first well episode, the guards pushed us back in ranks, and we continued up the road, with American prisoners of war going north and Japanese troops on the left going south. The road was paved, hard on our feet, but relatively free of dust.

Then a strange thing happened. Not long after we left the well, five trucks stopped and picked up some of us, as many as could get in, and carried us a few miles, maybe five or six, then stopped. Then the guards made us all get out. We never figured out the reason, but I never questioned the value of it, for it put me closer to the front of the line.

Not long after that, we began to have other groups of prisoners join us, men who had been captured elsewhere and were now waiting by the side of the road to join the march. This was making things more congested since it was putting more men in front of me, and there was still the heavy traffic of Japanese troops going south.

We marched till about nine o'clock that night. They put us in a compound in a barrio, maybe Pilar, I'm not sure. We'd already gone through Orion, I remembered that. Wherever this was, they pushed us into a compound, and kept pushing us in until we were so crowded we couldn't lie down to sleep; we could only sit and lean against each other in our weariness. It was dark and we couldn't see where we were, nor the person we might be stepping on or leaning against. I found a small bamboo platform and climbed up on it and sat down. From there I could look directly across a fence to where the Japanese soldiers were boiling rice in some big pots. I could see the fires under the pots and the movement of the men in the flickering light. I could smell the odor of the cooking food. Oh boy, they were going to feed us! I watched the steam rise from the pots and waited, the hunger welling up in me until it hurt, but none of it came our way. I watched as the pots were emptied, the men went away and the last of the flames flickered to embers. Then I sat on the bamboo platform and slept till morning.

At daylight the second day we were lined up and put out on the road again. Still no food. Though hungry and weak, I was in better shape than most of the men. I'd managed to avoid malaria, thanks to my mosquito netting, and I'd never required a great deal to eat. However, in the days since the war started, I had lost weight. I now weighed no more than the hundred and twenty pounds I'd started with.

We were traveling on nerves and fear; we didn't know what was going to happen; we never knew what was around the corner. One thing we were sure of—whatever it was, it wouldn't be good.

I FIND TWO FRIENDS

Early in the second day's march, just a few hundred yards down the road, I found Thompson and Alexander. Alexander had malaria and was struggling to keep going; he was so sick he had no strength.

Thompson and I swung Alexander's arms over our shoulders and we walked on. And on and on.

As a group we were suffering; there were very few who were well when the march started. Many had malaria; they were walking with chills and fever. Malaria, the scourge of the tropics, hit first. It is not just the mosquito that causes the illness; it is the parasite that goes through a developmental stage in the mosquito. The sickness begins with an overall sense of feeling ill. Shaking chills and fever follow. Delusion, coma and death can occur. Malaria can be accompanied by dysentery, and the urine can become dark. This can be suppressed by medication, but the symptoms can reappear later, even years later.

Dysentery was brought on not only by the malaria, but also from primitive, unsanitary conditions: polluted water, swarms of flies, no bathing facilities. Dysentery is not just diarrhea. It comes on abruptly with fever, nausea, vomiting, stomach cramps. The diarrhea can be a watery stool, often mixed with blood, mucus or pus. The body becomes dehydrated. The need for water becomes overwhelming.

Diarrhea had dehydrated many men until they were gaunt and hollow-eyed; diarrhea which wouldn't let up even when they were walking. If a man left the ranks for the bushes, he was likely to be shot for trying to escape. The other alternative was to mess his pants and keep going. Some were so sick they didn't even know when it was happening. Then in turn, dehydration causes loss of potassium which brings on weakness, faintness, abdominal pains. We were all suffering from heat exposure and extreme fatigue and were so weak from hunger we had little strength. Add all of this together with the Japanese atrocities—it is no wonder the men were dying!

Ray Thompson had picked up a musette bag somewhere along the way and had crackers and sugar in it. I kept trying to get him to open it up so the three of us could sample it.

"No," he said, "we'll need it worse later on."

I argued, remembering the can of meat and beans I'd added to the pile at Cabcaben. But it was his musette bag and he prevailed.

We marched without stopping until about two that afternoon when the guards ordered an abrupt halt. While we waited, a brand-new pair of shoes that someone had picked up by the side of the road was passed around to see if anyone could fit them. They were exactly my size, seven and a half D, and I surely needed them. I sat right down on the road, took off my old ones that had holes in the soles and were pinching my toes, and put on the new ones. I was soon glad I'd immediately changed shoes, as we were made to pile our belongings onto an ever growing pile by the side of the road. Onto that pile went Thompson's musette bag and the precious crackers and sugar.

We were put inside a barbed wire entanglement, the first of many we'd see before we were through with this seventy-five mile march. There we sat, the sun high overhead and most of us without any protection for our heads and faces. My steel helmet was hot and heavy, but it did provide shade and kept my red hair from attracting attention.

We sat there, not stirring, for at least two hours. Men began to pass out. I could hear them gasp, groan; see them shudder and crumple down, one by one, on either side, all around. When time came to leave the compound, if a man couldn't get up on his feet by his own strength, without any help, the guards made him stay there. Alexander couldn't rise. He tried. Thompson and I urged him, begged him, under the eyes of the guards, standing there with their bayonets poised. We couldn't touch him. They would have bayoneted him and perhaps us also. So we had to leave him there.

In an act of defiance, as we passed the pile of things that had been heaped there by the prisoners, tents, canteens, food, bedrolls, blankets—all things that would have made our agony less horrible and would have saved the lives of some of our men—I grabbed a shelter half, a part of a pup tent, as I walked by. Fortunately no guard saw me, so I rolled it up and stuck it under my arm and kept walking. That shelter half became my coat, my hat, my umbrella, my bedroll and my security blanket. I managed to keep it all during my imprisonment in the Philippines.

We walked. I'm not sure what words to use to describe our movements—plodding, struggling, staggering, hobbling—just trying to lift one foot and put it ahead of the other, then do it again, and again . . .

All through the night we walked. Sometime during this second night of our march, our third night of captivity, it began to rain, rain as it can do only in the tropics, hard, steady, soaking. I wrapped myself up in my shelter half. I didn't stay dry, but it helped hold my body heat, for as the tropical days may be hot, the nights are chilly.

Sometime in the middle of the night the column halted abruptly. I sat down in the road with the rain pouring straight down and went sound asleep. When it was time to move on, someone kicked me and ordered me to get to my feet. I don't know how I slept, for all through the night behind us we could hear screams. We never knew all of what happened, for most of the brutality (someone, I believe it was Lowell Thomas, called it the "orgy of Japanese crimes") happened toward the end of the line, where the weak were struggling, unable to keep up. For by now, if a man couldn't keep up with the line or fell out on the march, they shot him or bayoneted him on the spot. They made no effort to pick up the bodies, just left them lying there for all to see. I found out later, from those behind me, that the path we took became littered with the bodies of dead Americans, especially around the water wells, where the guards, infuriated with the mass of pushing humanity, bayoneted anyone within reach. Those in the rear said it soon became impossible to get to the wells without stepping over dead men.

It was well-named: Bataan Death March.

We continued. It was raining and I became cold. But I had my shelter half as a security blanket, and like a baby I went to sleep. We weren't moving fast, just moving, like a great wave, only much more slowly. Moving, plodding, stumbling and sleeping as I walked. I'd wake up when one of the men would push me back into my place after I'd staggered against him. Sometimes one would have enough strength to shake me and tell me to stay awake.

Daylight came, the dawning of another day, but the sun shone down on a sad sight. We found another well, and I got about ten swallows of water in my canteen and got out of the way. While the others were pushing for water I moved myself forward a couple of rows. By now the march was strung over thirty or forty miles, with gaps between groups.

One day became like another. I can remember the first two days. We had walked the first day and spent the first night in a compound so crowded there was no room to lie down. We'd walked the second day and all night the second night in the rain. The third, fourth and fifth days and nights have run together. I can remember sitting inside barbed wire entanglements for an hour or two, sometimes at night, sometimes during the day. I would go to sleep wherever I sat.

Even though I was near complete exhaustion I never wanted to sit down in the middle of the road, for when that happened we always heard screams. The screams came from behind us, for by now those of us in the front were the stronger ones. We were keeping up. It was the ones behind, the weaker ones that couldn't keep up, that would fall out and couldn't get up that were being bayoneted or shot.

Oncoming troops were no longer bothering us; that was over. No more foot soldiers to bother us, just an occasional truck moving south. Now it was the guards, eliminating the weaker ones. And we were weakening at an alarming rate. Every time we stopped fewer were able to continue. Some time in those three days the guards began to ignore those unable to rise inside the entanglements. They made a strange distinction: if a man fell out on the road, he was killed then and there; if he passed out in an entanglement and was unable to continue, he was left there to die on his own. But this helped the men, for many of them, after resting a few hours, would be able to leave with the next group that came through. Some of the men did this more than once. It prolonged their march, but enabled them to live.

From the third day it was the same. Walk, stop on the road with the inevitable gunshots and screams. Walk again. A water well, rush in and out before you got trampled. Barbed wire entanglements, sit there in the hot sun while your companions pass out around you. Get up, walk again. Only there are fewer each time. Someone always got left behind. On forward, to the front. Don't ever stop, keep going, for if you stop, they kill you.

Sergeant Ervin told us later that he'd taken his last step and lay down to die. A guard raised his bayonet and was coming down with it: "I raised my hand to the tip of the bayonet and he stopped . . . I got up and finished the march."

Then, there was the changing of the guards. Every two hours a truck would come to replace the Japanese guards. You never got used to one set until another would come to worry you.

I wish I could say that the encounters at the wells got better, but they didn't. The men were suffering more than ever from heat exposure and extreme thirst. The sight of water still had a maddening effect upon them. Even though I was near the front, I was still seeing men clubbed with rifle butts and jabbed with bayonets, and I began to see more bodies at the wells. The march was lasting a terribly long time.

As we entered the fifth day, I was walking faster than most men. It was easier for me, of course. Only the healthiest were in front. Most had slowed, but I was like a race horse that takes a spurt at the finish line. I was running a race, literally. I didn't know what was ahead, but I couldn't see how anything could be worse than what was behind me. I wanted out of it. I was within a half-mile of the front of the entire group when we came into San Fernando.

The length of the March for me was five days from Cabcaben to San Fernando; I got into O'Donnell on the sixth day. For some it ran from two to three weeks, partly from being farther behind in the line and partly from having to stop and rest more often. As bad as the march was for me, it was worse for many. For the entire march we had no food and very little strength. I was close to the front, and most of the atrocities occurred behind me. At that time I was free from malaria and dysentery and was going on energy caused by fear.

We were not the first group to reach San Fernando. A small group was there in the small compound when we arrived. I assume the group had experienced better conditions—had been brought in on trucks, or had been captured farther north and had a shorter walk.

Maybe it's a time of day that's stopped in my mind like a frozen clock, but it seemed we were always arriving somewhere about four o'clock in the afternoon. That seems to be the time on the fifth day of the march when I entered the San Fernando compound. Men kept pushing in after me, straggling in. They kept pushing more and more. It got dark. They were still coming.

Things were confused in our minds even then, and after nearly sixty years it's difficult to be certain about things. I don't know whether all our original group came into this compound or whether they were taken elsewhere. Some of the men I'd been with I never saw again. Some were interned in other camps. Through the years I've run across men that I was certain had died and learned that some died that I thought had lived.

There was no order or method to any of this. We just crowded in and milled about, trying to find a place to rest. Again that night we could see the Japanese, with their big pots of steaming rice. Again we thought that at last we'd get a bite to eat. We didn't.

During that night something happened—a strange thing. Not an important thing, just something that started and ended within a few seconds, no more than a minute. But I remember it clearly, and I've heard it repeated over and over, by nearly everyone I've talked to who survived all this. During the night, as we were sleeping, sitting as usual as there was no room to lie down, we heard a terrible scream. Then as one huge body, we rose and started running, moving against each other in panic until we hit the solid wall of a building in the compound. Just as suddenly as it started, the screaming stopped. We, too, stopped just as suddenly, wide-awake and reasoning. Then as one solid mass we retraced our steps back to our places, sat down as we were and went back to sleep.

There were a couple of versions, maybe more, of the reason for the scream. Some say the guards killed a man. Others say no, a man screamed during a nightmare. The wall we hit was the side of a warehouse. We found out later that there were other prisoners inside this warehouse and that they had heard the scream, had jumped up and moved exactly as we did. Strange ...

TO O'DONNELL

It wasn't until the next morning that we in the compound realized there were men in the warehouse. We saw them the next morning as they were herded out and marched down to a railroad track where the Japanese crowded them into boxcars and locked the doors.

We were next. We were crowded in as they were, into other boxcars, but the doors were left open and two guards assigned to each door. The train moved slowly, going from San Fernando toward Camp O'Donnell. As the train moved through small towns, Filipino people lined the sides of the track and tossed food into the boxcars. They threw such things as rice balls, sugar candy and sugar cane joints. I got a piece of sugar cane, which I stripped down and chewed

chewed for the sweet juice. Juice of the sugar cane, the first thing I'd swallowed, except for water, in eight days.

We rode this crowded boxcar north, past Clark Field and on into Capas, a town in the Tarlac Province. The train stopped. We unloaded and were greeted by the Filipino Red Cross with buckets of water and allowed to fill our canteens. Then we lined up and marched another seven or eight miles to Camp O'Donnell. Along the roadside were buckets of water and baskets of fruit. The Philippine people, knowing our plight, had set it out for us. Some of the men got fruit. I didn't.

One thing stands out in my memory: I saw a Japanese guard send a Filipino man to fill a bucket of water for us. This was the first act of humanity from a Japanese soldier I'd seen, except for the reaction to my Bible, since I'd been captured.

CHAPTER 9

CAMP O'DONNELL

We struggled up a hill our last mile and looked over the hill to a strange and depressing sight. O'Donnell, where we were to be housed, was an unfinished and abandoned Filipino army camp. The buildings were little more than skeletons, some of them with no roofs. It was April 15, 1942.

It was even worse up close. We were forced in, pushed in as before, crowded as in the boxcars. There was no effort at organization. We milled about, trying to find a place to lie down and rest, somewhere in the shade, out of the way, where we'd not be stepped on. I found a spot out in the grass against an old mess hall, settled in and then discovered my canteen was empty. I knew I'd better find water now. I didn't want to go into the night without water, as we never knew from one hour to the next what was before us.

I asked someone where I could find water and was told to go over a hill, a few hundred yards away, to an open area. I did, only to find a long line of men waiting to get water from one little tap! I joined the end of the line. It moved slowly, but that didn't matter. I figured I had nothing better to do with whatever time I might have left. I had nowhere else to go and nothing else to do.

While I was in this line waiting for water, I looked back to see a familiar face. A young man was squatting there, much as the Filipinos do, quietly resting as he waited for the line to move forward. I stepped back and spoke to him.

"Say, I know you. Do you remember me?"

He peered up at me and said, "Nope. Don't reckon I do."

"Did you go to Paris High School?"

His interest quickened and he glanced up sharply at me. "Yeah. Yeah."

"And you don't remember me? Doesn't your grandmother live at a little place called Pinhook?" (This man's uncle, William A. Owens, was to later write a book that would make Pinhook famous, *This Stubborn Soil*.)

The man smiled, "Sure does."

"Well, we rode the same school bus when you would go out on the weekend to visit your grandmother."

He struggled to bring his long frame to a standing position and peered at me closely. Then his face broke into a wide grin, "By golly! Red Allen."

John "Peapicker" Owens and I had a good visit as we moved up the line. Then we eventually got our water and went our separate ways. I never saw him again until . . . but that's another story.

As we waited I got thirstier and thirstier and began to get impatient at the slowness of the line. So did some of the others. As time dragged on, those getting to the trickle of water began to push those already there out of the way, telling them they were taking too long. I suppose we'd have had a riot and the Japs would have rushed in and started bayoneting, if some of the stronger Americans hadn't stepped in and taken charge. They maintained discipline until everybody got water.

This was our introduction to Camp O'Donnell. There was no organization, no discipline. Just exhausted, sick men trying to find a familiar face. Thompson and I had left Alexander behind at a barbed wire enclosure. Then I'd gone off and left Thompson in my race to reach the front of the line. I'd not seen Cochran or Melton or Fisher since all this started.

The water line never stopped. There was always someone there trying to get a supply of water from the one tap. Shelter was a problem, too. The army camp was incomplete, lacking floors and walls in some places. Many of the buildings were roofless and offered no protection. We sought shade to get out of the hot sun, and a place to curl up in at night.

I was still holding onto my shelter half. I couldn't find a complete building to get into, but I had found a place to lie down, in some grass by the mess hall. I was so tired, so weak from hunger and so scared, that sleep wouldn't come. It started to rain. I soon saw my shelter half wasn't enough to protect me, so I entered the incomplete kitchen. At least it had a roof and the warmth of other bodies.

Too many bodies, I discovered. I worked my way in, in the dark, stepping over and occasionally on, recumbent forms, getting an occasional weak curse from the one I'd stepped on. Some were too sick or too weak to care. One spot, and one spot only, was vacant: the sink hole (literally, the space cut out for the nonexistent kitchen sink). I stretched my shelter half over this vacant area and curled up as in a hammock and slept the rest of the night.

Early the next morning those of us who could walk set out to try to find food. It was a disorganized situation, with each person trying to look out for himself. About midmorning, we found a kitchen where they were cooking rice, and I got in line.

On the first day of the march I had picked up a mustard sardine can that someone had abandoned. This was larger than the regular sardine can and more oval in shape. I polished it when we stopped to rest, until I had it clean and shiny. I figured sometime soon we'd get some rice, and I needed something to put it in. I waited for that day, but it never came. On the second night when it started to rain, I put my Bible with the pictures in it inside my sardine can and put it in my shirt pocket. There it had stayed until now.

I got out my sardine can, all shiny and clean, took my Bible out of it and had the can ready to use as a mess kit. There were several thousand of us to be fed. I don't know how many were in our line, but it was an hour or more before I moved my way up in line enough to get my ladle of rice, my first bite of food, not counting the bit of sugar cane I'd chewed on, since three days before I was captured.

This was the 18th day of April; since the 7th day of April I'd eaten one-half can of pork and beans. If food had not been available, the crime would not have been so bad. But we were made to discard what little food we had, and then had to watch as the Japanese cooked up their own pots of rice, never giving us any.

As the days passed we began to get a better feeding schedule. We were assigned to particular areas, and kitchens began to function. We got two or three ladles of rice a day, and about once a day we got cabbage soup.

The Americans cooked for themselves; the Japanese never cooked for the prisoners. The food detail was for the Japanese kitchen. Prisoners were taken out in trucks by the Japanese to towns nearby and loaded the trucks with whatever the Japanese could find: beans, rice, perhaps some vegetables. All this was used by the Japanese, not the prisoners.

After the second or third day, because I was still able to walk, I got on water detail. The cooks told us they would probably be able to give us an extra helping of food if we carried water for the kitchen. Twenty men went in pairs, with bamboo poles balanced on our shoulders and a couple of five-gallon cans swinging between us. The stream was close to a mile away, with Japanese guards posted at intervals. The water looked clear, and we dropped our cans in it and filled them. As we were filling there, we looked upstream and saw a small Filipino village with women doing their laundry in the water and a water buffalo or two standing in it, drinking and cooling off as they switched their tails to keep the flies away.

The water flowed down from a mountain farther upstream and looked clear when it got to us. We could only shrug and hope they boiled it thoroughly in the kitchen. We'd walk the mile back to camp, dump our water into the containers and head back for another ten gallons. Trip after trip, all day. Each trip took an hour. It was getting dark when we went in and asked hopefully if that was enough.

Not yet, we were told, it takes a lot of water for a kitchen like this. On we went, in the dark. We knew the way well enough, the path was well worn by now. We wanted to stop, to give up, but that extra ration of food was like a carrot before a stubborn donkey. At midnight we didn't see how it could keep from being enough, but we had noticed that after we'd had our nightly ladle of rice and the KPs had started washing up, the water level went down fast.

"Sergeant, isn't this enough?"

"Boys, in a couple of hours we got to start breakfast." Back to the cans and the river and the stumbling in the dark. It was getting daylight when we finally gave up. "Sorry, boys," the sergeant said, "we've not got enough food to go around to everybody. Can't give you any extra."

Burial detail was one of the most common duties. A road separated the American camp from the Filipino camp. The Philippine prisoners were losing even more men each day than we were. One reason was, of course, that there were more of them. They were unable to bury their dead as fast as they were dying. We could look across and see bodies stacked in rows, awaiting burial. They wanted help from us, but we couldn't help much as we were having trouble burying our own.

On burial detail the men dug graves in the morning, came in for their bowl of rice, then buried the dead in the afternoon. I had caught burial detail a few times before I decided to stick to water carrying. We'd dig a common grave, about twelve feet by twelve feet, strip the bodies and put them in, hoping they landed in a prone position. The Jap guards wouldn't allow us time to straighten the bodies if they fell upright or across other bodies. If they weren't properly placed, or if the water in the wet ground brought them to the surface, dogs would get into the graves and uncover them. We weren't allowed to have services; if a prayer was said, it had to be a silent one.

After a few days at O'Donnell, I began to search for someone from my outfit, and found my officers, Capt. Kelly, Lt. Rice and Lt. Noles, among others. They were quartered together and I was hoping to be able to stay with them, as it would make things easier for me. But after a few days orders came that all enlisted men be separated from officers, so I "packed" my shelter half and my sardine can and moved out, moved back to the mess hall where I'd spent my first night asleep in a place that didn't exist, a sink hole.

We had no place to bathe and water was scarce, as I knew first-hand. If we wanted water for personal use we had to hustle it up for ourselves. I managed to keep my canteen filled at the spigot, hoping it was purer than the water we brought in for the kitchen. We were getting food, but just barely enough to stay alive. There was plenty of work to be done and we stayed busy: food supply, water and burial details. My thing was water detail; I had grabbed it to stay off burial detail.

I contemplated escape while on water detail. I looked things over carefully, trying to size up the Filipino village upstream and observing how closely certain guards watched us and which ones were lax. I decided that if I could get a plan worked out, I'd try it. The odds were against us staying alive in the camp.

I'm not sure what our numbers had dwindled to before I left O'Donnell, but we were losing around one hundred a day. Most of them were strangers to me, but some were friends. I was told that a friend, the mess sergeant I had worked with on Bataan, had died. We had a bond in that his last name was the same as my first: Oliver. And we had found that we lived only a few miles from each other back home.

When we were on Bataan, he would take me along with him when he went to the bakery. This was the place where the army cooks did their baking, in the mountains near Mariveles. He'd drive about five miles from Cabcaben to Mariveles, then back, at night with the lights off, in a Dodge panel truck which we used to haul supplies.

Sgt. W. V. Oliver ran one of the kitchens at O'Donnell. I tried to get to work with him, but so many were trying to get to work in the kitchens that they had to issue orders to let no one in to see the cook. I think if I'd sent him my name, he'd have seen me, but I didn't press it. I left O'Donnell without ever getting in to see him. Only recently his sister informed me that he died, not at O'Donnell, but later at Cabanatuan.

Around the first of May the group in our "barracks," the incomplete kitchen, was called out, lined up, marched out of camp and put in trucks. Among the two hundred of us who went were Sgt. Finch, Art Rice, Jesse Knowles, Harold Christopher and some fellows whose last names were Keith and Davidson. We were taken to San Fernando, the town where the march ended. In fact, we were taken to the same compound we'd been herded into on the last mile of the March. This is where we'd all been wakened by screams and had moved as one man.

The stone warehouse was to be our barracks. I remember this place with special distaste. The floor was dirty, and while it was softer than the ground, it had a layer of dust four inches thick. Silt got into everything—our clothes, our eyes, noses, mouths. God only knows what germs were thriving there.

FALL OF CORREGIDOR

It was here that we got word that Corregidor had fallen to the Japanese on May 6, 1942. Corregidor—where General MacArthur had left his headquarters in Malinta Tunnel, had left the Philippines—was now in Japanese hands. Some of the men who had made it to Mariveles before the Japanese got there found a way across to Corregidor. Some found small boats and some swam. One of the 7th group, a soldier who later became a good friend, swam across and was captured on Corregidor. Forrest (Blackie) Brooks had come in from Albuquerque and we met when we joined his group at Angel Island.

By the time we had gotten to the southern tip of Bataan, the Japs were everywhere. Even though the extent of my swimming was in Granddad's stock pool, I'd have made an attempt to get to Corregidor if I'd thought there was any way I could have made it. Now we learned our friends there were dead or captured also. It was hard not to be bitter. But I'd try not to think of that. Think of one thing only: survival. I'd show MacArthur, and Roosevelt, and the whole damn Japanese army. I'd show them all. I'd survive.

But I wasn't so sure I'd survive after I'd been in this warehouse a day. Dysentery hit us all. Hard. It was my first sickness, but it hit the others even harder than it had before. For four days I lay sick in body and sick at heart. I felt bitter. Bitter and betrayed. We'd been put on this island and abandoned. Back at Clark and Cabcaben we had kept hearing General MacArthur, on the radio, telling of his "gallant Filipino forces," never mentioning that the Americans were there, fighting and dying. Then we heard President Roosevelt's view that we'd already held out longer than he'd expected, so we knew no help was coming. It was hard not to be bitter. Remember, Red Allen, you're going to survive.

Our sickness was debilitating; we were extremely weak. The toilet that we were using so frequently—it almost seemed we lived there—was an open pit at the end of the warehouse, outside, covered with timbers that we would walk out on and squat. We were so weak we could hardly hold our balance long enough. One poor soul (evidently one who had come before us; we didn't know him) had crawled out on the timbers, lost consciousness and fallen in.

We pulled him out and buried him.

CHAPTER 10

BRIDGE OVER THE RIVER PENARANDA

We left there the next day, knowing that Corregidor had fallen and that our friends who had dared to swim to the rock were now either dead or prisoners. We boarded trucks and rode to the town of Gapan on the Penaranda River. After we left San Fernando aboard the truck, we traveled a long time. It was night when we got to Gapan. It was raining, and I had dysentery. I was in bad shape.

As sick and weak as we were, we were assigned to a bridge building detail. Bridge repairing would be more accurate. A steel bridge had crossed the Penaranda River, with five spans. Now one span was destroyed on one side, and two more on the other side, next to the banks. We learned we'd been brought here to replace one steel span with two wooden ones, and the two spans with three spans of wood. Two spans in the middle of the river were still intact.

We would be on this detail for fifty-two days, staying in a schoolhouse. The schoolhouses were all abandoned by the Philippine people, and now were used by the Japanese as headquarters and barracks for prisoners.

We unloaded from the trucks that first night in the rain and went in to lie down to rest on the floor of the school room. At least it was cleaner than the filthy warehouse floor. The guards pitched us one dried fish per person, much as you'd toss a fish to a seal, or a bone to a dog. I couldn't see the fish in the dark, but I could smell it and knew immediately I couldn't eat a bite of it. But morning light revealed only a few fish bones left in my sardine can mess kit.

We bunked down, lay down on the bare floor. A shelter half is thin on a wooden floor, much worse than on bamboo. It wasn't long before we began to get sores on our hips, backs, shoulders and even on the sides of our knees when we slept on our sides. We were a bunch of rag-tag skeletons. There was no real flesh between our bones and the wooden floor, only sunburned skin.

Two hundred men lined up to go out on the bridge detail that morning. But I had a severe case of diarrhea and felt like I couldn't possibly work that day. So I made sick call. Since there wasn't anything anyone could do for me between bouts of dysentery, I walked over to the cook house (a natural gravitation) and was put on water detail, a chronic condition for me. So, out the main gate, down the road a quarter of a mile, under the eyes of a guard, of course, to a public well exactly like those we saw and fought over on the march.

There were two of us on this assignment, with the bamboo pole called a *yaho* pole. We carried water all day. Each time we'd bring a load, we'd say, "That's enough, isn't it?" And cook Jesse Knowles would answer, "Got to have more."

At the end of the day I inquired about conditions at the bridge. They had spent the day carrying gravel from the riverbed up the road. A man would get two or three shovelfuls in a sack, throw it over his shoulder and join the others, like a string of ants, with one line going up and one going down, the pile of riverbed gravel growing bigger all the time.

"Yeah," I pursued my questioning, "but what about . . . well, if you need a toilet?"

"A bush, Red, just like the rest of us."

On the second day I chose to go to the bridge. For fifty-one consecutive days out of the fifty-two, I worked at bridge repair.

There were two hundred of us at the schoolhouse, and, excluding the ones that had other duties, such as kitchen and water duty, and those on sick call, about one hundred fifty of us went out the second day.

The gravel and sand were taken from the dry riverbed and were being stockpiled to use to build the concrete piers to replace those that had been blown up. After a few days of carrying gravel, I was called on to carry water for one day. A guard came to me, and speaking broken English, told me to go with him. I went. I picked up the *yabo* pole and started with him. On the way, he spoke, "I am a Christian." Nothing more. He became a candle in a deep, deep darkness. When we got to Gapan he guided me toward a barber shop, motioning for me to set my bucket down outside the door. Then he took me inside and instructed the barber to cut my hair. I needed it; I hadn't had a haircut since the war started. I didn't get a shave, of course. It would be three years before I'd have enough beard to shave. While the Filipino barber cut my hair, the guard disappeared. I was a little uneasy; I didn't want to get shot by another Japanese soldier who thought I was trying to escape. Not that I wouldn't have tried if I could have figured out any way to get off the island.

I needn't have worried; my gentle Christian guard reappeared by the time the barber was finished. He handed me a big sack of candy and a bag of Filipino "stogies," long black cigarettes. My, what a gift! What a treat the candy would be, after weeks of rice. And the tobacco—I didn't smoke, but there were men who would give half their rations for a cigarette.

I was glad to get a haircut. What I lacked in beard I more than made up in hair on my head. Then, as now, I had a thick head of hair, and it had grown long and bushy. Needless to say, I watched for him the next day, hoping to be on the receiving end of the Japanese Christian's generosity. But he chose someone else the next day, and someone else the day after that, spreading his kindness as far as he was able.

After we'd stockpiled our sand and gravel, we started putting forms in the river bed. These forms were built on land and floated out and put in place before the pole footings were dropped in. We did this by raising tapered poles with pulleys and dropping them into the soft mud of the riverbed as footings for the concrete piers. This was during the dry season, and the water in the river was shallow.

To raise the poles, we'd all pull our ropes. The main weight was pulled by a long rope, to which all our shorter ropes were attached. On a signal we'd turn loose of our ropes and let the pole drop. I lost all the top skin off my hands, pulling the ropes, and it got to be very painful.

To drive a pole in the river bed, we had a tripod with a pulley on top to put a rope through. The rope was fastened to a several-hundred-pound metal driver and put through the pulley. The other end extended out into the river and branched out to fifty or more small ropes. We would each take a rope and when they yelled "pull," we would tug on our rope and pull up the weight, and on the command "drop," we would let the rope go, and the heavy weight would strike the top of the tapered pole. After a dozen tries the pole would be driven into place.

Our scaffolding was made of bamboo and the derricks, of timber, and with the use of ropes, weights, pulleys and prisoner-of-war manpower, we set the footings.

The cement for the concrete was brought into Gapan by train, two boxcars of it. Guards took twenty of us to the railroad station where we unloaded it. Two men got inside a car to hand the sacks to the men outside. They laid them across our shoulders, and we started to the warehouse which was half a block down the street. These sacks weighed ninety-six pounds each, and by that time I weighed no more than ninety-six pounds, myself. By the time we got to the warehouse the sacks seemed to weigh two hundred, and we felt we were walking on our knees. We were much too weak to be doing this work.

Twenty of us started, and we were told we'd unload both boxcars before we quit. As we worked and struggled with these heavy sacks our group got smaller and smaller, as the strength of the men gave out. Once a sack slipped from my shoulders, and I hugged it around with my arms, trying to keep it from touching the ground, for I knew I'd never be able to get it up again. I asked for help in getting it back on my shoulders, but no one was able to help me. When I finally managed to get this bag to the warehouse, I made sure it never happened again. I got each sack firmly planted across my shoulders before I started and held on to it for all I was worth.

We emptied the last boxcars at ten o'clock that night, with six of us still working. During this terrible day we were allowed water but no food. Those who fell out just lay there, with the guard paying them no attention. We got food when we returned to the school house barracks that night. A scoop of rice.

Once the forms were built and floated out and put in place for the piers, and the tapered poles were dropped as footings, it was time to pour the concrete. I'd never seen concrete poured the way we did it and was quite sure it wouldn't work, but it did. The bamboo walks were extended with a platform for the concrete mixer. The "mixer" being shovels, a thin sheet of metal and coolie Americans. We carried the sand, gravel and cement in sacks on our backs and dumped it on the sheet of metal in proper proportions, mixed it by hand and then pushed it off into the water inside the forms around the wooden pilings. Dry. It worked; it set up. Later as the concrete rose above the water line, we added water to it before it was poured into the form.

This was backbreaking work. Carrying, mixing, pouring. Carrying, mixing, pouring. We poured one pier, then two, on one side of the river; then we crossed over and built three more. After this was done, we built a wooden floor for the bridge and wooden stringers.

Another interesting method of construction, a method different from ours, was the measuring of material. Whereas we laid a timber, put a measure on it and marked it, then sawed on the mark, the Japanese built a big platform, put the measure lines on the platform for each size piece they wanted cut, then laid each piece of timber on the pre-measured line and cut it there on the platform.

The cutting platform was located at another schoolhouse, across town from our barracks. After we had cut the materials, we carried the timber on our shoulders from the platform to the bridge, a distance of a half mile. This was hard on all of us, especially the taller ones, as they wound up carrying the load. For example, if I, five feet ten, were put with a couple of six-footers, they wound up carrying my load. Men were passing out more often. Some had all the skin rubbed off their shoulders and were in such bad shape it wouldn't heal. I met some of the men later, after the war at POW conventions, and several of them had never healed. They still had raw sores on their shoulders, even after they had been home for several years.

The Japs finally realized this method wouldn't work and started hauling the timbers in trucks. By the time they were ready to put up the wooden stringers, our work force had been reduced by half, to one hundred. Some were sick; some had already been buried.

Three rooms of the school building were hospital wards. In ward two, the men were sick but could get around a bit. In ward one, they were too sick to move about. Zero ward was where they were taken to die. We had one crew at the bridge and one crew working in the scrap lumber pile, making boxes to bury American soldiers. I'm happy to say these men were buried in a Filipino cemetery; this was not necessarily true of most of the men who died in the Philippines.

I was helping with burial detail now; I couldn't get out of it as there weren't enough healthy men left. When we got back from bridge work at the end of the day, we'd find that the few men who were strong enough to use a shovel would have dug the graves. Then those of us who were on bridge detail would take the bodies to the cemetery for burial.

While the food we got on the bridge detail was poor, it was better than what we had at O'Donnell and better than what we'd have at Cabanatuan, our next camp. We got an occasional bit of pork to season the dry rice, and we were given some flour. Since we could not bake, we had no bread, but the cook could use pork and flour to make a gravy to pour over our ladles of rice. This made the rice easier to swallow and a great deal more tasty. While our servings were minuscule, the gravy enabled some of those who were sick to be able to eat and gain some strength.

Each morning we had a hot breakfast, a small bowl of steamed rice. And another day to look forward to. Yes, a day I was glad to see because I was alive. For each day the number who lined up to go to the bridge got smaller. We averaged burying one man a day. The bridge detail took fifty-two days; we buried fifty-two men. That was more than one fourth of the men who started on the detail. On the last day of bridge repair only thirty-two people lined up for work. As I had been determined to be at the front line in the march, I was also determined to be in on the finish of the detail; I was determined to live.

While we were at the bridge, one of our fellows got caught trading with a Filipino over the fence. The Japs tied him to a post in front of the building and left him there for several days. I worried about him so much. When we came back from work one day he was gone. I didn't know what had happened to him and was afraid to ask. I didn't want to hear of any more beatings and stabbings and shootings. It was many years later at an Ex-Prisoner of War Convention that I saw this fellow, alive and well.

The schoolhouse barracks at Gapan were a few blocks from the cemetery. I remember watching Filipino funeral processions during the time I was on the timber cutting job inside the town. The hearses were all horse-drawn and followed by a marching band, with a procession of mourners on foot following the hearse. In contrast to our mournful funeral music, the Filipinos sent a departed soul on his journey with lively, spirited music, such as one I recognized: *Beer*

Barrel Polka.

When we were helping cut the timbers for the bridge at the measuring platform, we had to go through the residential section of town in order to get from the schoolhouse which was our barracks to the other schoolhouse which was used as Japanese headquarters and work area. After about a week, as we were trudging home after a day at our slave labor, we saw a young Filipino man, not much more than a boy, practicing his trumpet, warming up, "getting his lip." One of the group shouted out, "Hey, can you play *St. Louis Blues?*"

St. Louis Blues was composed around the turn of the century by William Christopher Handy, a black man from Alabama. He started a new style of writing music, using the 'blues' songs of the Negro bemoaning his sorrow, and adding the syncopation of ragtime and the rhythm of the tango. The bands added the piano, trumpet, drums and came up with a pure American style, 'jazz.' It was and still is very popular with our generation, played on the trumpet, as 'Satchmo' Louis (Louie) Armstrong did it.

Oh, boy! The young Filipino man "cut down" on that and old Satchmo himself never played it better. It made chills run up and down my spine. I could hardly keep from crying as I thought of my Allen cousins who lived in the hills of Missouri, not far from St. Louis. From then on, every afternoon, as we walked toward our barracks, dreading another meal of rice and another night on a hard floor, this young man would watch for us. As soon as he saw us, he'd play his trumpet. *St. Louis Blues*, with all the pathos and brassiness possible, would follow us into the dark night.

There is one other thing I can remember without bitterness. When I was no longer on the timber detail and could no longer hear the young man with the trumpet, I could still see the beautiful sunsets. I'd shut my eyes so others could not see my tears, because I couldn't understand how the sunset could still be so beautiful in this hell we were living. There it was, the whole spectrum of eternity, heaven and hell, and for us no in-between.

We weren't so proud of this bridge as the British officers in the film, *Bridge Over the River Kwai*. Much of the work we did on this bridge was done in the same way it was done in the film. We didn't try to sabotage the bridge; we weren't given any opportunity to try. The Japanese engineers and guards never left us alone. And it's just as well we didn't weaken it. We, those of us surviving this ordeal, were loaded into trucks as the barriers of the bridge were removed and were the first to cross. We held our breath and crossed our fingers as we went over the bridge, hoping it would hold. Quite frankly, we weren't sure it would. Then, as we cleared the bridge, one bitter corporal spoke the sentiment of all one hundred forty-eight survivors, "Now, fall, damn you!"

CHAPTER 11

CAMP CABANATUAN

It was toward the last of July, 1942 that we were again loaded into trucks, transported across the bridge we'd repaired and taken "home." While I was there, working on the bridge, I wore out my coveralls, the ones I'd worn since the march began. Then I got a pair of khaki pants and shirt that had belonged to a boy who'd died. Now the shirt, from wear and tear, had been discarded, and the pants had worn out at the knees. I cut them off, making shorts. I'd lost my helmet after I got to O'Donnell, so my worldly possessions consisted of one pair of cutoff pants, worn-out shoes, a shelter half, a sardine can and my Bible. That was what I was taking back with me to O'Donnell.

But we didn't return to O'Donnell, for in the fifty-two days we were gone, the camp had moved to Cabanatuan, which is a few miles from Gapan. So "home" became an old Filipino army camp near the city of Cabanatuan. This must have been the largest Japanese POW camp, for it was divided into Camps One, Two and Three. I was in Camp One. When we were reassigned on returning from bridge detail, the group was, for the most part, the same men we'd been with at O'Donnell.

Our fifty-two days of labor earned us no points when we returned to camp. We were not allowed time to rest and recuperate. The very next day I was assigned to grass-cutting duty. I was handed a hooked bill knife and put in tall grass somewhat like our Johnson grass. It was hot out there in the sun, with no shirt to cover my tender skin, which was already blistered and dried by exposure during the bridge detail. In the tall grass almost no air could reach us.

Problems started then that I still have to contend with over a half century later. Large blisters formed on my legs and arms. I thought it was sunburn but the camp doctor said it was pellagra. Pellagra can be brought on by a monotonous diet, such as white rice. It causes rough, thickened blister-like lesions. It can show up on the hands, feet, face, even sometimes in the mouth and on the tongue.

The grass I was cutting was tough and tall and had to be cut from the fence, the Japanese explained, for security purposes. There had been rumors of escapes and attempted escapes aided by friendly Filipinos. This tall grass made excellent cover. I dare say more of us would have taken advantage of the situation if we hadn't been well aware that we'd been abandoned to our fate, with no hope of getting off the island.

During the time I was on grass detail, I cut the grass that grew inside the fence. This particular spot was within the hospital area. When we took a water break, I went into the hospital to see if I could find some of the friends I'd not been able to locate after I returned from Gapan. There in the hospital I found Clifton Cochran. When I approached his cot he looked up at me and smiled. He was so weak he could barely talk, so thin he was almost a skeleton. We talked for a few minutes. Big tears rolled down his cheeks, and he said, "Don't go off and leave me." I nodded, trying to comfort him, knowing all the time that if I didn't get back before the guard missed me I'd be done for. I stayed, though, until he dropped off to sleep. I guess he was asleep; he may have gone into a coma, or he may have ... I don't know. I do know that the next morning the roster reported that I had lost a dear friend.

I'd lost Cochran, but where were the others? During the time I was cutting weeds in the hospital area, I made repeated short trips in there, trying to find them. One day I found Alexander. "Hey, Booger Red! How you doin', fellow?" Same old Alexander, still the big brother.

"Oh, pretty good. I'm not in here," I answered, joking. We chatted as long as I could stay. I learned later he was paralyzed, unable to walk, yet he didn't mention it to me, just pretended it was only a matter of a few days till he'd be out there swinging the scythe with me. In less than a week we lost Alexander.

I also tried to find my friends Milton and Fisher. I'd not seen them since before the march started. I never did find them. I heard from various sources that they both died while on duty detail. One thing I heard saddened me greatly. I was told that Capt. Kelly died in Cabanatuan. However, I learned later that he died on a prison ship leaving the Philippine Islands. I get angry when I think of it; for all the problems he caused me, I still think he was one of the best friends I had there or ever had. He deserved better than this. They all deserved better than this.

I'd been on the grass-cutting job for several days when I came down with malaria. This was my first experience with it. How fortunate I'd been, how very, very fortunate. I'd gotten through four months of fighting on the front line, through the hell of the march, through O'Donnell and the bridge detail, only to be felled by some tall grass. It was during the night after I saw Alexander that I came down with chills and fever. I wondered guiltily if my bantering words were being brought home to me. The next morning I couldn't eat. This was the first time this had happened since the seasickness on board the ship that had brought us here (how many lifetimes ago that seemed!). And I knew very well that the inability to eat or retain food was the first step toward death.

After the other men had gone out on their different jobs, I crept over to the hospital area to get help. The chills and fever would be gone each day by the time I saw the doctor. That's the peculiarity of malaria. Chills and fever come in waves, in cycles, and if, even in lab tests, it isn't caught during a peak of this occurrence, it's almost impossible to detect.

This continued for five days. Chills and fever at night. Inability to eat at anytime. Sick call every morning and no help. I was getting weaker every day, and on the fifth day I barely made it off my bunk and down to the dispensary. While waiting, I blacked out. When I regained consciousness, I was sitting in a chair with the doctor standing over me.

"Boy, what happened?"

"I'm sick."

"Yes, I can see that. But there's not a thing in the world I can do for you. I don't have any medicine."

No medicine. I had malaria and no medicine. No quinine. What was I to do? I might as well join Alexander. He'd get a good laugh at my expense, wouldn't he? Well, we'd laughed together and we'd die together.

The doctor patted me on the back, shook his head and left the room as if no longer able to stand the sight of young men dying when he could save them with a few bottles of medicine. I was staggering to my feet to leave when I heard a voice.

"Red."

I turned and through the haziness saw a young soldier, a corpsman who had been standing in the background. I recognized him; his name was Black. We'd known each other on the front line and had become pretty good friends. "Red," he said quietly, and motioned for me to follow him. He went into a small room in the back of the dispensary, where he bunked. "Come back here, I want to talk to you." We went in and he closed the door. He reached into a cabinet and pulled out a medical pouch which he opened. I could see that it was full of capsules. "I've got enough quinine here," he said," to give each man one dose. That wouldn't do anybody any good. It would be a waste. I'm going to give you twelve capsules. Take one a day for twelve days. And for goodness sake, keep this to yourself. Don't tell a soul. Not anybody! If it is known that you have these and where they came from, we could get killed for them."

I promised him faithfully I'd keep them well concealed and not let anybody know about them. I kept my word. After taking one capsule a day for about three days I began to feel better and could eat again. Then I went back to the grass cutting, but continued to take the quinine capsules. After being back at work only a few days, I had dysentery again. Oh, was I sick. But sick or not, I cut grass.

Another drama unfolded here that I didn't fully learn about until years later. I was pulled off the grass-cutting detail one afternoon just before I was assigned to wood-cutting detail, to help move a guard tower on the hospital side of camp. We had stopped to rest and someone told me there was a fellow across the fence in the hospital area who was trying to get my attention. I saw it was my old friend John "Peapicker" Owens, the boy from home I'd met on the water line the first day at O'Donnell. I couldn't talk to him then as we were ordered to move on, but I could tell from what I heard that he was so angry he could do nothing but swear. It was years later that he told me I had saved his life. "What do you mean?" I was astonished.

"Well, you did," he grinned and told me this story. "You were helping move a guard tower in the hospital area." Yes, I remembered that. "I was in the hospital sick as I could be with malaria and dysentery and everything else I could pick up in the Philippine swamps," Owens continued. "And I decided if I was going to die, I would just go out and die by myself. While I was there I saw you standing by this tower. I tried to call you, but I wasn't very loud. You didn't pay me any attention. Well, I got so damned mad at you because you wouldn't answer me, I lay there and decided that if I had enough strength to get that mad, I wasn't as near death as I thought."

Owens had lived; he had been sent to Japan where he spent three years in a prisoner of war camp. He never recovered his health and always looked as thin and gaunt as he did then, but remained active until his death a few years ago.

We had saved a few sacks of flour that had been provided to

those of us on the bridge detail. It was used to make gravy for our rice. We took it to the kitchen in Cabanatuan. At the bridge we were feeding one hundred fifty men; at Cabanatuan we were feeding several thousand. It was obvious the flour wouldn't go very far.

One day, when I had come in for the noon bowl of rice, I was expecting to have sauce to go with the rice, but it wasn't ready. I'd thought all morning about that ladle of brown gravy. I was mouthing off to one of my buddies in line, complaining about how we go out and work and slave and bring food in and then we don't even get to partake of it; it all goes to somebody else, and on and on. Just as I turned a corner to go into the mess hall, a major was standing there. "Soldier, do you know who you are talking to?"

I said, "No, Sir." The truth of the matter was, I had been talking to my friend, not him. I didn't even know he was there.

"I'm Major So-and-So from West Point."

"And I'm Private Oliver Allen from Paris Junior College." We all go a little crazy sometime, and that was my time. Oh, it made him angry!

"Give me your name, rank and serial number; I'm having you court-martialed."

Now if that had been Capt. Kelly I wouldn't have worried about it for a minute. But this was somebody new, and I didn't know how many times he might have been whacked over the head with a saber, or how mad he was at the world. Fortunately for me, he must have thought better of it as I never saw him nor heard from him again.

The sergeant in charge of barracks asked me if I'd consider going over to the Japanese side on wood-cutting detail, cutting wood for their kitchen stoves. I'd split plenty of wood for Mama's cook stove; I figured I could handle it. "You go outside in the morning, cut whatever wood they assign, and come back at noon to eat," I was told. "Then go back out in the afternoon to cut wood for their evening meal, and then come back to your evening rice and go to bed."

There were two of us assigned to this task, and it really wasn't a bad detail. We got an extra bun for working outside the camp. I'm not sure why. The work was no harder; perhaps it was because we were deeper into enemy territory. Or perhaps this was a way to pay us for our slave labor, in case they were held to account.

A severe diphtheria epidemic had recently hit our camp, and many men were hospitalized and several died. Naturally, we were all apprehensive about it. I'd been on the wood-cutting detail only a few days when I awoke during the night with a severe sore throat. Panic swept over me; this was it! This was exactly the way the others had started. Forty-eight hours, that's what they said. Forty-eight hours one way or the other. You could survive, we were told. So far, no one had returned to barracks, but then, it really hadn't been going on very long ...

I got up from my bunk and went over to the man in charge of quarters and talked to him. Well, there wasn't much talk; my throat hurt too much. Then I paced the floor. Forty-eight hours ... Well, I wasn't going back to sleep. If I had only forty-eight hours I wasn't going to sleep any of it away. When morning came I'd make sick call. Maybe they'd have gotten in some medicine; maybe it wasn't as bad as they said; maybe ... At least I'd be with somebody.

I walked for hours, up and down, trying not to wake the others, trying to tell myself my throat was better, though I knew it wasn't. Finally, after hours of pacing, I was so exhausted I decided to rest just a minute. I'd lie down and rest just ...

Whenever I woke the next morning the officer in charge, a U. S. Army captain, was standing over me, red in the face, furious, saying things I preferred not to hear. The others had risen and gone about their duties. I had missed roll call. I guess the Japs must have worked him over, as he was working me over. All the time I was trying to get my bunk made and stand at attention he was yelling at me, telling me I was no good, that he ought to turn me in to the Japanese, that he ought to have me court-martialed for dereliction of duty.

On and on. All the time I was saying, "Yes, Sir. Yes, Sir. Yes, Sir." I was standing stiffly at attention, yet he was getting madder. I couldn't understand it. Then I realized I was looking straight at him with a big smile on my face. He thought I was either being insubordinate or had gone mad, but I was happy, for I'd discovered my sore throat was gone and I didn't have diphtheria after all!

There's no need to say I wasn't worried. If the captain decided to press charges, he could. I'd been threatened with court-martial before, by Capt. Kelly and the West Point major. But I thought the officer was making much ado about nothing. We were all together in this, just trying to survive.

Two days later when morning came we fell out, counted off, and Sgt. "Skinny" Ervin called roll. When I came in for my food at noon that day, someone said, "Red, you remember the captain who reamed you out a couple of days ago for missing roll call? They found him in his bunk. Dead. Looks like he died of diphtheria."

Wood-cutting lasted about six weeks. During this time there were some escapes and attempted escapes. As some of us were going outside our camp to work, the Filipino guerrillas were becoming more active in this area. I know we all thought about it and talked about it and even made little plans to join the guerrillas, but we had to face reality. The Jap guards gave us little opportunity to attempt escape.

During this time another group went on a bridge building detail. They, like us, were housed in an abandoned school building near the river where they were working. One night a group of Filipino guerrillas came into camp, killed the Japanese guards and tried to persuade the American prisoners to escape. Most of the men were too sick to go into the jungle, so those able to go refused to leave them as they knew those left behind would be punished. Except one. One man went with the guerrillas. As a result the Japs shot ten men, five on each side of the one who'd escaped. (They'd been given numbers.) One man saw his twin brother shot.

This escape was the reason we were all called together after work one evening and told that we'd been divided into groups of ten men. Every man was responsible for every other man in his group, and if any one man attempted escape, or showed any inclination to cause trouble, the other nine would suffer whatever punishment was meted out to the offender. If any man escaped, the men in his group would pay the penalty—meaning they would be shot.

Needless to say, this caused unrest and a great deal of uneasiness, as there were others like me who were working outside, going on work details, sometimes into barrios, hauling supplies, etc. Our chances for escape were better than those who remained inside.

In this situation I was fortunate again. When all the men in our barracks were counted out in tens, there were two left over. Sgt. Ervin, our barracks leader, said, "Allen, we'll be in the small group. You watch me and I'll watch you." That was fine. Sgt. Ervin was one of the old soldiers. He was in bad shape and couldn't have survived in the jungle if he'd been able to get there.

Grass- and wood-cutting lasted from the middle of July until the end of September. I'd gone through one touch of malaria, a couple rounds of dysentery and the diphtheria scare. But, all in all, I was doing as well as, perhaps better than, most of the prisoners. I had decided from the first I'd survive.

TOTORA MARU

In October 1942, we were all ordered out of the barracks and marched to a rail station, located somewhere in the Cabanatuan area. They put us into boxcars and shipped us to Manila. From the railroad there they herded us into trucks and took us to the dock area.

I remember getting into Manila that night. We were taken to Pier 7, the same pier where we'd landed in the Philippines almost a year ago. It was the seventh of October, 1942.

From the truck we moved into an old terminal. It was no longer in use, having been bombed and shot up during the fighting. We lay down on the floor to try to sleep, not knowing where we were going, or, for that matter, if we were going anywhere at all. After we'd settled down for the night, the guards brought in buckets of dried fish and put them on the floor, where we could get to them. This was the first food we'd seen since we left Cabanatuan, and I knew I could eat it. I'd done it before.

I ate it, all I could get, because I'd learned from the beginning: eat all you can get when you get it, because you can never be sure when, or if, there'll be more.

The next day we were moved out of the terminal shell and put aboard a ship, the *Totora Maru*. The ship that took us off the islands has been called a "hell ship." There were other hell ships; this was not the only one. The temperature in the hold was oven hot. The men around me were becoming nauseated from the heat and vomiting. Some were glassy-eyed and passing out. My second attack of malaria came upon me, and I began to have a chill. As soon as the chill passed I made my way up to the deck. I figured if I was where I wasn't supposed to be, and got pushed around and maybe shot, I would be no worse off than I was going to be if I didn't get some help soon. The ship was preparing to steam out of port when I found an American doctor.

"I'm in terrible shape, Sir. Isn't there anything at all you've got for me to take?"

"Private, when I came on board this ship I had nothing, but just a few minutes ago a Japanese doctor gave me a gallon jug of liquid quinine. It's a terrible dose, but if you think you can swallow it, I'll give you a bottle full. Take one swallow each morning as long as it lasts. I'll give you enough for about ten days."

Feeling that once again I was most fortunate, I went immediately and drank a swallow from the bottle. Anyone who's never tasted liquid quinine doesn't know what bitterness is. It locks the jaws. On the second day I took another big swallow, and on the third day

I missed my round of chills and fever. I continued to take the life-saving doses as long as they lasted.

We were aboard the ship for thirty-three days. Thirty-three days, coming in and going out of ports, much of it while bobbing up and down on the rough seas like a cork. We didn't know where we were going. In fact, much of the time we didn't know where we'd been. It is possible the ship was heading for Korea when we left Manila and roamed around trying to avoid American ships and submarines. Or perhaps they were awaiting orders. Heaven only knows. We were somewhere in the China Sea, and I know we went in and out of Formosa several times.

Dysentery hit us hard and sanitary conditions were primitive. Our toilet consisted of a set of planks hanging out over the ship, on which we squatted, letting the waste go into the sea. There were no bathing facilities. The only water we saw was what we drank and the ocean.

We developed scurvy, a dietary disease brought on by lack of vitamin C, which causes a rawness in the mouth. For the first nine days we were fed one sack of hardtack a day. Every morning we were given a cloth sack containing a dozen of these. Hardtack is a very hard cracker; the men couldn't eat them.

One of my friends, one who had been on the bridge detail when the men were shot and who was in the 19th Bomb Group with me, had given a Japanese guard five pesos to get him something to eat. The guard brought him a five-pound can of oleomargarine. The friend told me he'd share it with me if I'd help him take care of it. When he had to go topside and couldn't hold it, I did. The first nine days he and I had all the hardtack we could eat. The men with scurvy gave theirs away, and with all the margarine, we did better than most.

After the ninth day we began to get small portions of rice, occasionally with sauce or a vegetable once a day. The men began to eat better and gain a little strength.

I was bunking just below top deck, and there was another deck below us. I never went down there, so I can't tell of it first-hand, but the reports made me glad I wasn't there. It was bad enough where I was. The heat was suffocating. Our "bunk" was a thin piece of bamboo matting on the floor, and these mats were so full of lice we couldn't sleep. They crawled all over us in the daytime and bit us at night. We continued to be sick with malaria. Everyone on board took a fresh case of dysentery after a man tossed his messed-up pants on top of the drinking water tank and they fell into the water.

We weren't part of a convoy and had no escort as we left Formosa the last time. We'd sailed onto the high seas when suddenly we heard a commotion above us and heard men yelling for life preservers. We rushed up as fast as a group of sick emaciated men could rush, to see two torpedoes heading for us broadside. The Japanese skipper was older and evidently experienced and on his toes. He maneuvered the ship, swinging it around expertly, and the torpedoes skimmed by, just missing us.

After thirty-three days, we reached our destination. On or near the ninth day of November 1942, we landed at Pusan, Korea.

CHAPTER 12

PRISONER OF WAR IN MANCHURIA—
MUKDEN AND MKK

Early November 1942, Pusan, Korea. Snow had already fallen there, and we disembarked and lined up on the dock in a howling wind. Since a pair of shorts was the only clothing I had, I wrapped my shelter half around me for protection. We stood there, lined up, shivering, not knowing our destination. "Join the army and see the world." I don't think this was what they had in mind.

We'd been on the dock perhaps five minutes when army trucks pulled up beside us and Jap soldiers began to throw down big straw bundles. Straw. What in the world for? Then they cut these straw bundles open, and we could see heavy fur-lined clothing: caps, coats, shoes, overcoats. Heavy underwear and socks, heavy uniforms. Brand new clothing. Unbelievable. We knew this must be a joke. They'd taunt us and then take them away.

No. We were all outfitted in these warm clothes and put aboard a train. No, not a boxcar or cattle car, but second class seats in a heated train. And given food. Not hardtack or dried fish, but three meals a day of rice and vegetables in lunch boxes that guards brought aboard at intervals at stations along the way.

On November 11, 1942, we ended our trip. We were now at the

place where we would spend nearly three years. The train stopped at Mukden, Manchuria (the Japanese called it Hoten, Manchukuo), a place I'd never heard of before. This was a large industrial city, and a large railway center, a city of a million population, south of Harbin. We saw little of Mukden while we were prisoners, but later learned it supported an aircraft factory, munitions and arms factories, several textile mills, canneries, breweries, saw mills, furniture factories, a foundry, as well as the machine tool factory where we worked.

We were ordered off the train and marched three miles out of town to an old Chinese army camp, which was a sort of dugout. It was built half in the ground and half above ground. We stayed here nine months before we were moved to a new camp. The dugout buildings were warmer than buildings above ground, and this helped because we had very little heat in the barracks.

Our fur-lined caps were the first to go. Some man wasn't wearing his, so the Japs said if we weren't going to make use of them we didn't need them, and they took them all. Next it was the coats; they gave some reason. They didn't really need reasons; they could take them whenever they wished. And they did. Before winter was gone, all our warm clothes had been taken away on one pretext or another. The fur-lined clothing was, in all probability, given to their own troops.

In place of the fur-lined coat, I was issued a trench coat, a light wool coat big enough to go over a back pack. Since I didn't have a pack, I could wrap up in mine. Much later, before we were liberated, I got a heavy wool coat that had been sent in by the Red Cross.

Our camp, the "old camp" we came to call it, was within two hundred yards of the Trans-Siberian Railway, with trains whistling through at all hours of the day and night, going from Mukden to Harbin to Vladivostok. I remember very clearly the steam rising from the engine, and the sound of the wheels on the rails.

A barbed wire fence encircled the entire camp, with another wire, a single wire, inside that. A single wire seems harmless enough, but it was the cause of death of at least one man. He innocently hung a blanket on it to air and was beaten so severely that he died. The Japanese said he was attempting to escape. After that a rope was stretched inside the single barbed wire. The penalty for crossing the rope was death.

Life in camp was routine in that we still had work details. Coal duty was my first one, bringing coal to the barracks, but mainly to the kitchen. I was on this detail with Nick Carter of Arkansas. Then there was the food detail, carrying food from the warehouse to the kitchen. It also meant going through potatoes and picking out the ones that were rotting. No, we didn't throw them away; they were the ones we cooked.

Then we began to be called out for what we thought was the purpose of our being there: free labor. In recent years we have learned that there may have been a different reason.

Ford Motor Company had built an assembly plant in Mukden. The Japanese had taken it over when they overran Manchuria. This was called MKK. I never did know what the letters stood for. We thought we were there for the purpose of converting the plant to a machine tool factory—setting up equipment and then running the factory after its completion.[1]

In addition to this being a factory, it was also a trade school for Japanese and Manchurian boys. They looked to be about twelve years old when they came. It must have been at least a four-year program of apprenticeship, as all the youngsters who came there about the same time we did were still there when we left three years later. These boys attended classes in the mornings and had on-the-job training in the afternoons.

From the dugout camp to the factory was three miles. We walked there each morning, often in weather forty degrees below zero, then back in the afternoon. We ate breakfast at camp and mid-day meals at the factory. The evening meal was ready when we walked back at the end of the day.

My first weeks at the factory were spent in helping set up machines and tool equipment in the lathe department. Into this area came a group of newly-arrived Japanese boys. When they first began their apprenticeship, they were given a hammer and a piece of scrap metal, about a half-inch thick, two inches wide and three inches long, one that would fit into a vise. They spent the afternoons hammering metal. I suppose they were learning to use the hammer. After a few afternoons we were ready to swear it was designed as torture for the prisoners of war: bang, bang, bang, hammer on metal, all afternoon by thirty Japanese boys. It was equal to Chinese water torture.

The boys were cruel to us at first. They followed the example of the Japanese soldiers we had met on the march. They threw rocks at us, spat on us, called us names we couldn't understand but didn't have to guess the meanings. We ignored their insults as much as possible, and it wasn't long before the kids began to make overtures of friendship, once they saw we weren't ogres. They were allowed a day off once a week and could go into town. Once, after they came in from their weekly outings, one boy brought me a little bit of candy. It wasn't long until we became quite attached to the youngsters. They, too, were away from home and lonely and needed a kind word and a smile every now and then. When I was reassigned, I missed the contact with the youngsters, the humanity they displayed.

The MKK was made up of four large factory buildings, and each building had four large overhead cranes, thirty feet wide, which ran the length of the building. After we had finished setting up the lathes in the building where the Japanese and Manchurian boys plied their hammers, we moved to another one. In this one we poured an entire floor, a concrete slab about four inches thick. We worked on one large section for several days. We weren't allowed to do the finish work; all we could do was the carrying, mixing, hauling and dumping, much as we'd done on the Penaranda River bridge. We poured this large section; the finishers had smoothed it off; and we left it to return to the camp. During the night the heat in the factory went off, and in that frigid climate it didn't take long for the concrete to freeze. During the next few days we had to break it up, chip it out in pieces, haul it out and start over. We didn't grieve over it. Anything that delayed the operation of the factory hindered the Japanese.

Into this same floor we had to cut a hole for a planing machine. It was a monster, this machine was. The foundation we had to build was supposed to be seventy-five feet long, fifteen feet wide and about ten feet deep, solid concrete. It was this foundation that we later looked upon with pride as our greatest achievement. Of sabotage.

It took several days to pour this concrete as it was being done by hand. Each day when the Jap guards and workers went to lunch (they always ate first) we were left with one guard to a section. It was no trouble at all for one, or several, of us to distract the guard. Being taller than the Japanese, we could just stand between him and what our men were doing. We were methodically gathering up everything loose and heavy enough to sink into the soft concrete that we had just poured, and dumping it in. Our problem was to be sure that it all sank out of sight. We gathered hammers, chisels, even picks and shovels, if we could pitch them in with something that would keep the wooden handles down. If one person couldn't lift something, like a lathe, he found three or four guys willing to help. We even used the overhead crane once to lift a huge lathe into the concrete. We were taking a chance on getting caught. Fortunately, this never happened. I'm sure the Japanese suspected, but how could they prove anything without tearing up the concrete? I feel reasonably sure the MKK plant in Mukden, Manchuria, if it still exists and anyone is curious enough to investigate, is the most expensively reinforced piece of concrete in the world.

This was not our only bit of sabotage. Anything that would hinder or slow down a Jap project, we did, if we could be reasonably sure of not getting caught red-handed. One example was the rock detail to which I was assigned. There was a huge pile of stone and broken boulders between two of the buildings. Each stone was so

large it was all one man could do to handle it. I never learned why
the rocks were there, where they came from or why we had to move
them. But move them we did. The Japanese built a narrow gauge rail
track and provided two flatbed dollies. We loaded the beds as full of
rocks as we could and still push them and started out. There were
eight or ten men to each flat car. As the track ran from between the
buildings, it made a sharp left turn. The first day we'd loaded and
made a couple of successful trips, but on the third trip, as we round-
ed the turn, we were traveling too fast, and the car accidentally
jumped off the track and fell over on its side, spilling the contents. I
guess the idea flashed into all our heads at the same time; we looked
at each other in agreement. The men in the car behind us saw the
situation and caught on quickly.

We righted the flat car and put it back on the track, and slowly
and laboriously replaced the fallen rocks. The guards grew impatient
with our slowness and ordered the men with the second car to help
us. They'd had to stop, of course, and wait until we got out of the
way. They were lounging on the ground and resting. "No," they shook
their heads indignantly. "They spilled it. They pick it up."

About two hours later, the second group took the first car, and,
after having experimented on the previous loads, knew exactly how
fast to go, and at what angle to start shoving. What a shame! They
spilled theirs, too. We sat down to wait for them to reload. No, we
wouldn't help them; they hadn't helped us. The entire thing, the
loading, the trip, the unloading, took an hour. We managed to get one
good rest in the morning and one in the afternoon.

We varied our method to delay suspicion. Sometimes the second
car would jump. This meant the first car would go to the dump,
unload their rocks, and return, but then it couldn't get past the overturned car. They'd wait until we reloaded, then turn around and push
their empty flat car back to the dump with us.

I learned later that as time went on and the rock pile grew
higher, the men had to go up a rise and down the other side. Work-

ing outside in the winter in Manchuria is hell frozen over. So, for an occasional rest in the sun, protected from the north wind, away from the eyes of the guards, the trips began to take longer and longer.

I say I learned this, because by that time I was no longer with them. One day a runner had come saying I was wanted in the factory headquarters. The guys were worried as they watched me go, for whatever I was guilty of, they were also. We couldn't understand why I was picked out from the rest. I always figured my red hair and freckles were the cause of a lot of my troubles. I'd been told early on that the Japanese were especially cruel to redheads.

I walked toward the building, trembling. Well, I thought, I was living on borrowed time, anyway. There were several times in the past year I should have "got it." After all, a man's luck is bound to run out sooner or later. I stood before the factory manager and waited. He peered at me through round spectacles as he talked with the aid of an interpreter.

"The Manager says he has been observing your work."

Uh oh. My heart stopped beating and my knees shook. Was it the lathe I'd thrown into the concrete, or had I been seen shoving the dolly?

"The Manager says he is pleased with your work and you are assigned to the kitchen."

I was so braced for the ax to fall I didn't comprehend. I just stood there, I'm sure, with a stunned look on my face.

The manager uttered a loud harsh remark and the interpreter said, "The Manager says to quit standing there like a blockhead and report to the kitchen immediately."

I was moving before he stopped speaking, for reason had returned and I was jubilant. The kitchen! The plum of assignments. To be where the food was! And where it was warm!

CHAPTER 13

TRAGEDY

The factory was warmer than the barracks; we could stop our shivering for awhile during the day and get some feeling into our extremities. But when I went to work in the kitchen I felt I'd gone to heaven. It was so warm and steamy and comfortable. And that's where the food was.

It was well over a year before I learned that I had gotten the job in the factory kitchen by accident. A man who worked in the kitchen had promised his friend that when a space was vacant, he'd recommend him. When they sent for number 361 they got number 362 by mistake. Me. Number 361 was Wayne Herbert who bunked next to me. He was my friend and didn't tell me I had his job.

Herbert worked in the bus section, which housed several wood-burning buses. Each bus had a burner on the back in which were burned small blocks of wood. They would get these blocks burning, then cap off the burners. They used a bellows much like a blacksmith's bellows to get the fire going. A peck of wood produced about fifteen miles of power. The driver would "fill his tank" by throwing on three or four sacks of wood blocks when he took off on a run.

These buses were used mainly to transport civilians who worked in the factory. The Japanese and Chinese workers who lived in Mukden were picked up and brought to MKK to work each morning and taken home after work in the afternoon.

It was the duty of the American prisoners of war to chop strips of wood into small blocks to burn in these buses and to see to their upkeep generally.

Through the nearly three years we were in Mukden, many things happened, mostly bad things, tragic things. Not only to us prisoners, but to others as well. The building that housed the buses was also where the wood was supposed to be made into charcoal. The wood was usually used without charring, as this process took too long. These blocks of wood produced more smoke and ash than charcoal would have, so charcoal was preferred.

This bus house, or garage, was near the factory kitchen where I was working. The factory president was the only one who rated a gasoline-propelled vehicle, so there was a fifty-gallon drum that held the fuel that was used in his car.

Early one afternoon, the American prisoners who worked there were outside the barn, rounding up wood to chop into blocks as fuel for the buses. There was one American left in the garage, when a Japanese electrician, with six Japanese boys who were his apprentices, went into the building.

It was midwinter, and the building was cold inside. The man found a smudge pot and put some small scraps of wood in it and lit it in order to get warm. It smoldered a bit but wasn't putting out enough heat to suit him. He hovered over it, trying to warm himself. Impatient, he tipped the fifty-gallon drum of gasoline over the smudge pot.

As soon as the gasoline touched the spark it ignited. The barrel blew up with an explosion that shook our windows. The American prisoner had seen the Jap trying to tip the gasoline and had started for the door. He didn't make it and was blown through a window. He was scratched and bruised but suffered no serious injuries.

The Japanese man was burned to death, and the boys were aflame all over. The kitchen staff ran outside at the sound of the explosion and began grabbing boys to extinguish the flames. I took my overcoat and wrapped one boy in it, then doused him in a wooden barrel full of water which was just outside the kitchen door to use in case of fire.

As I ran for the first aid section, the little fellow reached up and lifted the skin which had fallen from his brow over his eyes. He looked me straight in the eyes, then dropped the skin back again. It was several weeks before he came back, all scarred and sick-looking. He sought me out and smiled at me in recognition. From then on I was his good friend.

Later, the factory president, in the presence of Colonel Matsuda, the camp commander, presented six of us with citations and a carton of cigarettes each, for our actions. Nearly thirty years later I got a call from a man who, on Sabbatical, was in Paris, Texas, to hold services in one of our local churches. When my wife and I went to their hotel to meet them, I walked in and recognized his face immediately, though I'd never known his name. He was one of the six POWs who'd helped save the boys. So I had a reunion with Leslie Funk, who with his wife had returned to the Philippines as missionaries.

WE LEARN TO COUNT

There were several Japanese officers assigned to our camp who reported to Col. Matsuda. One of these was Capt. Ishitawa. He was one of the meanest officers in our camp and the sloppiest in looks. He was the embodiment of all the propaganda pictures seen during WWII. He was short and fat, and his saber lacked a couple of inches dragging the ground when he walked. But he sure knew how to use the weapon. He would work us over with his saber, still sheathed in the scabbard. It wouldn't cut, but it sure hurt. When he talked, he bellowed like a bull, so we called him "The Bull." When The Bull was on duty, which was every sixth day for a twenty-four hour hitch, we knew things were going to be bad and we weren't going to get much rest that night.

One incident occurred at the factory at the end of a day. Our procedure was to come in the main gate at the end of the day, line up and count off to ensure all were present and accounted for. Then the head honcho would report to the Jap officer of the day and we would be marched to the searching line, after which we could be dismissed for the evening "meal." On this particular day the officer in charge was Capt. Ishitawa, The Bull. As we lined up and were counting off, he screamed something in Japanese. We couldn't understand, so we stopped. Ishitawa bellowed again, then yelled for the interpreter. The interpreter came running, and after hurriedly conferring with Ishitawa, said, "Capt. Ishitawa said you will count off in Japanese."

The American in charge said, "Tell Capt. Ishitawa we don't know Japanese."

Ishitawa bellowed, "You will learn Japanese." So, The Bull walked up and down the ranks, yelling out numbers in Japanese; we'd repeat it. Then he'd start at the beginning, and we'd count off in Japanese until some poor soul didn't know his number, and Ishitawa would give him a good whack over the head with the saber and scream the number. Then we'd start the count all over again. Maybe we'd get to twelve or fourteen before someone forgot and we'd have to start again.

This started about six o'clock in the evening. It was ten o'clock that night before we quit standing in the snow, counting off in Japanese and getting hit over the head with a sheathed saber. We finally went inside when Ishitawa himself got so cold he couldn't get in a good whack anymore.

Nothing we did in camp ever satisfied him, and he had many ways of letting us know. One night in my bay, or barrack section, The Bull found some salt one of the prisoners had brought into barracks, and he got every one of us out of bed, about thirty of us in all, and lined us up around the room. He slapped the first man in line and made him pass it on. If one of us didn't slap his neighbor hard enough, The Bull would slap him the way he wanted it to be passed on.

He would make us double time around the camp for nothing at all, do push-ups until we couldn't do any more and stand at attention for hours. Almost every night that he was on duty he would come through the barracks about one a.m., bellow for everyone to get up for roll call and make us count off in Japanese.

One night he lined us up, stood in front of one man and jabbered something. The man answered, "Yes, Sir." The Bull knocked him down, and when he got up Ishitawa jabbered again. The fellow said, "Yes, Sir," again, and down he went again. This went on several times, until the sergeant told the poor prisoner, "Stay down. If you get up he will just knock you down again." The interpreter arrived soon, and to our astonishment told us The Bull wasn't saying anything at all, just making sounds.

It was something like this all the time. He left our camp about a month before the war ended. I believe it was a good thing he did.

CHAPTER 14

FOOD AND KITCHEN STORIES

I was never considered a cook in the army. My job was strictly KP, mostly washing pots and pans and mopping floors. We served only the noon meal at the factory kitchen, with the first serving being at eleven o'clock. That is when the Japanese and Chinese had their meal. (I use the words "Manchurian" and "Chinese" interchangeably, as they were Manchurian by nationality and Chinese by race.)

The Japanese ate on one side of the mess hall and the Chinese on the other. Then the Americans and other prisoners of war ate at twelve o'clock. There were British, Australian and some New Zealand prisoners, these three groups totaling perhaps two hundred.

The factory supplemented our mess, so the food we got at the factory usually had a few more ingredients in it; it was not quite as watery as the food we got at camp. The base for our food in Manchuria was not rice; it was what the Chinese called *chimbee*, which is a mixture of grains—maize, sorghum and such. It looked like what Mama fed her chickens. This made a good base for our soup, as long as we got a few vegetables to put in it. We had carrots, potatoes and Chinese cabbage. We had some eggplants but that doesn't go well in stew; we wished for oil so we could fry it.

Work in the kitchen was routine, but it was life-saving routine. We began our day rising early, dressing in the frigid barracks, eating our bowls of corn meal mush. We'd line up outside, answer roll call and begin our hike to the factory. We were cold on the hike as our fur-lined clothes had been taken away and we'd been given lighter ones. We of the kitchen staff began our work peeling and chopping vegetables.

After our day's work, the camp guards would relieve the factory guards. We'd line up and count off and start our three-mile hike back to the camp. We'd get there cold; have to line up outside the fence and count off; then march in line again through the gate into the camp compound, and count off again. Then we were dismissed to go to our barracks, where our bowl of soup was waiting. We had one scuttle of coal at night after work, but it was not enough to warm the barracks. Men working on details outside might never get warm.

PIGS

The Japanese started a pig farm. We'd been there only a few months, but it was quite evident we weren't getting all the protein we needed. I don't know whether the pig farm was the Japs' idea, or whether our adjutant asked for it as a means of supplementing our diet. The kitchen force was given the task of taking care of the pigs and the pens, in addition to our other duties. We were supposed to feed them table scraps. There was no way we could have enough scraps for that purpose, so the factory added some bran and ground corn, and we attempted to fatten the hogs.

The kitchen force was expected to take care of the pig pens and keep them clean, taking turns at this chore. One fellow, a friend of mine, was made "honcho." When it fell my turn to help and I went out to work, my friend the honcho was sitting down, issuing orders. "Start at this end, and when you finish cleaning those pens, move around to ... "

"Hold it," I interrupted, "and which ones are you cleaning?"

"Oh, none. I just see that *you* do it."

I threw down my shovel and marched back into the kitchen and told the sergeant that I refused to clean pig pens while the honcho sat on his rear, giving orders. I was asking for trouble, and I knew it. But I had to put up with enough gaff from the Japanese; I felt it was time to draw the line. To my surprise the sergeant said, "Forget it." I didn't clean a pig pen then or later, as I was never put on pig pen detail after that.

When we eventually got a hog ready to slaughter, the Americans were given the job of butchering it. The prisoners of war were entitled to the head and feet, while the Japanese would take the rest of it! The Japs complained that we cut the head too low on the shoulders. We explained to the interpreter in all innocence that this was the American way of doing it, cutting it down on the shoulders. We were ordered, quite positively, to do it the Japanese way and cut the head off right behind the ears.

So be it; we would find other ways to get food.

The American cook set up a bakery in one corner of the cook house and did baking for some of the Japanese officers who had learned to like American food. Some of them had lived in, and been educated in, the United States. The interpreter Ihara was our most valued customer. He brought in ingredients: flour, shortening, sugar, flavorings, etc. We made cakes, cookies, tea cakes, whatever we could from the ingredients he furnished. The agreement was that he would get half of the yield; we got the other half for doing the work. That was agreeable with him and it worked fine. Of course, there were twenty-seven or so of us in the kitchen and our share wasn't great. But even one cookie from a batch is better than, for instance, a dried fish.

For the reader to understand and appreciate our thoughts and actions through this entire ordeal, he or she must know this: For any man or woman who was prisoner of the Japanese, from the moment of capture to the time of freedom, life was always hanging by a thread, a very fragile thread. It took very little to antagonize some of the guards. We had no defense. Whatever came into their minds they could do. They had to answer to their superiors, of course, but we never found a Japanese officer who would punish a soldier for mistreating a prisoner of war.

Sometimes we got into precarious positions because of something someone else did. That didn't matter to the Japs. If you were in a group where one person did something to rouse the ire of the guards, all suffered. It was hard, sometimes, to think, to rationalize, to judge, as our hold on life was as a spider's web. Our first, and sometimes only, instinct was self-preservation.

SAUSAGES

I was caught up in such a situation one afternoon when ten of us from the kitchen were told to go to the warehouse and move food to the commissary where the local factory employees could go to buy food. There was a boxcar load of meat we were to move, big sausages, similar to sticks of bologna. Two men carried a big basket which was loaded with these long rolls of meat. Somehow one basket didn't get to its destination. After the detail was finished I was slipped a stick of meat with the explanation that there was one for each of us on the detail. I took it. What else could I do, give it to the Jap guard as I'd done with the hand grenade? It would have had about the same effect. Besides, there were men who could use it. Men at the camp weren't getting much to eat. To divide it between the men in the barracks would be only a bite apiece, but to us, a bite of manna. But how was I to get it back to camp? We were searched each day before we left the factory. Well, then, I'd divide it here in the kitchen.

I kept it under my coat till I got back to the kitchen. Before I went in, I slipped it under a pile of coveralls that were bound for the laundry, which were piled on a shed just outside the kitchen door. After the Japanese left and we were cleaning up, I'd bring it out.

Less than thirty minutes later a guard came through the kitchen, went straight to the laundry pile, felt under it and got the roll of meat. I was quaking in my boots and at the same time cursing myself for not obeying my own rule: have food, eat it--right then and there. I guess what stopped me was the size of the sausage. I learned that night that the guard had gone directly to all ten sausages, no hunting or searching. We now knew for certain something we'd suspected, that we had a "rat" in camp.

COOKING OIL AND MILK

Another time our efforts to find food got someone, an innocent person, in trouble. The Japanese had issued six fifty-gallon barrels of soybean cooking oil to the Jap kitchen, and lined them up against the wall. We were sharing their kitchen, though the Americans did no cooking for the Japanese, just cleaned up after them. They had their own cooks, and Wong, a good old Chinese man, was head cook.

Every day when the kitchen would get steamed up, we would siphon about ten gallons over into our cans to use to fry eggplant, potatoes and sometimes corn pone. We craved this fried food, and it was just not on our menu, according to the Japanese. Everything was going fine; nobody stopped us, until the oil ran out. Three hundred gallons of oil, used in two months. The Japanese factory manager hit the ceiling and Wong lost his job. He could have stopped us; he could have told the Japs we stole it, but he didn't. He took the blame for wasting the oil and lost the job he needed to take care of his family. Thank goodness, it wasn't but a few months after this happened that we had a chance to help him. As soon as the war ended, we sent for old Wong and returned him to his job in the kitchen. I suppose he worked for the Russians later when they took over the factory.

We took these things in order to try to stay alive. The Japanese and Chinese Manchus were getting plenty to eat in the factory mess hall. They got more and better quality food. We Americans were starving to death. Even though I worked in the kitchen and was in better health than most, I was down to ninety pounds. Many of the men were thinner than I was, gaunt to the point of being skeletal.

I dare say if we'd had even a little bit more food we'd have left the Jap food alone, but I'm not sure. They were so cruel to us; they liked to torture us, so we really looked for ways to get back at them.

There was one fellow, a Russian who had fled Russia during the revolution and had come to Manchuria. He had a dairy farm and delivered fresh milk to the factory kitchen each morning. He brought it in on his little cart in ten-gallon cans. He set the cans down in the kitchen, in a water trough to keep the milk cool. Late in the afternoon, the secretaries would come down with small containers and pick up milk for their bosses to take home.

The milk was left unattended all day, just asking to be taken. So we were taking out about a gallon a day and putting a gallon of water in its place. That went on for a while. We were never accused of taking the milk. In fact, I doubt we were ever suspected, but the Russian lost his milk contract for selling watered-down milk. We were sorry about that, but not so unhappy as when Wong lost his job.

PUMPKIN PIES

The matter of the pumpkins turned out a bit better. The Japanese got in a truck load of pumpkins for their kitchen. These were stacked just outside the Jap kitchen quarters, in plain view of our kitchen area. We decided we'd like a little pumpkin, too, so every day it was one American's job to go out to the stack and bring back to the kitchen one good-sized pumpkin, preferably without getting caught in the act. For several days I'd enjoyed the fruits of the others' crimes, and it was suddenly my turn to snatch the pumpkin. I didn't really want to, but I knew I had to, so I did. And just as I started in, I met the interpreter in the kitchen door.

"Ah," he said, looking from me to the pumpkin, "I see we're going to have pumpkin pies today."

"Yep," I said, turning fiery red. I went on in and never looked back. Fortunately, Ihara was the interpreter who'd been bringing in sugar and shortening and other ingredients to make cookies. He'd been getting his share of pumpkin pies.

Even with our scrounging and stealing (yes, stealing, and sometimes getting caught and punished for it) to try to get every bite available for the prisoners of war we fed, most of us suffered from malnutrition diseases: beriberi, scurvy, pellagra.

Beriberi, a thiamine deficiency disease of the peripheral nervous system, is characterized by partial paralysis of the extremities, emaciation and anemia. Scurvy is a disease caused by a lack of Vitamin C, causing spongy and bleeding gums, bleeding under the skin, and extreme weakness. Pellagra, a chronic disease caused by niacin deficiency, is noted for skin eruptions, digestive and nervous disruptions, and eventually, mental deterioration.

When you are as weak as we were, anything that comes along can kill—and did. Many died from malaria, dysentery (this seemed to be with us all the time), pneumonia and other things that many could have survived if they had had enough to eat and proper medication.

THE BOY AND STEW

There was one young Manchurian boy who worked at the factory that I began to notice because he sat at the table and wouldn't eat. He would push away his bowl of *chimbee* and sit there until it was time to go. He never ate and just seemed to be wasting away, so thin and pale. I knew how he felt. *Chimbee* with only a pickled vegetable as a side dish can be pretty hard to take. We cooked our food in a different way. We put it all into a stew. It was tastier that way. I began putting some of our stew into a bowl and slipping it to him. He ate that and in a few days was looking better, though still not healthy.

About that time the Japs began to find fault with things in the kitchen. They did this at different times for no reason that we could see. We had no way of knowing, since we weren't getting much news from the outside, but we thought perhaps this happened when the war was going badly for them. We told ourselves that; it made their cruelties easier to bear. The Japs had been coming down hard on us, and I was afraid that if they caught me feeding the boy I'd get into trouble, and the child would also.

So one day I didn't put the food out and one of the cooks said, "Red, your boy is waiting for his food." In a minute another said, "Allen, the kid's out there." I told them what I was afraid of, and they said to go ahead, they'd keep watch. After that he always got his food, for not only was I watching for a safe time to put his food on the table, so was the whole kitchen force.

Then one day he didn't appear. We never saw him again. We never learned whether he was moved to another place to work, or whether the youngster was seriously sick the whole time and had to be sent home. I hope our feeding him helped give him strength to handle whatever came next.

LEE AH

There were many Chinese and Manchurians working in the

Japanese kitchen, but we had little contact with them, so I don't remember them. Except one. His name was Lee Ah. He was small and had a young-looking face, so we thought of him as being younger than he was and referred to him as a boy. Lee Ah had the biggest ears I've ever seen on a human, nearly as big as my hands. But that isn't what makes me remember him; I remember him because he was so mean. He hated the Americans and showed it in every way possible. He was supposed to be working under Wong, but he was insolent and arrogant and would tell lies to get us in trouble. This was unusual, as most of the Manchurians we met were, if not friendly toward us, at least polite.

We finally had all of it we could stand. The ceiling of the dining hall was supported with steel columns. One column had electric wires running through it, and evidently had a short in it. When we'd get to cooking up the watery food, the hall would get steamy and the columns got damp. When we'd accidentally touch this column we'd get a pretty good shock. One morning when Lee Ah was being particularly obnoxious, we all lined up and held hands. On a signal, the fellow on one end grabbed Lee Ah's ear, and the one on the extreme opposite of the line touched the column. Lee Ah left the ground, dangling by the ear, shaking and quivering from the electric shock.

We don't know the reason for it, or what the shock did to his brain, but from that day forward Lee Ah couldn't do enough for the Americans. He was always underfoot, doing and fetching. He learned to speak pretty good English, and when the war was over he became the interpreter for the Americans to use when they wished to speak to the Chinese help, especially old Wong, who had returned to his job in the kitchen.

The kitchen detail was a prize detail, but it wasn't all roses. The most unpleasant task was to clean the dining room. The Japanese and Chinese ate first, then we did. But we usually had to clean the place after they'd eaten just so we could use it. The Oriental eating habits were different from ours and not just because they used chopsticks and raked the food into their mouths. They were sloppy eaters. Much of their spilled food wound up on the floor. If they spilled food on the table and wanted it out of the way, they simply raked it onto the floor. But the thing that made the job so repulsive was that they spat on the floor, as a matter of course.

When we cleaned up after them, if we had any appetite left, we could sit down and eat in a clean mess hall. I'm not sure it could ever be called sanitary, but we did the best we could.

CHAPTER 15

WAYS TO BE FREE

Sometime in the spring of 1943, while we were still in the old barracks, the Japanese brought in some athletic equipment—footballs, basketballs, volleyballs and baseballs with bats and gloves for recreational use, all from the Vatican. This really pleased us, though we weren't in any shape for sports. We certainly didn't have the extra energy it required, but we had the need of it. It would be a diversion. We needed something that would take our minds off our dreadful conditions.

We had to use the equipment on our own time, which meant after we'd come in from the factory and before lights out. A few of us who were still reasonably healthy divided into teams, practiced a few days, organized a tournament and were all set for some baseball.

Within a week after we'd started our tournaments the Japs came around and took our equipment. As far as I know, they didn't give a reason for taking it away. I thought it was because we were too lively and too exuberant with our shouting and yelling, and the Japs figured we weren't yet subdued to their satisfaction. I learned much later the reason given to the British prisoners of war was that some of their men escaped, and the escape had been planned at the game! After our vigorous protests, they left some of the volleyballs and basketballs that we could bounce individually, but couldn't use competitively. These balls came into use in an entirely different way later on.

Since America was built on the idea of freedom—individual freedom, freedom of the spirit—and grew by the endeavors of individuals "spreading their wings," it is difficult, if not impossible, for Americans to be completely subdued by any people or ideology.

We found ways to free our minds, if not our bodies. Even those confined in detention cells would bear their torture in silence. Many were there for minor infractions of the rules, rules many times made up on the spur of the moment to provide another excuse for cruelty. Most would bear the beatings in silence, not giving the guards the satisfaction of subduing them completely.

We made up small ways to be free. For example, gambling. Some of the more religious fellows chided us for gambling in the barracks. Big deal, I thought, gambling with Japanese yen was like using play money. It was virtually worthless. The card games helped me relax, got my mind off my hunger pains, off my cold hands and feet, off the beatings I'd seen that day at the factory, off the fellow down the aisle who never returned after going to the hospital.

We were allowed one scuttle of coal per stove each evening after returning from work. There were four sections to each barracks building and each section had one small stove. One scuttle of coal provides little heat when the temperature outside is below zero. And the barracks had no heat since the previous evening. After returning from MKK we'd eat our little bowl of soup and have about two hours when the stove would be used.

The fellows using dice would throw a blanket over a table so they wouldn't make any noise and attract the attention of a Jap guard. Then we'd get out the cards. I played blackjack; it was the only game I ever learned. The place really got to be a small casino. But we certainly weren't doing much financial dealing, not with Japanese yen. We worked all month for four yen, and in trade we could buy one bun or one cigarette for two yen.[1] So it's obvious their value was nil. When I won at cards I used my yen to buy bread; when I lost I'd trade my small issue of cigarettes (I didn't smoke) for yen to gamble with.

All this was against the rules, of course. It wouldn't have been nearly so enjoyable if the Japs had approved. We had an alarm system; we fellows took turns being lookout. When a guard approached, the lookout ran through the barracks calling, "Air raid, air raid." Then we quickly put the cards and dice away, yanked the blankets from the tables and folded them on the bunks where they belonged. We would be innocently lounging on our bunks or sitting at the tables when the guard walked through. We didn't fool them completely, however, for soon some of the wittier guards came through saying, "Air raid, air raid!"

Later some of the talented men put a small band together. A few instruments came through with those who had come from places other than Bataan and had been allowed to keep more personal possessions. Some of the clever fellows built their own. We had a violin, a guitar and a bass fiddle that were "homemade." Then some of the singers got a small choir together and barbershop quartets and such. Since I am not talented in music, I could only appreciate their efforts and applaud them.

The Japanese allowed this, we believed, for propaganda purposes, as Red Cross inspectors came into the camp a few times while we were there. About once a month our band and choir were allowed to get together and do some of the old tunes we loved and remembered. A friend of mine, Bill Hewgley, who was also from the Paris, Texas area, would sing *Love Letters in the Sand* as a duet with an Englishman's *'Til the Lights of London Shine Again.*

RULES

Back to the realities of a frightful existence of suffering. Roll call in the Mukden camp was scheduled for six a.m. Breakfast was scheduled for six a.m. Rising time was also scheduled for precisely six a.m. This is just one of the many unreasonable, senseless rules we were required to follow. So we had to try to get up, eat our mush, and be in line for roll call at the same precise minute.

This confusion provided many instances for guards to punish offending Americans. Punishment ran the gamut from missing the morning bowl of mush, to standing at attention in the snow for hours, to beatings, to detention in the guard house. Punishment rarely fit the crime. It all depended on the individual guard, on his mood, entirely.

This nonsense went on for three years. Many of us would rise at five-thirty, dress quietly, eat our bowl of mush as soon as it was ready and slip back into our bunks in order to be able to answer roll call at precisely six o'clock. Hoping, of course, that we didn't get caught. Each barracks had four sections, so those in the farther sections had a little more time and could manage this feat easier before the guard got to them.

The first winter in Manchuria, while we were in the old camp, when we fell out for roll call in the morning we also went through a searching line. This was another place where we could get into trouble. We always tried to make sure our pockets were perfectly empty; even a small inoffensive bit of paper could be turned into a "secret message" for escape purposes, and so forth.

I must admit that sometimes we did things that would have been punishable in an American camp. The volleyballs and basketballs, part of the sports equipment sent by the Vatican, had laid useless for a long time when some of the men found a rather illegal use for them. They took the bladders out of the balls, slipped them into the factory and brought alcohol and antifreeze from the factory into camp. They managed this by putting them inside their clothes next to the skin, so when they were "frisked" the full bladders felt like parts of their bodies.

Of course, the Japanese could not help but learn of it. They would have been stupid if they hadn't, for the men were getting drunk on this. Punishment for getting drunk was usually detention in the guard house.

In the winter of 1944, not long before the air raid in December, one of the men came in from the factory drunk. Because of the punishment, we didn't want to see the fellow get caught. So those of us near him in line tried to keep him upright so he could stand roll call. The Japanese probably wouldn't have noticed this, but our "white rat" was still hard at work.

Of course, the Japanese knew a man was drunk and who it was, but instead of pulling him from ranks and taking him to the guard house, they decided to play one of their little games. It was "Tell On Your Fellow Prisoner" game. They played these games often. They pulled us out of the barracks that night, had the entire barracks standing in snow, in shoes but with no overcoats, trying to get us to tell who it was.

Nobody would tell. The Japs said we could go back to our "warm" barracks when the guilty one stepped forward and admitted his guilt. Nobody stepped forward. We'd had to do this sort of thing before, and there was tacit agreement that no one ever told on another person. We stood there until just before midnight when the guards finally got so cold they let us go in.

They didn't punish the fellow who was drunk. To do so would have been admitting they knew who he was all along and were playing a game with us. They had to pretend they didn't know who the culprit was in order to save face.

THE FACTORY

We marched to the factory four men abreast, close file, with our hands out of our pockets. Of course, some men suffered from frost-bite as a result. It was always a relief to us when we reached the factory in the mornings and were turned over to the factory guards. They were usually Manchurian Chinese, and while they had to answer to the Japanese in charge and the Jap in charge made an occasional appearance, usually the atmosphere was more relaxed. Unless someone created a severe infraction of a rule, the Chinese left us alone.

There were instances when the Jap guards came through and beat men severely, sometimes just for trying to protect themselves from Japanese acts of violence. We soon learned which guards were the meanest and tried to stay clear of them.

The Manchu guards wore uniforms similar to Jap uniforms, but were distinguishable from them. They never scolded or yelled or attempted to beat us. If they saw something that displeased them, they went to the senior American and told him and let him handle the situation.

The pressure and tension in the factory would increase when a Jap guard came around. We didn't know when he would, for no apparent reason, walk up to one of us and hit us over the head. We weren't free of Japanese people at the factory, just relatively free of Japanese guards. There were Japanese civilians working there, as well as Chinese and Manchurians. There were Japanese engineers, machinists, teachers, students and others. Most of the groups had a leader, but as long as we weren't deliberately causing trouble and were working, they didn't bother us. It was only the Japanese soldiers.

We weren't making anything that was particularly helpful to the Japanese war effort at MKK. Some Americans, as well as some British, who went to the armaments factory in Mukden refused to work. Many of them spent months in solitary confinement as a result. But we at MKK were secretly sabotaging so much, there were times when we got a gleeful satisfaction from what we were doing.

After I started to work at the factory mess hall, I knew what was happening at the factory from hearsay. I heard enough to know that the Americans were trying to put them out of business. The matter of the reinforced concrete I mentioned earlier was typical of what they did in the factory during the three-year period we were there.

For example, the machine shop was making German-type index machines. In the thirty-four months we were there, they turned out two of them, and the parts of one wouldn't fit the parts of the other. They were still on the loading dock when the war ended. These machines had been made from the same blueprints and were supposed to have standard interchangeable parts, but nothing was the same. For example, the men would deliberately cut a shaft too small, then have to make adjustments on the parts that fitted on the shaft, then have to make adjustments on the parts that fitted those parts. If the machine ever broke down, every part to be replaced would have to be manufactured especially for it.

The machines they were working with were constantly "breaking down" and having to be repaired. And tools got misplaced, etc., etc., etc. The Japanese became aware of what was going on. They brought in several hundred soldiers inside the shops to watch the men, to keep them from doing these things. In some cases there would be two soldiers watching one man operate a machine.

But the soldiers didn't know whether the prisoners of war were doing their work the right way or the wrong way, so that didn't change things. In fact, the men were making more pipe stems than they were making parts for machines. One enterprising fellow turned out a miniature train, piece by piece, under the eyes of the soldiers.

Finally, a Japanese engineer who spoke perfect English came in to put a stop to these things. After two weeks he left, saying it was the biggest example of sabotage he'd ever heard of, and there wasn't anything he could do to stop it as long as the prisoners operated the machines.

At the end of the day at the factory, we were made to follow the same procedure as in the morning. We fell into ranks, then the honcho, the factory guard, marched us to the factory exit. The long building had lanes running through it, and each group was assigned a lane. We came out at the end of the lane and were searched by the Japanese guards. We fell into our four-man ranks, then counted off in Japanese and marched off to camp. At the main gate the officer who was to take charge of us came out and we had to count off again.

If we were all there, if none had managed to escape while walking four across, as close in ranks as we could be, with Jap guards thick around us, then we could go inside. Once inside, we were lined up again, searched again and then led into the changing room where we were supposed to shower and change our clothes. At least that's what the room was built for. We were allowed a bath once a week, at an assigned time. If we missed that time, we waited another week for a bath.

After all that we could go to our barracks and huddle around the minuscule fire in our section to try to thaw out our frozen fingers and toes.

CHAPTER 16

THE SICK AND THE DEAD

It is impossible to be completely accurate about statistics, and since we never knew the exact numbers, our figures are estimates. It is believed that an estimated 81,000 soldiers—12,000 Americans and 69,000 Filipinos—surrendered on April 9, 1942. It has been estimated that fully 10,000 prisoners (including 2,300 Americans) died from malaria, exhaustion, starvation, thirst, suffocation, beating and murder on the March. However, because of the breakdown within the Army's organization, the losses suffered may never be known. Within two months of the surrender, however, 21,000 men disappeared.

On the march from Bataan we lost many Americans; some say 600 to 1,000; others, 2,500. Different sources quote different statistics. At Cabanatuan we were burying well over one hundred men a day. There were about 6,500 men there, so I did some figuring the week I was on burial detail and decided that if it kept up, in thirty days over half the camp would be dead. In sixty days the whole camp would be gone. I figured I had sixty days to live, because I was going to be the last to die.

But it tapered off; when we left Cabanatuan we were burying about fifteen men a day. Not all the prisoners in Cabanatuan left the Philippines. I understand that the men who stayed there were later liberated by an American cavalry unit that drove right through the

Japanese line, loaded the men on *caraboas* and carts borrowed from the Filipinos, and went right through the lines. The only casualties were a prisoner who died from a heart attack, and several soldiers, including a doctor.

On board ship many died. I don't know how many, as we never knew what happened outside our immediate area. When they died on ship, they were simply dropped overboard. In our own area in the hold of the *Totora Maru*, we lost close to 175 men in the thirty-three days we were afloat. At Pusan we left 175 men who were too sick to travel. Of that number 75 died. The men who died at Pusan were cremated, and when the 100 who survived came into camp, they brought 75 little white boxes. They were buried with our other dead in the spring of 1943.[1]

We arrived in Manchuria in November, 1942. During the winter of 1942 and 1943, we lost a lot of men, at least 375. We had thought that coming to a cold climate would alleviate the tropical diseases. We thought we could tolerate them better. This easement was slow to come. Men kept dying of dysentery and malaria, added to pneumonia and diseases brought on by malnutrition.

Most of those who died had been captured in the Philippines. We made crude boxes from scrap lumber found in the dugout camp. The men who died that winter were put in these boxes and stored in a warehouse. When the spring thaw came and we could dig graves, these frozen bodies were buried in a Manchurian cemetery.

Digging graves for so many dead became a dreaded ordeal. The winters are severe, and the ground stays frozen at least two feet deep. When it was time to start burying, we would get scrap lumber, each one of us with a load in our arms, then go to the cemetery where we built a large bonfire on the spot where we were to dig. When the fire burned out, we would get busy and dig there while it was still thawed, before it froze again.

As soon as we'd dug all the thawed area, we'd build another bonfire and while it was burning, we'd return to camp for our noon meal. After that we'd get another load of scrap material and go back. We'd build a bonfire and dig, build a bonfire and dig, until we had the grave done. We had to work fast once we got a spot thawed, for it would start freezing again as soon as the heat was removed. It usually took several days to get the grave dug. This was a mass grave large enough for many men.

I was never on a detail to bury the bodies. I built boxes and dug graves, but never put the bodies in the ground. It was my opinion that all bodies were buried in the boxes. But that is not so; I was told later that they were buried in common graves just as they had been in the Philippines.

The rate of death seemed to taper off somewhat by the spring of 1943. But Americans continued to die needlessly all the time we were there.

In February, 1943 after we had been in Manchuria about three months, I came down with my third attack of malaria. I'd made the march off Bataan without food and little water and managed to be on my feet when it ended. I'd gone on work details with severe dysentery. But malaria is really something to contend with. So far I'd been lucky; in both my other attacks there had been somebody around to provide me with quinine when many others didn't get it.

I made sick call this time and was told there was no quinine available. The Japanese doctor who had been providing quinine to the prisoners was no longer able to get any. I couldn't work at the factory; I didn't have the strength to march the three miles there and back. So I had to make sick call, to go through the motions of getting help even though I'd been told there was nothing to be done. If we stayed in camp without being in hospital, we were harassed by the guards. I knew that to survive, I not only had to be free of malaria, I had to be free of guards.

I'd been through sick call three times. I was leaving the hospital area this third day when I heard a loud, "Pssst!" I turned and saw a soldier lying on his bunk, motioning for me to come to him. "Hey, kid. Need quinine?"

Wasn't it obvious, from my sunken eyes and the sallow skin that had shrunk on my bones, that I needed quinine? I nodded numbly, each nod of my head causing a heavy throb.

"I've got some. What you got to trade?" I shook my head; I had nothing.

"How about food? Got any extra buns?" I thought a moment. Food was a valuable commodity. I'd learned early in the war to take all the food you can get and make use of it. I didn't like giving away my food. But on the other hand, I was getting a little more than most of the others. And what good was all the food in the world if I didn't get this malaria in check?

I nodded. It was a deal. Every night I'd bring him my nightly ration of food and in turn he would give me one quinine capsule of the hoard he'd accumulated from not taking what had been given him. In a few days I went back to work, but I didn't quit trading my food for the quinine until I'd taken all the medicine he had been given in the hospital.

Again, I'd been saved by great, good fortune. Many years later, thirty-three years later, to be exact, I had my fourth attack of malaria. I was hospitalized with extremely high blood pressure. This was followed by pneumonia; then, while I was weakened, another violent attack of malaria. It was interesting that my doctor in the U.S., Dr. Courtney Townsend, who had been an army doctor during the war, was the only one on the staff with the experience to recognize it as malaria. None of the tests showed malaria. I came out of this fourth attack as thin and gaunt and ravaged as I'd been in 1943 in Manchuria.

During the first winter in Manchuria many Americans died, and they kept on dying all the time we were there, though the rate of deaths declined. There was usually no medicine available. There were American doctors, but no equipment. I had a tooth pulled without a shot and a finger lanced without any medication, not even an antiseptic. It was reported that there was one bedpan for several hundred patients with dysentery, and many of them died from pneumonia as a result of running to the latrine through the snow, often barefoot.

Our medical facilities were crude. I was never an inpatient in the hospital, but I know that very few that went in ever came back to barracks. The doctors were competent and could have done a great deal to alleviate our suffering and to save us, if they'd had the things they needed.

My finger that was abscessed got so bad that red streaks were running up my arm into my chest area. The doctor said it had to be lanced immediately or I was liable to lose my hand, and even possibly my arm. He had no disinfectant, no pain killer. He washed it with soap and water and cut into it as I yelled to the high heavens. I was to soak it in salty water to keep it soft and to aid in the healing. But I had no salt. The hot water I used helped; it healed, but there is a hard scar.

The first winter we were in the new camp, men were sick with colds and sore throats, losing their voices. One morning a big tall guy spoke to me in a whisper, "Good morning."

I answered in a whisper, "Good morning."

He picked me up and was going to work me over for imitating him, until a friend stopped him. "Hey, fellow, leave him alone. He's lost his voice, too. Half the camp's talking in whispers."

He put me down and apologized.

Just a few weeks before the end of the war, I had a bad toothache. We had a doctor who was doing what he could under the circumstance. He looked at the tooth and told me he could fix it in just a few minutes back home. Only a small spot of cavity was visible, but it went directly to the nerve. Couldn't I wait? No, I couldn't, I told him. I'd stayed awake the entire night before and I wanted relief. I told him to go ahead and pull it; I couldn't stand it any longer. He tried to talk me out of it, and I wish I had listened. He pulled the tooth, without the use of any sort of pain killer. How did I know that three weeks after I insisted he pull the tooth the war would end?

CHAPTER 17

DAILY LIFE

After we'd been in Manchuria in the dugout camp less than a year, we were moved to a new camp that was built specifically as a prisoner of war camp, and where we stayed until our liberation two years later. The morning and evening walks to and from the factory were now about half a mile, easing that burden a bit. The buildings were new and cleaner, but harder to heat with our one daily scuttle of coal.

These new barracks were two-story buildings. In my building, the U.S. Air Corps prisoners were on the lower floor, and the U. S. Navy and prisoners of other nationalities were on the floor above. We were moved about as time passed. The American officers were housed separately; we had little contact with them while we were there.

In the Philippines, the only toilet facilities we had were straddle trenches. In Manchuria, the old camp had a change room and a bath house with showers. In the new building there was a long row of wash basins at the end of each barracks. These were made of concrete and had taps with cold water only. There we would wash our mess kits, which were metal bowls. I had gotten rid of my sardine can after we got to Manchuria and were issued bowls. Each man would wash his bowl and set it on the shelf near his bunk and have it ready for the next meal.

The toilets were in a room adjacent to the wash area. There were no stools as we use, but straddle trenches as in the Philippines. In summer months, flies swarmed as a result.

We worked every day except for one day a month, which we used for laundry and straightening up the barracks. Our hours between work at the factory and lights out were spent inside the barracks, tired and often hungry, with little to do to amuse ourselves and relieve the tedium, except for the gambling and an occasional concert by the band and choir. We had plenty of time for talk. There were few subjects we didn't cover.

Since we didn't know what was happening about the war, we latched on to rumors and made plenty of guesses. We planned our futures, hoping we had futures. One fellow and I decided we'd go into the egg business. We spent days talking and planning, figuring every possible way, and didn't see how we could keep from making a fortune. There was one man in our barracks who had raised chickens, so we had him look at our figures. He looked them over, pursed his lips, nodded his head and handed our notes back to us. "Well?" We were anxious to get his opinion. "What do you think? Did we figure right?"

"The figures look pretty good, but ..."

"Yes?" Why did he have to be so slow to tell us the good news?

"You forgot one little item."

One little item. That couldn't be so bad. We'd figured it carefully, so it couldn't be anything major. "What is this little item?"

"Chicken feed. You forgot to feed the chickens."

We talked mostly about food. It was impossible to have a conversation without sooner or later getting around to food. Mama's food. Wife's food. Grandma's food. What the best restaurant served back home. And invariably, someone in the back of the barracks would yell, "If you don't shut your mouths, I'm gonna shut 'em for you!"

We had Englishmen on the top floor of our building, and we

fought the Revolutionary War over, several times. The British started off being rather snobbish to us, but after a while turned out to be pretty good fellows.

We talked about wives and sweethearts; what we'd do if we went home and found they'd been unfaithful. It was the young ones who were so sure what they'd do. Then some old timer would say, "Well, how good have you been? Have you stayed true? If you expect a woman to be faithful, she has the right to expect the same of you." That would really start a debate about the double standard.

Some of our debates got rather heated. We were like sick children; it took very little to make us peevish and irritable. There were occasional skirmishes, but nothing to worry about. No one was strong enough to hurt anyone else. I can remember standing up in my bunk yelling at someone (I can't remember whom) about something (I can't remember what), telling him what I'd do (whatever that was) *if* he wasn't too cowardly to fight.

The subject that came nearest to us, though, was death. After all, who had seen more of it? Who before had ever lost so many good friends in such horrible ways? We talked about it, what it really was, about the hereafter.

Our biggest debate, though, was about predestination. "You don't die till your time comes."

"Yeah, but if I decide I'm tired of living and go out and put a gun to my head and pull the trigger and kill myself . . . ?"

"Then it was your time."

When the men really got nostalgic, they thought of their mothers almost every time. I guess we thought about them a lot, for most of us had plans about what we were going to do for our mothers when we got home. We had lived in the Great Depression and knew that our mothers had sacrificed for us. One fellow had planned just exactly what he was going to get his mother for her house: a new stove, a refrigerator, a sink and water piped into the house so she wouldn't have to draw water from a well. He told us about this over and over; he had it planned right down to the last detail. When the war ended and we got all the letters that had been held in the Japanese office since 1942, one of the first letters he opened brought news of his mother's death. He'd done all that planning, and she'd been dead nearly three years.

There were many letters that came to us, but very few got to us until we were liberated. At the end of the war, I had fifty-four letters, some dating back to 1942, that had been in the Japanese headquarters all this time. Some men had as many as two hundred letters.

There was surprisingly little talk of sex. We were too weakened to have any kind of sex drive.

It was hard to find a subject that most of the men agreed on, but one that most of them were in accord about was that if we were women instead of men, more of us would have survived. We believed that women could have withstood the suffering better and would have adjusted to these difficulties better than men.

There was no way we could get to know all the two thousand men working in the factory. We didn't socialize; this was drudgery, not pleasure. Unless we worked closely, or were in a barracks together, we weren't likely to get to know someone. When a man died, it was easier if it were some nameless fellow who worked near you than to lose another friend. Working in the kitchen gave me an opportunity to see the faces of many men. Later, I would be able to recognize a face without having a name to put to it. But as the years passed, after the war, our faces would look quite different from the emaciated skeletons we were then.

The bulk of the men in our camp were Americans who had been captured in the Philippines. There were also some Englishmen, Australians and New Zealanders, who came in from Singapore.[1] There were probably two or three hundred of these three nationalities, plus a few who came from the Dutch East Indies.

We always knew when a visitor was coming, as we were ordered to get busy and clean up the camp, spruce it up a bit. Winter clothing would be issued to us, then as soon as the visitors—usually the Red Cross—left, it was promptly taken away.

Red Cross packages came into camp, but we received very few of them. In fact, I got one package the whole time we were there and had to share it with another fellow because there weren't enough to go around. In reading a British officer's diary after the war, I learned the British and Australians regularly received small bits of these packages, but we didn't. I don't know what the American officers got, but the enlisted men in our barracks certainly did not receive Red Cross packages.

It is evident, from what we found and learned at the end of the war, that not only the Red Cross packages, but our own private parcels from home, were rifled as they were inspected. We were aware of this, since when they were given to us, they were open and strewn about. Unexplainable things happened in regard to the contents of these packages, things we couldn't understand then and still have not been able to make sense of years later. For example, in packs of playing cards, the fives were all marked in some way, such as with red dots. One man opened his package to find a set of dominoes. He discovered the double five had been cut in two and glued back together. Since our packages were handed to us open, anyone could have taken things out, or added to them, at their discretion.

One fellow who'd just received a package from home looked at the things in his parcel and then looked up with an expression of astonishment on his face. Five white feathers and five yellow feathers were scattered among his belongings. "Feathers! This is ridiculous!" he sputtered. "My folks wouldn't put feathers in a package. Why, it's silly!"

"Maybe, well . . . maybe," someone suggested weakly, "maybe they're pipe cleaners?"

"I don't smoke. Never did!" It was a mystery and remains one.

A package arrived from my folks at home just a few months before the war ended, in the fall of 1944. It contained toilet articles and a very good supply of razor blades. It also contained something very special, Dad's razor, the one he had used when he was "over there" in World War I. It was army issue and still in good shape. How wonderful, I thought, all those razor blades and that razor, but I still didn't have a beard. In fact, with our poor diets, beards were slow in growing, as well as the hair on our heads and our fingernails and toenails.

There was also a pair of shoes in the package, the military low quarters type, just my size. They came from the shoe store where one of my old professors worked part time. He had donated a pair of socks, with a note tucked in the toe. Thank goodness it was still there when I got the package. The note was written on a blank check from one of the banks back home. If the Japs had found the note, the least they would have done was to take the package. It might have been just as well if they had taken the package, for not only did I not need the razor and blades, when I got the shoes from home, the Japs took my other shoes. So I spent the winter in low quarter shoes that fit so well I could wear only one pair of socks with them.

It wasn't long before my feet were frostbitten. My toes and heels were so sore I couldn't stand to touch them, much less wear shoes. I had a friend who worked in the cobbler shop in the camp, and he traded shoes for me. He gave me a heavy pair, a pair large enough that I could wear several pairs of thick socks with them. Earlier, I had made mittens from a blanket to keep my hands from freezing when we were marching the three miles to and from the factory with our hands out of our pockets. Now I made some leggings from the blanket and wrapped my feet.

I was still having trouble with my feet when I came home after the war was over. It took months for me to be able to walk without a hobble. I had no feeling in my toes for a long time after the war and the feeling has never completely returned.

The shoes stayed in camp until the war was over, and then the friend gave them back to me. They proved valuable, though, in the long run. One man, between the time we were liberated and when we left Mukden, gave me twenty-five hundred yen to get to wear them to town one night. This amounted to about ten dollars.

The American attitude to life and toward society was so different from the Oriental one that it was almost impossible for the two ideologies to live together without clashing. The Japs had the guns, so we had to tread lightly to avoid curses, beatings, detentions and other punishments for "crimes" we didn't know we were committing, and usually the offenses were so minor as to be ridiculous. The overriding fact of our daily life was that we were prisoners—subject to the whims of our Japanese guards.

We weren't allowed to smoke away from an ashtray or to smoke after lights out. We were ordered to salute the Japanese officers and soldiers, bowing to them every time we met. We were in a constant state of dread. Never relaxed. For if we relaxed we were sure to do something to offend the Japs. This does not apply to the civilians with whom we came in contact; they were nice enough under the circumstances.

It was the military. It seemed their belief was that when they put on a uniform they were given open-ended license to torture, murder, terrorize; that it was almost their duty to do these things, as if it were expected, a part of their commitment. We understand those minds a bit better now in view of what has happened and is happening in the world today, but in the 1940s, it was hard for us to comprehend.

We went without water when it was available. We went without food when Red Cross packages—thousands of them—were near at hand (a warehouse full of them, we learned at the end of the war). We were beaten just for being alive and stood for all sorts of indignities that no human should ever have had to endure.

The worst was hunger. Hunger isn't just an unpleasantness or a pain. It's a real sickness. It left scars, physical scars, that we'll bear to our graves. It left scars, psychological scars—some still open wounds—that affect us and our families and friends.

CHRISTMASES

Since we had no contact with our officers, we had no access to a chaplain and no religious services. I can remember the Christmases quite well. Christmas 1941, the war had just started; we'd evacuated Clark Field and had moved south to help fill in the lines. I remember the half can of meat and beans and thought how good it tasted.

Things were worse the Christmas of 1942. The day was no different from any other day except we sang carols in the barracks that night. I lay in my bed and thought about home. Did they get the letter I'd sent out in February on the submarine? Did they know what had happened to us in the Philippines? Was there any way they could know now whether I was dead or alive? I thought of the orange that number 361, Wayne Herbert, had brought to me from the factory. I ate every bit of it, peel and all. I was not in the kitchen that first Christmas we were in Mukden, but I understood the men sang carols and weren't bothered by the Japanese as a result of it. I went to sleep wondering what Mama had cooked for Christmas.

We of the kitchen staff began our morning on Christmas, 1943 peeling and chopping vegetables, like every other morning. We had lots of conversations around the table. I guess the best times around the table were at Christmas time. Oh, we didn't have turkey and ham and mince meat pie, nor any of the things we would expect to have at Christmas at home. No, we had *chimbee*. It was the singing that made the difference. Oh, it didn't sound all that good; as for myself, I can't carry a tune. It was the songs and what they meant.

There were Chinese children who worked at odd jobs around the factory, and they would occasionally find a reason to come near the kitchen area. We sang *Silent Night, O Little Town of Bethlehem* and *Hark, The Herald Angels Sing*, all religious songs. These young-sters would put their hands to their eyes and shake their heads to indicate that these were sad songs that made them want to cry. They had heard us sing *Jingle Bells*, so they would speak in their soft, high-pitched, sing-song voices, asking us to sing *Jingle Bells*. They liked the happy songs.

On that Christmas Day we did a brave, and perhaps foolish, thing. One of the men had an American flag that he had managed to bring in with him. He must have come from Corregidor, as the men on the march could never have brought it in. So, foolish or brave, we displayed the American flag on Christmas Day, 1943. We hung it up in the barracks and sang patriotic songs and carols and had a wonder-fully good feeling. Our rations had been doubled for the day and we felt less empty than usual. It was a day to remember, the day we got to see our flag again. Even if it was patched and faded, it was the Stars and Stripes.

Of course, it wasn't long before the Japanese came and took it away. The white rat had squealed. No particular punishment was meted out. I guess they thought taking the flag was enough. It was.

Years later, I took a class of students to the Hall of State at the State Fair Grounds in Dallas and saw this same flag on display. There it was, all patched and faded, and underneath was the story of that Christmas Day, 1943. The owner of the flag had had it returned to him after the war and again, had cleverly managed to keep it hidden when we had to get rid of everything, including fleas.

Christmas of 1944 was different. We had no way of knowing about events on the outside, but we could often see a change in the Japanese attitude and felt that this bad attitude indicated that things were not going well for them. That may not have been true, but we comforted ourselves with these thoughts. Christmas 1944 was not so happy; we were not allowed to sing carols. By the Christmas of 1945 we were free of this hell and back home. Some of us were.

THE BEGINNING OF THE END

CHAPTER 18

BOMBING OF MUKDEN

Mukden, Manchuria was a large industrial city and a prime target for the United States Army Air Corps based in China. On December 7, 1944, an anniversary date, a beautiful sight appeared over our horizon. It was the flight of one hundred twenty American B-29s. We had warnings that brought us from the factory to the camp. We stood outside and watched the sun reflect off the silver "eagles." It never occurred to us to seek shelter in the trenches we'd dug around the edge of the barracks; we were enjoying the sight too much—bombs falling on the factory where we worked, on the armaments plant, on the aircraft factory, on all the things located in Mukden that would benefit the Japanese in war.

Flying in formations of twelve, ten flights came over, one after another. Unhappily, we saw one plane go down and saw parachutes falling to the ground in the wake of the flaming plane. On one of these flights, a group of twelve planes came over our camp as we waved and cheered. Then unexpectedly, one lone plane veered sharply to the right and dropped two bombs, right on top of our camp. We started running for cover.

Many didn't make it to shelter. To the best of my memory, thirty-five prisoners were killed outright, and approximately forty-five were wounded. Some of the wounded died later. Again, as many times before, a miracle occurred, for I was in what could be called a no-man's land. Where the bomb hit the bodies were mutilated. The shrapnel rose over me and hit the men beyond me, leaving me scared but unharmed, twenty feet from the bomb crater.

It was a beautiful sight, those planes, and the last sight some of us saw. I saw some of the men who were killed outright; they died with smiles on their faces. One was a special friend that I'd worked with for over two years. His face was black with powder burns, but his teeth were shining with a happy smile. Some were cut all to pieces with shrapnel and still died smiling.

Considerable damage was done to Mukden. One aircraft factory was completely destroyed. There were no Americans there as they had refused to work in anything that would help the Jap war effort. What was left of that plant was moved to one section of our factory. Many of our men were sent to the guardhouse because they refused to go to work there. Perhaps they were wrong. With our expertise at sabotage we could likely have put an end to the Japanese air power, once and for all.

The bombing of our camp was a good chance for propaganda, the Japs thought, as they instructed us to write messages to be sent by short wave to the Air Corps in China, where the flights had originated. But they were disappointed, and in some cases furious with our response. Our attitude was "Keep 'em Flying!"

One man, who lost an arm and got shrapnel in his skull as a result of the raid, wrote something like this, "One of the most beautiful sights I've seen since WWII started was the flights of the B-29s over the camp where I am held. In your air raid of Mukden a bomb hit our POW camp. As a result I lost an arm. If that's what it takes to win the war, I have another arm." Needless to say, the messages were never sent out.

Shortly after the bombings, the B-29s began to come over at very high altitudes, but didn't drop bombs. We thought at that time they were doing photography to determine the extent of their damage and to locate other war equipment manufacturing plants for future targets. That's what we thought then. We have reason now to believe they were trying to locate the 731 Germ Warfare Laboratory, "Unit 731," as it's called.

THE "HONEY CART"

My duties in the kitchen came to an end, I'm sorry to say. That was a black day for me, for I felt it was truly the beginning of the end. The reason was not my doing. It was simply that after the bombings most of the factory was inoperable and there were fewer people working there. Consequently we were feeding fewer people in the kitchen, and the kitchen work force was cut.

I was put to work at odd jobs, just whatever came up. I was glad to do that in order to stay away from the camp. This odd-jobbing went on until August of 1945. I had no way then of knowing the war would end in two weeks. Thank God it did, for at this time my life expectancy was going down fast.

I had been working with a survey crew; my job was to hold the surveyor's pole. It was tiring, boring work, and I was sick. Sick with malnutrition, sick with tape worms, sick with dysentery, sick with hunger. So weak, I could hardly stand. So I leaned against a gravel pile to support myself. It seems that we're all allotted a certain number of minor miracles, and mine were all used up. While I was resting, a feisty little self-important Jap guard came by and saw me. He accused me of sitting down on the job and promptly took me to camp to stand before the camp commander.

Speaking through the interpreter, the officer called me all sorts of vile names and accused me of being a malingerer, a low life, anything that he could bring to mind. My punishment was severe. First,

I was made to stand at attention before the officer's desk. This was one o'clock in the afternoon. Every time I'd move he would hit me with his saber. Soon my muscles began to ache, then to throb. I was in agony, in agony from my tortured muscles and from the numerous beatings with the saber. By late afternoon I was numb. And grateful. I could no longer feel the muscles nor the whacks of the saber.

At eight o'clock the officer said I could go and left his office. I tried to move, but couldn't. I stood there, as a statue turned to stone. Sometime later the interpreter came back in and found me still there. He told me the officer said I could go. Then he left. I stayed. Thinking I'd not understood, he came back again and found I'd not moved. Again he said I could go. I said I understood. I could talk, but my body wouldn't move. He pushed me over onto the floor and left me there. Once I was no longer in an upright position, the blood began to flow, and I gradually got feeling into my body. I moved an arm, then some fingers, then a leg and an ankle and so on until I could get up and hobble.

The interpreter came again and this time he took me to the headquarters building. There I stood before another officer. Some of the officers could speak English but insisted on using the interpreter. This one did also. "I'm not sending you to the guardhouse because that is too good for you. You shall be put on probation and will remain on probation as long as you are here."

Probation meant wearing a piece of wood saying "probation" in Japanese. This was the Jap version of the scarlet letter; you were a pariah. It meant you rose before the others; you came in after the others; and you did all the dirty work that everyone else refused to do. I went to my bunk and lay there and wondered if the struggle to live was worth it. All through the march I had struggled to survive and to avoid the worst of the terror by trying to reach the head of the line. I fought to live on the hell ship; I held on again when so many men were dying. Small blessings were life-saving miracles that came at just the right times. Had I struggled and suffered in vain?

It would have been easier to have given up and died early, like the dear friend whom I had visited in the Cabanatuan hospital who had refused to eat because he couldn't stomach "that old stuff." Well, I'd stomached it, gagging at times on bread made of flour and maize when the flour cooked and the maize stayed raw and soured. On rice that had been discarded by the Japanese because it was too wormy, on potatoes that had frozen and spoiled on thawing. But I'd forced it down *and lived* . . . well, survived. I'd done it, against all odds. I was still alive. Damn it, I'd show these bastards. Let them do their worst. I will live!

But doubt returned when dawn came and I was assigned to the "honey cart." That was the job that had been relegated to the lowest of the Manchurians who came into camp to work. And they had refused it. Prisoners had been put to work on this job before and gotten so sick they couldn't handle it. Others had taken the guard house rather than the honey cart. I was determined. No matter how sick I got, I was not going to give up.

This job involved cleaning out the toilets, using a long dipper and putting the filthy mess into a wooden cart, then pushing the cart to a farm where there was an open pond, a big hole where this was dumped. I opened the trap door and the excrement slid out into this hole. Later we, another poor human who had also been put on this duty and I, would have to reladle it from the pond and put it on the plants as fertilizer.

It was just as well our punishment kept us out later than the others, as the men in the barrack wouldn't let me get near them. I was able to bathe and change clothes after I came in each night so as not to offend them with my odor. How did I stay sane in this?

After the Bataan March, the intense sorrow at losing dear friends, the hell ship, after arriving in Manchuria, the senses were still bombarded. Even on our three-mile march from the factory and back, we kept seeing things that shocked us—we, who by now should be immune to shock. There were dead bodies all along the sides of the road, lying unattended. We asked about them at the factory and were told they were probably paupers, beggars who had no one, no family to miss them or to see to their burial. We kept seeing them day by day, as they lay there, frozen, and as time went by parts of the bodies would be missing, eaten by dogs or other animals.

Stay sane? Sane amidst insanity? Were we deceiving ourselves and had we already died? Was this hell? Stay sane? I don't know. I had joined the Army Air Corps to learn to fly in the blue skies of the heavens and had instead been brought down to handling human waste.

Then redemption came! It was on an August morning two weeks after I'd been put on probation that we were suddenly, without explanation, run into camp. I had just started out with my honey cart. I dropped my ladle and left the cart where it was. I didn't worry about how I smelled, as I knew something was in the wind. Whatever it was, it was more important than the smell of a sewer.

We knew the war was winding down. The Jap interpreter at the factory who had been educated in the United States, and was occasionally friendly to us, had told us to be careful when the war ended. The Japanese were to distribute to each man an extra bun and a baked potato and start us on a march. We were to be shot, mowed down as in an execution, and their explanation to the world would be that we had attempted escape. We believed the interpreter, for the Japanese were capable of doing just that.

CHAPTER 19

FREE AT LAST

Earlier in the summer of 1945, we had a sudden, almost overnight inundation of rats. Rats were everywhere, scurrying through the barracks, running over us as we slept. Not only did the suddenness of the onslaught make us suspicious that they'd been dumped on us, but the fact that there was no food in the barracks made us almost certain they were. I could understand hungry rats converging on a place if they could find food, but in our barracks there was never so much as a crumb of food. If there had been, we would have eaten it ourselves. Overnight, hundreds of rats. It wasn't normal. I counted as many as ten rats at one time on the floor near my bunk.

But the rats weren't the worst of it. We could fight off rats to some extent, but the rats were infested with fleas and very soon so were we. They got into our clothes, in our bedding, even into the walls, it seemed. We weren't able to get rid of them. The fleas were particularly hard on me and my thin skin. I'd weathered the Philippine sun without a shirt on my pink back. I'd withstood the gales of three Manchurian winters, and now the fleas were devastating me.

On the 14th day of August, 1945, after we'd had our midday bowl of soup, the air raid sounded. We heard the siren, and all prisoners were rushed back to the barracks from MKK and the farm. In spite of my filthy condition from being on the honey cart, I went inside with the others. We knew something big was afoot.

Were they ready to send us out with the extra bun and potato on the march they'd planned? We'd been warned by the interpreter Ihara, and we knew the kitchen had already prepared the bread and potatoes. To be forewarned is to be forearmed; we'd already decided that we would not go on the march. We were going to overpower the guards and take their weapons. If we were going to die, we'd try to regain some of our dignity when we did it.

There were bars on the windows of the barracks, not metal ones, but wooden slats. A slat was broken off one window and we could see outside a little bit. An older Air Corps man called me over to the window and said, "See those parachutes coming out of the sky?" Parachutes? Yes, I saw parachutes! A plane was going over, and different colored parachutes were falling.

"See the different colors, red, orange, yellow?" he asked. "If that's an American plane, the colored parachutes will be bringing down supplies. It will circle and then those colored chutes will be followed by white parachutes that will carry men."

Almost as he said it, the plane circled, and beautiful white parachutes floated down. Six of them, six white parachutes! I let out a cheer that must have been heard all the way to Mukden.

Very shortly the whole barracks, the entire camp heard the news. Americans had parachuted in! Yes, it must be. What did it mean? We began to move about, talking, almost ecstatic, yet afraid to be too hopeful. No guards bothered us; we weren't sent back to work. What did it all mean?

I thought about the men in the building just outside the camp. These were almost sure to be the crews of the B-29s that fell over Mukden in the December 7th air raid. But we'd not been allowed any contact with them. We in the kitchen prepared their food, took it to the gate and left it there. They came to the gate, picked up their food and took it to their barracks. When they finished, they'd set the empty containers at the gate. After they'd gone we'd retrieve them.

We tried several times to send messages, making false bottoms in the wooden buckets and inserting notes, but they never found them. This really puzzled us, their not being brought into the camp proper with the rest of us. We couldn't think of any logical explanation for it. What did it matter if they told us what was going on outside? There was nothing we could do about it.

As no guards were patrolling our area, we left the barracks and went down behind the hospital building where we could see better. From there we had a view of the main gate and could see anybody that came in or went out. I got down as close to the front as I could.

We waited there, after seeing the cloud-white parachutes drop, perhaps thirty to forty-five minutes, when two Japanese trucks pulled through the main gate. We could see colored parachutes piled high on top of something—the supplies they dropped, I supposed— whatever that might be. The second truck came in, and we could see white chutes and Americans sitting on top of them. Years later, when we met some of these men again we were told there were five men, not six, but I remember seeing six parachutes.

The Americans hopped off the truck and lined up in front of the headquarters building, wearing full khaki uniforms and 45s strapped to their sides! Their 45s still in their holsters! Col. Matsuda had his men line up, and the American Major and the Japanese Colonel saluted each other, and the American officer gave his men "at ease." Then he glanced over toward us and raised his hand in a "high ball" sign. And we went wild. Absolute abandonment! Like a buffalo stampede, and just as dangerous, we were running and jumping and hugging and crying. And I was right in the middle of it, putrid smell and all. Later, as I went to the change room for a bath, I decided it had been worth waiting for after all.

Several years later when I was working towards my masters degree, I was asked to tell about the liberation as part of a class lecture. When I finished, a man in the back of the room raised his hand and spoke, "I was in an American Air Base in China. I knew these men who went into your camp; they were volunteers."

We'd heard earlier that when the end came, the prisoners of war in Mukden were to be done away with—a forced march and execution. These men were sent to prevent this happening, he said. The men had volunteered to drop into enemy hands four to six hours before the camp commander knew of the Japanese surrender, in order to prevent wholesale slaughter. (Many years later we met some of these men, including the pilot who flew the plane.)

After that, nothing happened until the next morning. We calmed down a bit and began to wander back to our designated areas. But I never returned to stay in our barracks after that. After I'd bathed and changed, I stayed outside. I was determined not to have another flea bite. I stayed outside and walked and talked with the others who, like me, refused to go back inside the flea-infested barracks. We disregarded the rules to be in bunks with lights out at nine o'clock. We could see guards walk through the barracks every once in a while, but they never said a word to us about going in. They didn't curse us or hit us. We definitely knew something was different tonight.

Three of us went into the change room and on into the shower and bath house that adjoined it. There were windows in the back of the bath house that opened opposite the Headquarters building. We climbed into the windows and peeped over the fence. Yes, there in Col. Matsuda's office were the Americans, moving back and forth, their 45s still strapped to their sides. We were getting higher and higher, the exhilaration of uncertainty and anxiety for good news was almost unbearable.

(In the fall of 2001, shortly after the September 11, 2001 attack on the Pentagon, our Mukden group had a reunion in Washington, D.C. There, we again saw Hal Leith, one of the men who parachuted into the camp. His memory of these events differ a little bit from mine. He says they did not get into the Japanese Commander's office at first, and they were wearing their holsters, but the guns were not in them. In my excitement, that was an easy mistake to make!)

But no one came to our side of the fence or spoke to us. The only sign of recognition we'd had was the Major's okay sign. We walked up and down the parade ground and talked about every conceivable possibility. We thought the war must be over, or very near it, but the thing that had brought it to an abrupt halt, the bombing of Hiroshima and Nagasaki, was beyond our imaginations. We'd been out of the world for more than three and a half years; we had no idea that the world we'd go back to would be so utterly different from the one we'd left.

THE RUSSIANS ARE COMING

About eight o'clock the next morning, our top-ranking officer, General Parker, was called to Japanese headquarters. He stayed there approximately one hour, but it seemed half a day. At nine a.m. on August 15, 1945, Gen. Parker came inside the walls and spoke to us. It seemed it took him thirty minutes to say what he could have said in two words, "It's over!" He told us that we were liberated from the Japanese by these American Air Corps men, but we were not to leave camp, as the Russians were invading Manchuria. There was still a war going on outside, and for our own safety we must stay until the Russians arrived.

Twenty minutes after Gen. Parker told us this, the Americans entered our camp. We were anxious to question them, but Gen. Parker told us to leave them alone as they had necessary jobs to do in order to get us processed and on our way out of there. We didn't have to be told twice. We moved back and watched.

One of the Air Corps men started getting the names of the Americans in camp as fast as he could. Another man had radio equipment and was setting up a communications post. They were also putting up a PA system, with speakers all around camp. When they finished this, they started playing records. Some were "oldies," ones we remembered. Some were new ones, war-time songs we'd never heard before. The one I remember best is *Sentimental Journey*. It must have been everybody's favorite, for in the days before we left Manchuria, it was played over and over and nobody complained.

We still wanted to talk to someone who knew what was happening in the world. As the parachutists didn't have time to talk, we felt the Air Corps men held in the building just outside camp were our next best bet. Those men were allowed to come over to our camp, and we bombarded them with questions.

They told us all they could, about the American invasion of the Philippines, about the war in Europe, everything that had happened prior to December 7, 1944, when they had become prisoners of war. Oh, there was so much we wanted to know. After all, we'd been out of the world for almost four years. Four long years of our lives, of our youth, gone forever.

Evening came on August 15, and the communications people put up a big screen on the wall of the hospital and started showing films. They showed them half the night, and I saw all of them from the top of one of the buildings where I'd crawled. Not only could I see the movie on the screen from there, I could see a world outside. I can't remember what films I saw that night; I was too excited to concentrate.

On August 16, B-29s started coming in from somewhere—Okinawa, I think—loaded with food and other supplies. They had stripped their bomb bays and put in racks loaded with supplies. Believe me, that was a sight to see, those B-29s flying low over us, dropping food, not bombs. These supplies didn't come down as well as they should have, for when the racks came out of the bomb bays, about half the chutes would rip loose and supplies were scattered all over the place. One of the fliers from China got to a radio and called a pilot, "Man, you're wasting half the supplies you're dropping!"

The answer came from the pilot, "Don't worry, friend. There's more where that came from, and we'll see you the same time tomorrow!" Then he wagged his wings and flew away.

Sure enough, they came again. For two days they bombed us with parcels of food and clothing and other necessities, more than we'd seen the whole time we were prisoners. We didn't really believe they could bring us more than we could eat; they could never bring that much.

Of course, there were medicines for the sick, though in many cases it was already too late. The cooks got busy and started feeding us Spam and corned beef hash, canned vegetables and fruit cocktail, three times a day. We didn't turn up our noses at it. To us it was the best food we'd ever had in our lives. We sat down with our plates full for the first time since December 7, 1941, determined to eat it all and have seconds.

We made some startling discoveries. None of us could eat more than a few bites; we filled up too quickly. I saw one soldier sitting, staring at his plate, with tears running down his cheeks. He was crying because he couldn't eat it. Our diets had been so inadequate for so long, our stomachs empty so much of the time, that they had shrunk. There was simply no room for the food we were now getting. Sometimes men would sit for a couple of hours at the table, eating a little, then waiting a while and eating a bite or two more, trying to do what we had done for years—eat every bite on the plate. Never leave a bite. It was a habit hard to break.

When the supplies broke loose as they were being dropped from the plane, they went flying all over the place, through the tops of buildings, into the countryside. People who were watching ran for cover. Some were injured because they couldn't get to safety soon enough. I was running from one of the racks that came circling down out of a bomb bay, with food and clothing parcels still tied onto it. I stumbled and fell into a pile of gravel outside the camp. The rack and its burden fell right on top of me. It could easily have crushed me, but it hit the top of the gravel pile and tilted to the ground away from me. I didn't get a scratch. Another minor miracle.

I did get hurt later, though, as a case of canned goods had gone into a bit of swampy ground and got sucked down and covered up. I stepped on it, not realizing it was there, and cut my foot pretty badly on a can that had broken open. A friend that I was with at the time saw all the blood and grabbed me and started running up the road about fifty yards to where a Chinaman had a vehicle. I'm not sure what it was, perhaps a cross between a three-wheeled bike and a rickshaw. My friend pulled the startled Chinaman off the seat, pushed me onto the back and started peddling toward camp with the outraged Chinaman running as hard as he could behind, yelling and shaking his fist.

We rushed into the camp hospital and got my toe fixed up. We gave the Chinaman back his bike and loaded him with cigarettes, candy and chewing gum. He rode out of camp with a wide grin on his face.

The Chinese and Japanese civilians were as anxious as we were to get their hands on this manna from heaven, and we were having to fight them off. I was so anxious to get one parcel I stepped right into a "honey pool" that some Manchurian was stockpiling for his vegetable garden. And I had thought I was through with all that!

I lay on the ground that August night on Manchurian soil and looked up at the stars and thought of the folks back home. I wondered how Mama and Dad would feel when they got the news I was coming home. I wondered if Clif ever went into service, and if he were still alive; I thought of cousin M. L. and hoped he'd get home soon so I could see him again. Well ... it had been a struggle ... many times it would have been easy to give up ... but I didn't.

Now, no more being hungry, no more beatings and standing attention until I was numb. No more Manchurian winters, no more rats and fleas, no more having to rise and eat and stand roll call in one instant. No more having to put up with ridiculous rules and undeserved punishment. Best of all, no more honey cart! Soon I'd eat steak instead of watery soup and would be able to taste Mama's caramel pies. I was going home!

CHAPTER 20

TABLES TURNED

We were given our mail that had accumulated in the Japanese store room. I got fifty-four letters, some of them dating from six months after I'd been captured. I sorted mine by cancellation dates and read them in order. Word came out that the Japanese had intending burning, destroying our mail, but the American parachutists had prevented it. I don't doubt it for a moment.

All my letters were from my mother, and all said about the same thing. She was a homebody, and her interests and those she wrote of were of the family and friends in the Springhill community. What could a mother say to a son she hadn't heard from in three years? The first word Mama got about me after I was captured was when a propaganda group came into camp and let us write a short message to be sent out on short wave. We thought it would be a waste of time, that they wouldn't send it, and, even if they did, no one would receive it. But another miracle happened, an Air Corps sergeant, stationed in China, an off-duty radioman, picked up the message and sent a letter to my family. That was the first word they'd heard from me since they'd gotten the letter sent out on a submarine when I was on the front line in Bataan, February, 1942.

Years later I read a diary kept by a British officer who had been in our camp. He kept mentioning the Red Cross parcels they were getting and how many letters the Americans were receiving. If he hadn't mentioned events I knew about, the Jap officers I knew, I'd have sworn we weren't in the same camp. The only Red Cross package I saw the whole time I was there was the one I shared with another man. If Red Cross packages were designated for us, they got sidetracked. I do know that at the end of the war there was a warehouse full of these packages that the Japanese and Chinese civilians looted.

Very soon, about two or three days after the Americans dropped in, the Russians reached our camp. They were a new breed to us and about as strange as the Japanese had been. They marched boldly into camp, brought the Japanese guards into the parade ground, lined them up, and ordered them to stack their weapons (remember those piles on Bataan!). The Americans lined up opposite the Japanese. The Russian officers went through the ranks and chose a group of Americans, marched them forward, issued them a rifle and ammunition and told them to take the Japs prisoner and march them off to the guard house.

I don't know, of course, but I imagine the Japs felt that we would bring retribution on them for all their atrocities and must have been greatly relieved when we didn't. Col. Matsuda and all the officers and enlisted men remained our prisoners while we were still there.

After the Russians took over the camp and the Japanese were imprisoned, we began to move outside the camp. These excursions weren't without hazards, however, and we were warned against certain things before we were issued passes.

A group of Chinese had worked at the factory and in the factory kitchen, and since I had been in both, I was acquainted with many of them. Wong was a good cook, and he was put in charge of the American kitchen, with other Chinese working in the kitchen under him.

There was the Chinese boy, Lee Ah, working in the kitchen with whom I had worked closely until he had to go home to "take his bride." He wasn't happy about this. She had been chosen for him as a child, and he had never seen her, but he followed the time-honored Chinese tradition. He'd learned a few American words and had found out that wasn't the way we did it. He left the factory wistfully saying he'd like to try it the American way.

Lee Ah reappeared at the end of the war, and we used him as an interpreter to tell the Chinese helpers and other workers what to do. This did not relieve the American cooks, supply sergeants and others of their duties; it just took a lot of the burden from them.

Our treatment of the Japanese after they were taken prisoner was a true classic, concrete example of our national philosophy. We could have retaliated in kind, an eye for an eye, but we didn't. I suppose if we'd been fighting for our lives, it would have been different. Now we had the upper hand and could wreak any vengeance on them we wished, but we didn't. I often wondered what thoughts went through the Japanese minds. I think they were confused. If the situation had been reversed, they would have retaliated.

I never stood guard duty over the Japs, but I did catch a guard duty I didn't relish. In fact, I hated it, dreaded it. Frankly, I was frightened by it. There was a munitions factory in Mukden. Some of our men were going there getting souvenirs. The Russians set a few of us as guards over the factory to keep our own men out. I was afraid one of my buddies wouldn't take the whole thing seriously, and go on in past me. Would I shoot him as a result, or would the Russians shoot me because I didn't?

Another miracle. It didn't happen. My stint was over without incident, and I quit sweating and breathed a great big sigh of relief.

CHAPTER 21

SEEING MANCHURIA AS A TOURIST

American ex-prisoners of war were being flown out at the rate of about fifteen a day. Some of them went by air all the way home, and as a result got home several weeks ahead of me. I was not sick enough to make it necessary that I be flown out.

So many things were happening at this time; everyone was so excited. We were getting plenty to eat, cigarettes, chewing gum, clean clothes. We could even leave camp and see the town.

My first visit to Mukden was on foot. Like ninety-five per cent of us, all I knew of the city was our camp and factory. The day I chose to leave camp and go into town, I simply followed the crowd. The population of the city was probably a million, so a person could walk forever and not see it all of it. I was meandering around, going nowhere in particular, when I found myself at a warehouse, a large Japanese warehouse. In it were cases and cases of beer. I had never drunk much beer, but I was liberated and wanted to celebrate. I was very much surprised to see there, the Chinese boy, Lee Ah, who had left camp to marry.

He helped me load his two-horse cart with twenty-eight cases of beer, and hauled it to camp for me. It was an unusual cart. Instead of putting both horses in harness side by side, he had one horse in front of the other. We had started on our journey to camp when a Russian soldier walked over and stuck up one finger. I didn't want any trouble so I handed him a bottle of beer. He swung his gun around and pointed it at me, yelled and moved one hand in a square movement, using unmistakable sign language. I gave him a case immediately. We'd gone only a few yards farther when another Russian soldier stopped me and stuck up one finger. I was pretty sure what he wanted, so I gave him a case.

I got back to my bunk in the change room with twenty-six cases of beer, and it was a pretty popular place for a while. Anyone who wanted warm beer could help himself. Even Lee Ah, who hauled the beer into camp, didn't go away empty-handed. There were a lot of discarded uniforms, mostly heavy British, Australian and Dutch uniforms, so we loaded his cart down with woolen uniforms, and he went away happy.

My next trip into Mukden was with a friend. We were just wandering around, seeing the sights—walking the streets because we were free to walk the streets. We happened upon a street, several blocks long, that was filled with bars and hotels—bars on the lower floor and rooms above—all deserted. This was the Japanese "red light" district, where Manchurian women had been put for the use of the Japanese soldiers. We left there in a hurry and went on to see other things, remembering we had orders to get back to camp before dark. There was danger of ambush, as there were Japanese who were angry at the loss of the war; there were Chinese who would rob us for very little; and there were Russians who, we were told, needed no reason at all.

The latter proved to be true. My friend and I started back to camp with plenty of time to get back in daylight. Two young Russian soldiers, each looking to be eighteen or nineteen years old, pulled up beside us in an American jeep and signaled us to get in the back. They'd take us to camp. We got in the back and were driven to within a hundred yards of the gate, when suddenly the driver wheeled the jeep around and headed in the opposite direction. They took us to the far side of the city before they stopped, waved goodbye to us, and sped off laughing heartily.

It was way past "lights out" when we finally got back to camp. We had a lot of difficulty with the guards, who thought we were making up the story as an alibi. I never got into a vehicle with a Russian soldier again.

One of our fellows, a fellow of Czech descent, didn't feel that way. He disappeared one day, and after we had worried for a week believing something dreadful had happened to him, he showed up in camp, happy as a lark. He'd met a Russian pilot, and since they could communicate, they became friends. He had flown to Russia with the pilot for a brief holiday. He visited with the man's family and returned to Mukden when the Russian returned to duty.

Col. Matsuda had a 1935 Ford V-8 that was propelled by a carbide burner which was set on the trunk. Eagerness to be out of our long internment wasn't confined only to enlisted men. Three officers decided to take the Colonel's Ford and make a sightseeing tour of the city. They'd hardly started on their tour before they fell into a tank trap that had been built in defense against the Russians. The officers wound up in the hospital, and Matsuda's carbide burner ran no more.

Like the bear that went over the mountain, we used our passes to see what we could see. In our meanderings we wandered down to the railroad tracks, a busy place, to watch the trains come and go. We watched as the Russians loaded everything from the factories where we had worked that was worth moving; not just things from the factories, but everything of value they could get loose. They were so busy shipping goods out and had the rail lines so tied up, we had to wait for them to finish before we could leave camp to go to Port Dairen, where ships were waiting to take us home.

We watched as the trains came in, bringing in soldiers and equipment for the Russian takeover. We were fascinated by the soldiers, both men and women, lounging on top of the equipment piled on flat cars. We'd never seen women soldiers before.

My friend and I left the railyards and found a familiar Chinaman who took us to the warehouses where the Red Cross packages had been stored. The warehouses, once full of these parcels containing food and clothing, originally meant for us, were now in the hands of Japanese and Chinese looters. We weren't surprised by the looting. We'd have been surprised to see the packages there. After all, in a city of a million people, overrun by the Japanese, then by Russian troops, where people die on the streets and are left there to be eaten by dogs, what else could one expect?

CHAPTER 22

GOING HOME

Finally our waiting was over—it was time to leave. We were ordered to get our gear together, and the Russians started sending in trucks, hauling us to the station. One train load went out, then another train moved in. I was on the last truck to leave the camp. There must have been two thousand Manchurians standing outside the camp, people we'd grown to know and like. We were shedding tears, American and Chinese alike, as we waved goodbye. We waved as long as we could see each other.

We were taken to the same station we'd come in on, boarded the same kind of train we'd ridden to come to Manchuria. We didn't use the same port, Pusan, Korea, where I'd stepped off the hell ship from the tropics clad only in a pair of shorts, into a frigid gale straight from Siberia. Instead we went to Dairen.

The train moved so slowly; there were times as it traveled up hill, we could have gotten out and walked by its side. Chinese lined the side of the railway as we went through villages, waving to us. Most of us had our barrack bags full of cigarettes, candy and chewing gum. I had twenty-seven cartons and I didn't smoke. I started throwing out a pack of cigarettes to the crowd, then a bar of candy, or a pack of gum. The others were doing the same. When the train stopped at Dairen, the southern port on the China Sea, some two hundred miles south of Mukden, I didn't have a pack of cigarettes or chewing gum left. So what? Who wants to take twenty-seven cartons of cigarettes from Mukden, Manchuria to Paris, Texas, when you don't smoke?

At Dairen, two ships were docked. One was a hospital ship, filled with some that had been sent out ahead of us, the sicker ones. The ship I boarded was a troop transport. It was equipped with landing barges, with twin engines and twin props. It was made to maneuver fast, to move troops in fast and get out. Large barges were fastened down on the deck, with some of the smaller barges hanging over the sides, along with life rafts.

Our enthusiasm and exuberance was about to be dampened, literally. As we went up the gang plank to the ship we were ordered to get rid of everything. Everything! Cigarettes (wasn't it noble of us to give all that away!) and clothes (just issued when the war ended). Where did all this go? We never knew. Maybe left on the docks or incinerated or thrown overboard at sea, or possibly sent for fumigation. We never saw them again.

We were handed a bar of soap and a towel and escorted to the showers where we scrubbed from head to feet, then scrubbed again, under the watchful eye of a seasoned sailor. (Oh, the indignity of it all!) We had to get rid of years of filth, fleas and lice. I hadn't felt so clean since my Mama scrubbed me in a number three washtub when I was a small child. We were issued a suit of underwear to wear out of the shower, then taken to another room and given navy fatigues, a two-piece jump suit.

From Dairen we were headed for Okinawa, according to the sailors. Okinawa was the assembly point for Pacific area prisoners. We were to be further processed and sent home from there. We sailed all night and into the next evening, when we steamed into Buckner Bay. We'd come into port expecting to disembark momentarily. Instead the ship began to move, and we left port and went back out into the China Sea. What was happening? Naturally we were curious and very disappointed. It seemed a typhoon was raging in our area and was moving into Okinawa.

The safest thing for us to do was to ride it out at sea. To stay in port might cause us to wash aground and lose the ship. So much for them, but what about me? I, Oliver Craig Allen, who had been clever enough to avoid malaria on the front line when others had been eaten alive by mosquitoes, who had worked his way to the front of the Bataan march to avoid the severest atrocities, who had managed to get quinine each time he was brought low by chills and fever, who had been able to work in the life-saving kitchen and had survived the honey cart, was now brought low again by another attack of seasickness!

The typhoon hit. The ship rocked, lunged, tossed. I was flat on my back, holding on to my bunk to stay in it, sick, sick, sick. Sick at my stomach, seasick, deathly sick.

The rocking continued until around five-thirty in the morning, or whatever time it is when they sound their horns for rising and breakfast. Bunks were five deep and I was on top. I asked the friend across from me if he was going up for breakfast. "Breakfast. Are you kidding? It's all I can do to stay flat on my back," he answered mournfully. I agreed that even if we wanted breakfast we'd never be able to navigate ourselves out of this area to the galley, with the rocking and bouncing that was going on.

I had barely gotten the words out of my mouth when there was a violent explosion that shook the entire ship; the thing seemed to shudder. We were five levels down, and when the lights went out there was complete darkness. We were so far down daylight could not even have been pumped down to us.

When the explosion occurred we all started running, groping in the dark, bumping into bunks and walls and each other. It was pandemonium. Being on the top of five bunks, I ran in my shorts, never mind trying to find my pants, never hitting the floor, but on top of other men running for the door. I know when my feet finally touched floor, it must have been three or four flights up.

When we finally got up to daylight, it was a sight to see, with people running everywhere, waves lapping over the deck. We had to grab hold of the first solid object we could find and hang on to keep from being washed overboard. I grabbed a gun, a big cannon pointing toward the angry seas. I stayed there, shoeless, clad only in shorts, waiting to see if the ship would sink.

We'd hit a mine, or perhaps the mine hit us. Whatever, we had a hole in the side of the ship the size of a house, about midship, right in the engine room. We were there with no power, being lashed by high waves, helpless as could be. The damaged area was sealed off, and we were waiting to see if it was going to hold before we abandoned ship.

I clung to the gun for a long while. Then seeing that we weren't going to sink immediately, I got brave enough to go below for some clothes. By this time emergency engines were supplying enough light for us to see to move about a little. I found my pants and shirt, but I never found my shoes. I went ashore in Okinawa, eventually, without any shoes on.

After finding my clothes, I returned to deck, determined never to go back down there again. The several hundred former prisoners of war aboard the ship were the calmest of all, once we saw the situation. I don't know the psychology of this. Perhaps it was because we'd faced death so many times, we'd become hardened to the idea. The ship was new, having been commissioned a few months before, and the crew was young. This was probably, for some, their first crisis. Even they weren't frightened because only those with experience really knew the seriousness of the situation.

After the waves began to calm a bit, a friend and I set up quarters in a life raft. It was covered with a tarp, so it was waterproof. The galley couldn't cook food, so most of what we ate came from cold cans. But the raft had water and survival rations. We tried to figure out how to separate the life raft from the ship in case we needed to get afloat. It never came to that, for as soon as the storm passed four days later, a tug came and brought us into port again.

Years later, one of my neighbors, on hearing I'd been on that ship, told me he'd been a sailor in port when the ship was brought in, and everyone marveled that it had been able to stay afloat.

An even more remarkable tale comes from Lloyd Boatright, an ex-prisoner who had been with me in Mukden. He told me he was aboard the ship that "sank," the ship I was on. He had jumped overboard and was picked up by a tug. "They'd shoot me a line," he said, "but they'd be on top of a wave, and I'd be down, and it would miss. Then I'd ride to the crest of a wave and they'd shoot and then go down. Finally, after numerous tries, they got me aboard."

He reported seeing landing barges being tossed over the ship and several men getting killed. So, he'd picked up a life preserver and jumped overboard. He'd come home and lived twenty years or more believing the ship had sunk. And truly, it was another miracle.

We went into Buckner Bay and unloaded as fast as possible. We got on trucks again that took us—can you believe it—to Tent City. I never did get to stay in stone barracks.

Hardly had we got settled in our tents when we were surrounded by a dozen or more ex-prisoners who had been in Japan. "Where is he? Tell us! We want that son-of-a-bitch!"

We didn't know what the heck they were talking about.

"The white rat, the traitor! Old So-and-so." I didn't know the name and can't remember who they said. It seems they had gotten a newsletter the Japs put out that told of this Mukden prisoner who had worked for the Japanese there and had been quoted as saying how much he liked the Japanese and that he intended to live in Japan when the war was over. These men were out for blood.

It appears the traitor had actually been responsible for several men losing their lives. These blood hounds didn't find him, for we heard later he had been hustled out of camp when the Americans came in, was tried for treason and confined to Leavenworth. I suppose that is the truth, as I've not heard anything more about the matter.

The storm had hit Okinawa pretty hard. Airplanes on the landing field had been rolled over. The tents in Tent City had been blown away, but were now replaced and ready for us. Tents with cots, with mattresses and clean sheets. The mess hall was not far away. We had nothing to complain about.

I did have one disappointment, though. General Eubanks of the 19th Bomb Group had been sending in one plane a day and taking out the prisoners of war who were members of that group. They were picking up men who were part of the 19th, getting them released and flown to Guam, where they were reassigned to the 19th. Three days later they were in San Francisco. But as a result of the typhoon, wrecked planes cluttered the runways and the B-29s could not land. Consequently, I lost my quick ride home.

There wasn't much to do on Okinawa. We were all impatient to get home, so any diversion was welcome to pass the time. A Marine colonel came over to visit us. He commanded a group of planes that were on an aircraft carrier. "Would you boys like to see a show?" Would we!

The next morning at ten o'clock, without preliminaries and to our great surprise, something happened that at first sent us running for cover, as we thought we were in a bombing raid. With our reflexes being affected by years of our slow-paced primitive existence, we were slow on the uptake in recognizing this as the show the colonel had promised.

Those little planes came over a hill, flying in formation almost on the ground, and were on us before we knew it. They were flying so low one of them hit a flag pole and tipped it over. I was waiting for the plane to fall, but it kept its equilibrium and stayed in formation. If the colonel had wanted to start the adrenaline flowing in our sluggish systems, he had succeeded.

It was a week before the landing strip was cleared enough to get planes in and out of Okinawa. Unfortunately for me, General Eubanks was no longer sending in the B-29s for the 19th members. I flew out of there on a B-24, stripped down, with no seats or safety belts. We just sat on the floor anywhere we could find room, holding on to whatever was handy, on take-off and landing.

We boarded this airborne boxcar early in the morning and headed for the Philippines, just sitting there thinking about home, listening to the heavy roar of the engines. I was situated where I could see the propellers on one side. I was watching them with their invisible spinning, when poof!—a little puff of smoke—and one engine stopped. I looked down at the water below. We were eight or nine thousand feet up. Oh, Lord, what will we do? I prayed. I'd been in the Air Corps nearly five years and knew almost nothing about an airplane. All I knew about flying was what I'd learned in junior college back home before the war. What a waste of time, those five years. God, what a waste of time!

We were wearing parachutes. This came about as the result of a tragic accident in one of these planes that had preceded us. These stripped-down bombers still had functional bomb bays. As this particular plane was crowded, one tired man lay down on the bomb bay door to sleep. The door was accidentally opened and the poor soul fell into the sea. After that not only did the passengers wear parachutes, but they kept their distance from the bomb bay.

Very soon after I'd seen the puff of smoke and the engine propeller quit, the crew chief came back to us and told us not to worry about the one engine. These planes have been brought back from missions with only two engines functioning. "However," he explained, "we're returning to Okinawa because we can't get repairs in the Philippines, so we need to return to home base." We returned to Okinawa, got off the disabled plane and got right on another one.

I looked this one over as I approached it, and what I saw was not reassuring. It looked pretty beat up, like it had been around for a long time and had seen a lot of action. Along its nose were rows and rows of little bombs painted there to indicate the number of missions it had returned from. There were so many I didn't have time to count them.

I was really nervous about getting on it, for I wasn't sure it would stand the trip. Some other men had joined us, some pilots, three or four of them, young men. They had flown their missions; the war was over; and they were going home. After we got into the air and began to relax, I struck up a conversation with a pilot. I remembered, as if it had been in another lifetime, my ambition to be a pilot, an ambition that had been thwarted. It was hard not to feel a little envy and be a little bitter.

This pilot, on hearing my fear about the condition of the plane, began telling me its history. This plane was in his squadron and every pilot wanted to go out in it, because no matter what happened it never failed to make it back to home base. It might come home with a hole in it or some metal hanging loose and flapping. "Yes, sir," he smiled in remembrance, "it may sound like a tin barn, like it's going to fall apart, but she'll sure get you home." I went to sleep sitting on the floor, listening to the rattle of the old plane above the steady hum of the engines.

We were all pretty well exhausted when we got to the Philippines, hoping we could land soon and find a soft bed somewhere. It was not to be. A hard rain was falling; it was beating against the sides of the old plane and making it rattle worse than ever. The pilot didn't land, but flew and flew. We stayed in the air so long we were getting worried, afraid there was something wrong, that perhaps in the storm we were lost and couldn't find the landing field. What if we were over the ocean again and ran out of fuel? What good would parachutes do then?

We finally landed at Clark Field and never really knew what happened. The friend who'd jumped overboard in the typhoon explained years later that the reason for the delay was probably that they couldn't get the landing gear down. It flew until the fuel was gone and bellied in. Well, I was sitting on the floor and surely would have felt it if we'd bellied in. I do know that when we landed we stopped dead still. We didn't taxi anywhere, and the bus came and got us off pretty quickly. The rain was pelting so hard we didn't stop to look at the plane as we left it. Whatever had happened, the old girl had brought us home safely once more; she'd lived up to her reputation.

From the plane the bus took us to a Red Cross area where we were given coffee and doughnuts. There we saw the best part of the whole trip, the thing that made the trip worthwhile: American girls! For the first time in four years I saw a Caucasian female, with fair skin and blue eyes. I thought I was nearly home.

We were in line, moving up to get our refreshments, with maybe a smile and a kind word or two, when one fellow suddenly went wild. He let out a shriek and jumped over a booth and grabbed a girl. She shrieked, and we all moved to run to her defense, when we realized they were laughing and crying and hugging and jumping around. It was his sister. Needless to say, we enjoyed the reunion almost as much as they did.

While we were still having our coffee and doughnuts and basking in the family reunion, ambulances came and took us to an old transport. This transport had hinged seats that folded down from the sides of the plane, not the most comfortable seats in the world. I sat down, and the next thing I knew, felt the fellow next to me nudge me with his elbow.

"What's the matter? Have we taken off? Is something wrong?" I asked.

He laughed. "Fellow, we're at Nichols Field; we're in Manila. We're ready to get off." I'd fallen asleep as soon as I sat down and had slept through the flight.

Buses met us and took us to the 29th Replacement Depot, another tent city, which had been set in the middle of a giant mud puddle. Mud was everywhere; we waded in shoe-top-high mud to the latrine, and to the change room, where after a shower to clean off the mud, we waded in mud to get back to our water-soaked tents.

Our three weeks, or thereabouts, stay in Mud City was a time of mixed emotions. Three weeks in this unpleasant place seemed endless. I wanted to go home. I'd been liberated for nearly two months, and I thought it was time I went home. I'd been delayed at every turn. Why couldn't I get home as the others were doing?

I'd been there a day or two when I wandered over to a Red Cross booth for a bottle of beer and maybe somebody to talk to. I was standing there alone, sipping the beer slowly to pass as much time as possible, when a soldier walked up to me and said, "Red?"

I looked at him in astonishment and said, "Red?"

We two redheads grabbed each other much like the brother and sister in the Red Cross line at Clark Field. This was James "Red" Griffin that I'd gone to high school and college with. He'd come to the Philippines shortly before I arrived from Manchuria and was working with the finance division. He had been getting lists of arriving ex-prisoners of war and had the job of making partial payments to the men as they came through the processing center.

"Red, old buddy," he said, "I was about to give you up. I've been watching the lists and was getting to the end of them. I was getting worried."

Griffin had spent a couple of years as recruiting sergeant in our hometown and was pretty well up on the news of what had happened to the fellows we knew. We sat there and he began to tell me about the ones he remembered. "You remember England, don't you? M.L. England? Well, he got it at Guadalcanal. Nose gunner on a B-24, got shot and bled to death before the plane got to home base."

M.L.! Oh, God! So that was why Mama hadn't mentioned him in any of her letters. I'd wondered why. I was shocked and must have looked it. "Red, what's the matter?"

"M.L. He's my cousin," I managed to say.

"Oh, Red. I'm sorry. I didn't know."

M.L. Dead! My closest cousin and my closest friend. Born in the same bed at Granny England's, fourteen days apart.

Griffin looked almost as stricken as I felt. "Oh, Red, I wouldn't have told you if I'd known." It didn't matter, I tried to reassure him. I had to learn about it sometime. It was just as well I learned it now; it would give me time to accept it before I got home and found out other things.

But it did matter. It mattered a lot, for the last time I saw M.L. was the day before I joined up, and he tried to talk me out of it. He was going to buy a truck, and we could haul blocks and make some money. That way I would have the money to go to college. But no, I had a dream, a dream of flying, a dream I wouldn't let go. But the dream had gone as surely as a dream goes when you wake in the morning.

So that is why Mama didn't mention him in her letters; she told me all about the family and friends, but not about M.L. What would life be like back home without M.L.?

James Griffin had to work during the day, but he got off at five o'clock and we'd get together for a few hours. Often we'd hitch a ride on an army truck and go in to Manila. The drivers of the trucks wouldn't stop for you, but they'd slow down so that if you were agile enough you could grab a ride. Things were moving a bit fast for me, I had to admit, so my first venture at "catching a ride" was almost "missing a ride." If I hadn't been aided by Red Griffin I'd have been left standing by the side of the road. We'd hitch a ride back and get into our bunks about midnight. This was okay for me as I could sleep late the next morning, but it made it a little hard on Griffin who had to rise early.

We saw the sights in Manila, drank an occasional beer and talked. That's what I wanted most, to find out about everybody, to learn about the people at home so I wouldn't walk into too many surprises.

It was on one of our little junkets that I had my first experience with a new breed of soldier—a WAAC colonel, no less. We'd been approached by a flower vender, "Orchids, Joe. Ten centavos." Orchids! I was celebrating life, why not an orchid? Red and I each got one and stuck it in our buttonholes.

"Soldiers, I see you're a little bit out of uniform." I was startled at first; I'd never seen a woman soldier before, except the Russians on the flat cars. I pulled the orchid out of my shirt immediately. Then I got angry as I went on. How dare she pick on such a petty thing! An orchid in a buttonhole couldn't be wrong, when less than two months ago I was on the honey cart. Then it struck me as funny. What the heck, let her have her day. I started laughing and then Red Griffin joined me. We went our orchidless way, happy.

CHAPTER 23

BACK TO THE U.S.A.

Whilhile in the 29th Replacement Depot, I drew a partial payment of five hundred dollars. I thought I was rich, for I'd never had more than thirty or forty dollars in my pocket at any one time before. I was drawing sergeant's pay now. Sometime in the spring of 1945, a group of officers had come into our camp from a camp on Formosa. Among them was my friend Col. Laughinghouse. I'd gone over and visited with the colonel. He told me what he had learned about the war, and I told him the news I'd picked up around the factory. He never left his quarters and always seemed glad to see me.

One day Sgt. Hamilton made a list of names for promotions and asked me to take it to Col. Laughinghouse for him to sign. I did so, and the colonel looked at the list and asked, "Where's your name?"

"It's not there, Sir."

"Take it back to Sgt. Hamilton to put your name on the list and I'll sign it."

He offered to make me a lieutenant, but I refused because I thought that since I had to live with the other fellows I'd better stay on their level. I'd been promoted to PFC just before the war started, so when I came out I was a staff sergeant.

The day arrived when I said "so long" to Red Griffin and got my gear together to head home. "Here we go again," I thought.

From the same pier that I arrived at in the Philippines in October, 1941, the same pier I had shipped out on a Jap prison ship in October, 1942, I was leaving in October, 1945, heading home. I was leaving Manila at last, heading for the good old U.S.A.

The trip was one of tranquillity except for a few minor occurrences. A friend had bought a box of Philippine cigars and urged me to try one. I did, much to my discomfort. I thought a storm had hit and we were riding the waves again. Needless to say I spent a lot of time in my bunk the rest of the way home.

One of my buddies said to me one night, after I'd risen from my bunk and stepped up for fresh air, "Do you remember what happened going overseas four years ago? Remember, we went to bed on October 11 and woke up on October 13. We crossed the international dateline and lost October 12. Well, today is October 12." We got up the next morning to find it was still October 12.

We'd crossed the international dateline and recovered the day we'd lost four years before.

A few days before coming into San Francisco the officers started lining us up on deck, drilling us on how we were to leave the ship. We went over this a couple of times to be sure we knew how to do it. We steamed in under the Golden Gate Bridge at midday. There was a band playing on the bridge, and we were all crying like babies. We were going home. We were about to set foot again on American soil. Unimportant? If you think so, you've never been on foreign soil, denied the right to live in dignity.

As we approached the pier, we were all getting ready to march off in pure military style. We were going to march off like soldiers. The ship pulled in. We gathered our belongings and jumped into formation. The gangplank dropped, and suddenly we were ordered to drop everything and hit the gangplank. We stampeded like a herd of cattle.

The pier was lined with people waiting for their sons and husbands and sweethearts and brothers to come in. My folks weren't there, of course, as they could never have afforded a trip to California. But I got to meet the wives and children, fathers, mothers, brothers and sisters of friends. One friend, a corporal, discovered that his little brother whom he had left at home as a high school student, running an elevator for spending money, was now a major in the Air Corps, flying P-38s in the South Pacific.

I had no folks there to meet me, but I did have a letter from home, telling me they were waiting anxiously for my return. We stayed on the pier for a couple of hours visiting, then got on the buses and moved to Letterman General Hospital.

A DIFFERENT KIND OF CASUALTY

It was here at Letterman that I received devastating news about a special friend of mine, a friend I'll never forget. I'll call him Ben; I'll not tell more of his identity. We'd been on the front line together and got along well. When I was in the Pampanga Province on the Penaranda River Bridge building detail at Gapan, he was on another bridge detail just below us down river. He was the one who saw ten men shot by the Japanese because one man escaped with Filipino guerrillas.

When we left the Philippines aboard the *Totora Maru* we were together; he is the prisoner who shared his oleomargarine with me. He truly saved my life. After we got to Manchuria I went to work in the factory and so did he. I was working on the machines, and Ben was working in the office of the head engineer. I'm not sure what his duties were, but evidently some sort of book work, as he carried pencils and pens in his shirt pocket.

When I went to work in the kitchen, he would come down each afternoon somewhere around two o'clock to pick up a kettle of hot water to take back to the office for the group to make hot tea. While he was there in the mess hall, waiting for his water to boil, I'd set out some food I'd saved for him. It varied, never was very much, just whatever I'd been able to have extra. Whatever it was, it was food and he needed it. I felt that I was helping to repay his good treatment of me aboard ship.

This arrangement went on for several months, six or seven, perhaps. Then one day I had to leave the kitchen to go out on detail, so I set out his food before I went out. When I came back in later, his food was still there, untouched. The men asked, "Have you seen your friend Ben?" No, I hadn't seen him. "It's just as well. He came in while you were out, looking like a wild man. He took his pens and pencils out of his pocket and threw them in the fire, yelling, 'They're after me! They're going to kill me, and it's all Red's fault. He's been plotting against me all this time.' The guards have taken him back to camp."

This upset me so much I could hardly finish my work. When we got back to camp that evening, I'd just gotten to the barracks and hadn't even sat down on my bunk to rest, when a runner came and said the doctor wanted to see me at the hospital. I went immediately. The doctor told me to sit down. "Sit here and talk to me a minute before you go in to see your friend." He asked a few questions, about Ben's mental state, how he got along with others, if he'd had any particular troubles that I knew about. I told him what little I knew, about the bridge detail, and how he'd helped me.

Then he told me what had happened to Ben, pretty much repeating what the kitchen staff had told me, that he was raving and blaming me for plotting against him. "I know you feel upset about this, but don't feel guilty. You've done nothing to harm your friend. In cases like this, the person closest is often blamed. Usually a family member, in his case you, because you're the one closest to him. Now go in and talk to him. And try not to be too shocked by what you see. He'll have days when he'll improve and seem normal. I want you to come in every afternoon after work and visit with him. You'll be his closest touch with normality."

I thanked the doctor and walked down the ward, dreading what I was going to see. I didn't see him at first, as he was hiding under his bunk, peering out from under the blanket that was hanging down. "Come on down," he said.

I knelt by his bunk.

"They're going to kill me."

"No, they're not."

"Yes, they are. It's all your fault. I thought you were my friend."

" I am your friend, Ben. Nobody is going to hurt you."

"You've been plotting, I know. And you told the Japs all about me. I know you did."

I stayed and tried to reassure him, but I could see I was only upsetting him more, so I left. He was there every afternoon when I went in, hiding under his blanket. I'd visit a while and talk to him, but he still accused me of plotting with the Japs against him.

This was discouraging. I felt worse every time I went in, until one afternoon, about two weeks later I went by and found him sitting on his bunk, nonchalant, at ease, and as normal as could be.

"Hey, Red!"

"Hey there, yourself. You look good today."

"I feel good. I feel perfectly fine today. They said you've been coming to see me. Red, please don't abandon me. Don't quit coming to see me. When this hits—when I get—well, it's like a nightmare. Have you ever had a nightmare when you were little, and you think someone's going to kill you? You try to run and get away, but you can't. Well, this is the way I feel, except it's not a dream. It's real. I know it's in my mind, and I try to concentrate and talk sensibly, but I can't. I may be perfectly sane, then five minutes later it hits me again." I stayed as long as I dared, and we had a good long normal talk. The next afternoon he was under his bunk again.

For six weeks or so this went on, good days and bad. Mostly

bad. Then one afternoon I went by to see him, and he was not in his bunk. No one in the ward would tell me where he was, so I went to the doctor. He motioned for me to sit down; he sat across from me, looking tired and drawn. "Well," he said, "you'll not have to worry about coming by to see Ben any more."

Haltingly, and with effort, he told me. Ben had crawled out from under his bed during the day and suddenly, in a bold move, grabbed a saber from a surprised Japanese officer and paraded up and down the aisles, waving the saber back and forth, vowing to kill everybody. The ward was cleared out quickly. Patients, medical personnel and guards evacuated the place. This went on for some time. Eventually, after Ben had begun to weaken from this exertion, a British corpsman went in and calmly asked Ben if he could see the saber.

"Sure," Ben replied and promptly handed it over. He was immediately hustled to the guardhouse where he was placed in solitary confinement. Detention for an offense meant you got food and blankets every third day; for two days you got no food and no blankets in an unheated cell in the frigid Manchurian winter when the temperatures stayed from zero to forty below. But Ben had food and blankets every day. There he would stay, without me, without anyone being able to visit him, to comfort and cheer him. There he stayed with no contact with another person, except the Jap guard who brought his buns and soup, for over two years.

When the war was over and Russians relieved the Japanese of command, they released all the men in the guardhouse. My friend Ben was still surviving after two years in solitary confinement. The camp doctor called me over and asked if I'd see after him. They wanted him to have as normal an adjustment as possible before he returned home. So he was assigned to me. I got bunks from the hospital and set them up in the change room away from the fleas. He stayed in quarters there with me and seemed just fine. It looked good for him, and I was happy.

Soon a team of doctors called a processing crew arrived from a base in China or Okinawa, I'm not sure which. It was their job to interview all of us and determine which ones could wait for ordinary processing. The more seriously ill ones would be flown out as soon as possible; and others, like me, would go out by rail to a seaport and then leave the Orient by ship.

Ben and I were called to the doctors the same day, and he went in ahead of me. When I had been examined and returned to the change room, I found him there, ranting and raving, blaming me for all his troubles, saying I had told the doctors about him. I couldn't do anything with him; he just raved on and on and on. Finally I couldn't take it any longer and told the doctors to come and get him, I couldn't handle him. They put him in a room in the hospital that could be locked. He was flown out the next day. I never saw him again.

One of the first things I heard when I reached Letterman General Hospital was about Ben. It seems he went home and was so normal the folks never suspected there was anything wrong with him. He was on his way back to the hospital when he shot himself in the head in a hotel room. He left a note, "If I can't find it here, I can't find it anywhere." Another horrible victim of war.

TEXAS, AT LAST!

At Letterman General Hospital we underwent more processing, more physical exams. We were issued uniforms, and eventually were given passes so we could go into town. Some of the men were impatient, however, and slipped out of the hospital and went into town in hospital garb, dark maroon jumper and slacks. The MPs were as busy as could be, picking up soldiers in strange-looking uniforms, but they were fighting a losing battle. There wasn't enough official transportation to take care of the situation, so they began hailing taxis and putting men in them, with orders to the drivers to take the men to

Letterman. After the cabs had gotten a safe distance from the MPs, the men would buy the drivers off and be out on the streets again.

I'm reminded of kids off on a spree for the first time without parental supervision . . . I didn't attempt to go downtown. My timing hadn't caught up with me yet; part of me was still running on Manchurian time, back with the horse carts and *jinrikshas*. I wasn't all that anxious to buck traffic.

After I'd been issued a uniform and had my patches and campaign bars, my stripes and medals put on, I thought I looked sharp enough to go out in public. I had finally grown enough facial hair to shave, and that made me feel good. So I found a fellow I'd been with in Manchuria, and we decided we'd go see San Francisco. He said, "Trust me; I know all about this city." Ha!

We caught a streetcar at the hospital, and the first thing he did after we got there was to start hitting the bars. Pretty soon he was feeling good. I'd say, "Straighten up, here come the MPs." He'd rear back and walk straight. I'd not tell him when they passed, hoping to keep him erect a bit longer. But he'd realize they were gone and would relax again.

I got pretty tired of this; I'd come to see the sights, not bars. Soon he went into a bar while I window-shopped, and he gave me the slip. I decided I'd had enough of San Francisco and wanted to go back to the hospital. I tried to hail a cab, but the fleet was in—I think the whole U. S. Navy was in port—and there wasn't an empty cab to be found.

I was standing on a corner vainly trying to get a taxi. There was an older man and woman there, too, trying to get home. "Where are you going, soldier?"

"I'm trying to get back to Letterman General Hospital."

"There's no need to get a cab for that. The streetcar goes right to it."

"I know, because that's the way I came in, but I don't know which one to catch to go back."

"Go down the block," they instructed, "and get Car D. It goes right to Letterman."

I thanked them and walked to the designated place. It was about one o'clock in the morning now, and there were other people waiting there, including some of my friends. They were uncertain, too, as to which car to catch. Within fifteen minutes Car D stopped and I got on. I tried to get my friends to join me. Several of them said they'd already tried Car D, and it didn't help them a bit.

"I'm going to try it; I've got nothing to lose. I can't be any more lost than I am now, and at least I'll have a place to sit," I said.

I got on the street car, paid my fare and had another shock. The conductor was a woman, first one I had ever seen. This was a strange world I was coming home to. People got off and I rode some more. Soon the car was nearly empty, and I was still riding. Finally the conductor pulled to a stop and said, "Letterman!" I could have shouted. I got up and off, the last passenger on the car. It was 2:30 in the morning.

There was no early rising for me the next day, so later in the morning I went to see if my friend had made his way home. Yes, he was on his bunk, not remembering how he got back there.

Before I had a chance to go into town again, our ranks began to thin. We were put on hospital trains, going in different directions, taking us closer to our homes. The train I boarded had dining cars converted into hospital cars by putting in bunks. When we boarded, we gave up our uniforms and were given hospital pajamas, the afore-mentioned uniforms. A nurse was present in every car, and the trip was pleasant.

The train made a few stops along the way. At one, one of the nurses got off to get some whiskey for some of the men. She was slow and had to run to catch the train. Not watching, she ran into a telephone pole, and got on board with a bloody nose, but the whiskey was intact.

Sleep, eat, lie in bed and watch the scenery go by. Soon we

were in Texas, in San Antonio, which is several hundred miles from Springhill, but I was getting closer all the time.

Brooks General—that's where we were to have more physical examinations and get our passes to go home. Some passes were for thirty days, some for sixty, but all for home. They soon began meting out the passes. I was excited. I couldn't wait to get back to those big oak trees and the spring and Mama's cooking. But my pass was not among the others. Why? There were thirty of us who were denied passes, and moved to the old part of the hospital. Oh, the indignity of it all, to have to be treated for tapeworms. For a little over a week I was delayed going home while the worms were worked out of me.

After I'd taken the medicine to kill the worms, they had to be flushed out. The nurse came in with a big glass of Epsom salts. I refused to take it. No, ma'am. Every time the least ailment occurred to Clif and me, Dad and Mama had got out either the Epsom Salts or castor oil. Remembering the vow I'd made at March Field, when I'd run the length of Tent City, I flatly refused it.

"Suit yourself. But you're not going home until you do."

I couldn't get it down quickly enough. Me, who'd been ahead of everybody physically, to be the last one to go home. Because of tapeworms. I'd already written my folks telling them I'd be home; now I had to write again, saying I'd be late.

One day I had a nice surprise. Uncle Willie Fodge, with sons Norris and Jimmy, had come to take home another son, Caton, who was there for his discharge. They came by to see me.

My brother, who was teaching school by this time, couldn't stand it any longer. He got a substitute and bought a bus ticket for San Antonio. But others, wives and parents and brothers, had come in, too, and he couldn't find a hotel room. He came out to the hospital, and after a pretty emotional reunion, told me of his predicament. One of the nurses in our ward had been stationed at Camp Maxey, which is near our home, and we'd struck up an acquaintance.

I told her where I first heard of Camp Maxey, Texas. It was when I first got to Okinawa, before I met Red Griffin. I was watching truck after truck of young soldiers pull in and unload. They looked so young, like eighteen-year-olds, as I looked when this mess started. Out of curiosity I asked where they came from.

"Camp Maxey, Texas," one answered

"Camp Maxey?" I'd never heard of it. "Where's that."

"At Paris."

"Which direction from Paris?" It wasn't there when I left.

"North."

North. We lived north of Paris. Had the camp taken our place? "How far north?"

"Oh, about ten miles."

"Is it east or west of Highway 271?"

He thought a few seconds. "West."

I breathed a sigh of relief. Mama, in one of her letters, had said there was a rumor of a camp coming there, and surveyors had been out, all over the place, but she'd never mentioned it again. Good. My folks were still on the tree-covered hill. I'd be able to get water from the spring again. All was well.

When I learned that Clif had no place to stay, I spoke to the nurse and told her of Clif's need.

"Is there an empty bed in your ward?" she asked. Yes, there was.

"Then let him have it." So Clif stayed with me. Except for meals; he always went out for his food.

Each afternoon, after I'd taken my medicines for the day, we'd go downtown just to get away from the hospital and see the sights. To get a bus going downtown we had to cross Broadway, a wide and busy street, at a place where there was no traffic light. I tried, but I simply could not make it across all that traffic. So we walked to a light where we could cross to a bus stop. This was eight or ten blocks away.

"Heck," Clif said, "we're halfway there now. Why catch a bus?"

So every evening we'd walk our twenty blocks or so, eat a good meal and talk, which was our best enjoyment, anyhow. When we decided to go back to the hospital, we'd catch a bus the whole way because the bus stopped on our side of the street.

When I finally got my pass, after a week or ten days, we planned to travel home together. I had no idea that travel was such a hassle when you were out on your own. It seems that two hundred people were waiting to catch one bus. When it came time to get on, service men had priority, then women with children, then old people. If there was any room, all others came next.

I was going to wait for Clif, but he shoved me forward and insisted that I get on the bus. That wasn't what I wanted, but people were pushing forward, so I had little choice. I left Clif at the San Antonio station and waved to him as I left him standing there.

When we got to the Austin station, I thought my eyes were deceiving me. There was Clif. He'd gotten a bus and beat me there. When I got to Dallas I looked around for him, but couldn't find him. I didn't know whether he'd gone ahead on the journey home or was still waiting in Austin. My wait in Dallas was a long one, five to six hours. But I finally got a bus and arrived in Paris at eleven a.m. the next day. He wasn't waiting for me, so I knew he was en route. I put my bag in a locker and started out to find someone I knew.

Goodness, how different it all looked! It was five p.m. before my brother came home. By that time I'd visited with Uncle Marvin and Aunt Myrtle and wept over the death of M.L. I'd visited the Butler kin and arranged for a ride home.

It was December, 1945; I'd been away since May, 1941. I can't describe my meeting with Mama and Dad. It's still too emotional to talk about. But isn't it strange, in all serious times, there is almost always an amusing or ironic note. I remember thinking how high my Mama's voice sounded. In fact, all women's voices sounded unnaturally high. I had been so long without hearing a woman's voice, that after I was liberated I had to retrain my ears.

I was home. I never did learn to fly; I was much too unstrung, too unsure of myself, to try. My older son is a pilot and sometimes I go up with him. And that's enough. Not all dreams come true. But then, some do.

CONSEQUENCES

CHAPTER 24

AFTEREFFECTS

I had arrived at Brooks General Hospital at Fort Sam Houston in San Antonio, Texas, in early November, 1945. I got my first furlough, for thirty days, in December. After reporting back to Brooks in January for a checkup, I stayed there as a patient to try to get my physical and mental condition back in shape. I was discharged in June of 1946.

Recovering from three and a half years in a Japanese prison camp was not an easy task. When I was liberated I weighed ninety pounds, but weight was not my main problem. We had thought that food was all we needed to put us back into perfect health. Before we left prison camp, after we were liberated, we found that we could eat very little food. Doctors told us our stomachs had shrunk over the years, and it would take time to overcome this problem.

We had been out of the regular routine of life, so it took a long time to adjust to some of the most simple things, such as trying to cross a busy street. Stress was one of the hardest things to overcome. I was married in 1947, two years after I was liberated. At that time I weighed one hundred twenty pounds; one year later I weighed one twenty-five.

I still have trouble with my feet. My feet were frozen in the winter of 1944; numbness set in and made it hard for me to walk. My toes lost their feeling, and I still have some numbness in my feet.

Nightmares are something most of us have had to contend with even until the present day. I have been on medication for high blood pressure for twenty-five years and was forced into early retirement because of hypertension. But with the help of medication, I have passed my eightieth birthday and have hopes of many more.

Another problem I have is with my skin. When I came home I had large scaly spots on my body. I use medication to try to keep these under control, and several skin cancers have been removed. My exposed skin, on hands and face, has reddened over the years, whether from high blood pressure or the exposure of my fair skin to the sun, or a combination of both, I'm not sure.

When I was discharged, my brother Clifford asked me what I planned to do, and I replied I thought I'd like to go to school and get a degree. He suggested I try teaching a year to give me time to decide what line of work I wanted to pursue. He secured me a position, and in the fall of 1946 I began teaching school.

I met my wife, Mildred, during this time, and we were married in June, 1947. We would teach during the school term and go to college during the summer. We did this until we both had Bachelor of Science Degrees and Master of Education Degrees. We have both returned to college, off and on, and done some post-graduate work.

In 1957, we became the parents of two wonderful boys (one adopted and one born to us, ages four months and four days apart). They were a blessing to us, especially as we had lost a baby daughter three years previously. We hired nannies for the boys, Danny and Tim, until they started kindergarten. Unlike some parents who can't wait to get the kids out of their hair, we always enjoyed our boys and loved to have them with us. We still do, for that matter.

When the boys were about five years old we began to attend the American Ex-Prisoners of War conventions during the summers. These were held in different places and afforded us a chance to travel throughout the United States. It also gave us a chance to get in touch with some of my old buddies; I renewed friendships and made new ones. Some of the friends who attended these get-togethers, along with their wives and children, include these men from 7th Materiel, 19th Bomb Group: Hurshel Reeves, Forrest Brooks, Russell Gill, Ray Thompson, Edwin Preston, Larry Hamilton, Dorman Ivey, Robert Kay, Lloyd Mulkey, Sammie Young, John Turner, Johnny Knight, Francis Gabour, Bob Palmer, Charles Baum, Harold Christopher, John Hatfield, Kenneth Luton, Billy Ayres, Robert Bailey, Carl Egner, Roy Allen, Luther Allen, Miller Barnes and Lawrence Hamilton.

Soon after Mildred and I were married, I had the opportunity to introduce Mildred to Sgt. "Skinny" Ervin at one of the first AXPOW meetings held in El Paso. We also visited with Col. Laughinghouse at his home in Tucson, Arizona.

Others that we saw at these get-togethers were people I'd been with at Mukden. They included: Art Rice, Everett Waldrum, Jesse Knowles, Leslie Nichols, Orville Padilla, Glenn Stewart, Leo Padilla, Weldon King, John Rowland, Joe Brasel, Clifton Sharp, Ira Wallace, Henry Harlan, Harold "Nick" Carter, Dean Smith, Paul Lankford, Frank McDaniel, William Russell, Harry Dunlavy, Charles Dragich, Greg Rodriquez, Jim Bogart, Robert Brown, Albert Allen, Robert Rosendahl, John I. Stout, Art Campbell and General Robert T. Taylor, a chaplain. Arthur Christie of Wales and George Gunning of York were two British men who also attended our Mukden reunions.

At our reunions of the American Defenders of Bataan and Corregidor, we see many of those mentioned above, and also others, including: Thomas Gage, John Snellen, Bynum Cook, Leon Gray, Elbert Hampton, Grady Inzer, Shelby McAllister, Gordon Smith, Dewey Spriuell, John Owens, Sam Siegel, Talmadge Wallace, Ralph Rodriquez, Walter Tucker, Conrad Langley and Lt. Col. Hattie Brantley of the Angels of Bataan. Several of these are members of our East Texas Chapter of AXPOW.

We have known so many people who were prisoners of war of the Japanese and many who were German prisoners. We are fond of all of them, but it's hard to remember all their names. Many of our dear friends mentioned above have passed on in the years we have been getting together, telling our stories, laughing and crying, but they remain in our memories.

Some of the veterans' organizations to which I belong include the *American Ex-Prisoners of War, Disabled American Veterans, American Legion, Veterans of Foreign Wars* and the *China-Burma-India* group. I was invited to join this last group, not because I had fought in that area, but because I had spent three years during the war there. I appreciate their thoughtfulness in including me. One other group that I am now a part of is the *Battling Bastards of Bataan.*

In 1969, we moved from Richardson, Texas, where we were teaching, to the hillside at Springhill, where I was reared. My brother and I had a business together, which he was operating, but his health was failing and he needed help. My wife and I started teaching in the Paris schools shortly thereafter.

At this time our sons, Danny and Tim, were ready to start junior high school. They finished high school in Paris and went to Texas A&M University. They left us to ourselves in our beautiful new home we'd built on the tree-shaded hill, near the old spring which had become our water supply, sitting on our big screened-in back porch and contemplating how good life is.

For physical exercise and to contribute something worthwhile, I started doing my bit for the community by cleaning and mowing the little cemetery where five generations of our family are buried. It had been allowed to grow up; it badly needed cleaning and clearing, and became a challenge for me. After a couple of years, others became interested. We now have annual reunions of people from the community and those who once lived there. We have accumulated a perpetual care fund that takes care of the maintenance of the cemetery. It is beautiful, well taken care of, with new fences and an entry gate.

Our older son Danny is a nuclear pharmacist and has two laboratories, one in Tyler and the other in College Station. He went from A&M to the University of Houston Pharmacy School. For his nuclear training he attended the University of Southern California Medical Center in Los Angeles. He and his wife, Georganne, have two wonderful (of course!) children, Adrienne, now sixteen, and Andrew, age seven.

Tim went from A&M to Baylor College of Medicine in Houston. He became a pathologist and practiced medicine with Baylor. He later attended the University of Chicago Law School where he received his Juris Doctor Degree and is now practicing medical law. He and Fran have two daughters (who are also wonderful!), Caitlin, age six, and Erin, who is four.

After Mildred retired in 1982, we enlarged our garden to two acres and really went to work. It was good for me and quite a change from teaching. We enjoyed our teaching days, but now we were glad to be able to spend our time on the hillside. We were so busy we didn't have time to do much traveling. We started a hobby— genealogy. Most of the traveling we did was to try and trace the family trees, meeting many family members and making new friends.

In 1983, reunions of Mukden survivors were begun by Greg Rodriquez and his wife Lois, of Henryetta, Oklahoma, at the suggestion of their son, Greg, Jr. They are to be highly commended for doing this. They hosted the get-togethers for the first two years. But now it has grown, and we're having them in many different places throughout the United States.

Since these reunions were started, we have been fortunate to meet several new and interesting people. On December 7, 1944, when the 120 B-29s bombed the city of Mukden, we saw two of the bombers go down. One blew up from a direct hit by a Japanese plane; the plane just flew right into the bomber. The survivors of these planes were brought as prisoners to Mukden and housed in a building outside the camp. We have now met one of these prisoners, Walter Huss. He and his wife Ellie have attended some of our reunions, and we keep in touch.

We were fortunate, also, to attend a reunion in Baton Rouge a few years ago, to meet the pilot who flew the plane for the men who dropped in to liberate the Mukden camp. Pilot Paul Hallberg told us about the flight, and also that he had to make a return trip to Mukden to bring in a wheel and tire for a plane after the Russians had punctured a tire. He left the wheel and returned to his air base in China, taking with him some of the now ex-prisoners.

The leader of the team that liberated our camp, who was dropped in with the others, the one who gave the OK sign that excited me so, is Hal Leith. After Hal and his team secured our camp from the Japanese, he had to find Generals King and Wainwright. He brought them out in time to attend the surrender on September 2, 1945, on the battleship *Missouri*. We keep in touch with these new friends to let them know how much we appreciate the brave thing they did.

Not all the things we learned during these years was good news. A startling and disturbing bit of information was uncovered regarding the Mukden prisoners, thanks to Greg Rodriquez, Jr. It is our understanding that young Greg, after seeing his father suffer from recurring illnesses which puzzled the doctors, began a search for the cause.

It seems that there was a "Unit 731" near Harbin, a city north of Mukden. There the Japanese were conducting biological experiments. It is believed they used Chinese civilians, Russian prisoners of war and possibly Mukden prisoners of war, both American and British as guinea pigs.

There has been some publicity about this, and the general public is becoming aware of it. Some ex-prisoners tell of getting shots at the hospital for reasons they could not understand. Several have reported such strange occurrences as feathers being rubbed beneath their noses to spread germs.

It is now understood, as I have long suspected, that the inundation of rats and fleas in our camp was one of the ways of introducing something into our bodies. We are aware that the prisoners of the Japanese died sooner than the German prisoners.

It has also been reported that the Japanese scientists who worked at Harbin used their findings to start their own drug companies after the war. A television crew from NBC went to Henryetta, Oklahoma to the Rodriquez home in 1995 and interviewed several ex-prisoners of war from Mukden on this subject. They included Greg Rodriquez, Art Campbell, Leslie Brown and myself. An hour-long documentary appeared on *60 Minutes* later that year.

I have been interviewed by newspaper and television reporters through the years. I have spoken to high school and college classes and am still doing so. My wife has been interested in this cause and was at one time editor of our AXPOW Bulletin. I also have been guest speaker for the *Veterans Day* program at the VA Hospital in Bonham, Texas.

It gets harder and harder to give satisfactory interviews. The interviewers get younger and younger as time goes by, and many appear to know nothing of the history of our time. Some will say, "Just answer my questions," and don't know what to ask. One young lady even asked me, "What does 'POW' mean?"

In December of 1991, I was invited to attend a Governor's Conference on World War II at the University of North Texas in Denton. This was called "Texas Goes to War" and was to commemorate the fiftieth anniversary of the beginning of the war. I appeared on a panel discussing the physical and emotional stress of being a prisoner of war and the adjustment in its aftermath. On this panel with me, was a civilian missionary and six other former prisoners of war. I also appeared on another panel which included an admiral and a colonel who were also former prisoners.

There were several other panels, including those on such subjects as science and technology in war, war on stage and screen, fashions in dress during the war, music and other arts. One panel was made up of representatives of the different women's groups: WASPS,

WAVES, WAACS, the Nurse Corps, women pilots and others. Various panels included the Tuskegee Airmen, survivors of Pearl Harbor, The Lost Battalion, submariners, the home front, the female labor force and just about any subject relative to the war. The name of the panelist I remember best is that of Tom Landry.

Interviewers made tapes of several of us as individuals; these tapes were run in the lobbies and could be seen on closed circuit television by those not attending the conference.

In 1990, we reluctantly sold our Springhill home and moved to Tyler. My hands had become disabled with arthritis, and I could no longer handle the tractor and other equipment needed to maintain the place. Added to that, Danny needed me to help out occasionally at his Tyler laboratory. We miss our country home, but are in a very nice neighborhood. We have good neighbors and are not far from our church, shopping centers or medical facilities. Best of all, we are not far from our grandchildren.

In the fall of 1998, Mildred and I traveled to Fresno, California, for a Mukden reunion. On the way we stopped to visit with Ray Thompson and his wife. Ray and I were the only survivors of the six close friends, meeting first at Tent City at March Field. Miller Barnes and Harold Christopher and their wives joined us for dinner one evening. What a wonderful reunion we had! A few months later we received news that Ray had died. I am so happy I got to see my dear friend one more time.

CHAPTER 25

I RETURN

In the spring of 2000, I had an opportunity to return to the Philippines. My wife had been urging me to make a trip back, hoping I would see that after nearly sixty years things were different, that it was all over. The group called the *Battling Bastards of Bataan* were preparing a tour on the anniversary of the fall of Bataan, to dedicate a monument at the old O'Donnell camp. A friend, Barrington Beutell, who is stepson to General Edward King, asked me to accompany him. After only slight hesitation, I called to accept.

We left Tyler on March 29 and flew to Dallas. Then we went nonstop to Tokyo on a Boeing 777, which, believe me, was quite different from the planes I flew in when leaving Okinawa. From Tokyo we flew to Manila, where we were picked up at the airport and taken to the beautiful Manila Hotel. The next day we were met by a friend of Mr. Beutell, Jim Litton, who with his driver, escorted Barrington, his sister Jean Beutell Abrams, former POW Tillman Rutledge and me on a tour.

Our first stop was the old Bilibid prison where many Americans were kept while they were prisoners of the Japanese. It is run down but still in use, containing many criminal prisoners. In some cases the families of the prisoners live there also.

Our next visit was a place of great contrast to our first stop.

This was the beautiful Manila American Cemetery and Memorial. Located about six miles southeast of the city, it covers over one hundred acres. It is the largest cemetery built and administered by the American Battle Monuments Commission. In this cemetery are buried over seventeen thousand of our military dead, representing forty per cent of burials originally made in temporary cemeteries on New Guinea, the Philippines and other islands of the southwest Pacific area. In Section Ten of this cemetery, there lie buried 1,100 of my comrades-in-arms, men who died on Bataan.

On the next day, the first of April, the four of us hired a van and a driver for a tour. We visited the San Fernando Air Base south of Manila. This air strip had been built by American prisoners of war. Tillman Rutledge, one of our four, had been a prisoner helping to build this strip. Tillman got passes for us, and we had an escorted tour of the base.

Mr. Beutell, his sister and I joined the tour group on Sunday for a tour of Fort Santiago. This fort served as military headquarters through the regimes of the Spanish, British, Americans and Japanese. During World War II, it was a dreadful place where hundreds of men and women were jailed, tortured and executed by the Japanese military police. It was destroyed by the American forces in the 1945 Battle of Manila, and restored as a public park in 1950. This is part of the Walled City.

From Fort Santiago, we visited the San Agustin Church, an old monastery now converted into a museum. Then we went on to the University of Santo Tomas, the oldest existing university in Asia. During the Japanese occupation of Manila the university was transformed into a concentration camp. American civilians and the brave American nurses (*Angels of Bataan*) were imprisoned here.

One day we took time off from our tour and went shopping. Then we visited Pier 7 and South Harbor. This is the pier that was so familiar to me. It is the one I entered when I came to the Philippines in 1941; it is the pier where we were put aboard the *Totora Maru*; it is the pier where I left the Philippine Islands to go home in 1945. The number has been changed; it is now called Pier 13.

On Wednesday, April 5, we checked out of the Manila Hotel and left with the tour group for Cabanatuan. This was also a memorable day for me, as on the way we went through Gapan and found the site where I worked for fifty-two days on the bridge-repairing detail. The old bridge is gone and a new one built in its place. However, there was enough of the old bridge in the river bed for me to locate it; there were concrete pieces lying in the bottom of the dry river bed.

From there we went to Cabcaben and found a beautiful memorial with a granite wall that contains thousands of names of soldiers who died there. I found names of some of my own 7th Materiel buddies on the wall. The only thing left of the old camp where I was imprisoned is the concrete footing of the water tower.

Clark Field was on our tour for the next day. I saw very little that looked familiar, but I have very vivid memories about the place. Only the Fort Stotsenburg parade ground and the officers quarters looked the same, even after nearly sixty years. We were taken to see the former quarters of Gen. King but were not allowed to go inside. We could take pictures of this attractive former residence. I'm not sure what it's used for now, as there were Filipino military guards all around.

From Clark Field we moved on to Capas. This is where the train we rode from San Fernando (in boxcars) stopped. The old brick railroad station still stands, and is a museum. The rails are gone except for one lone rail of which, of course, I took a picture.

We went from Capas to O'Donnell for the memorial service. As I rode the bus with our other tourists, I recalled the walk we made, up and over a hill, to look down on a sorry sight. All this is gone and is no great loss as far as I'm concerned.

On the Filipino side the people have built a monument to their defenders. They very kindly allowed the Americans to build a monument on their grounds, within walking distance between the two.

We attended the Philippine ceremony as guests. When their ceremony was over, we moved to the American monument where there were reserved seats for the four ex-prisoners of our group: Richard Gordon, Tillman Rutledge, Philip Coon and myself.

We four were privileged to unveil the monument dedicated to the American soldiers who died there. This was a great moment for me, and for all of us, including several people who had relatives who had died there. It contains sixteen hundred names of Americans who survived the March, only to die in Camp O'Donnell. After this moving dedication, the Philippine people graciously served a meal to the whole assembly.

The next day our tour group left our lodgings at Clark Field to go on to Subic City on Subic Bay. However, at Clark Field we had met a British camera crew who was making a documentary on the Bataan Death March. We were accompanied by Barrington Beutell and Mr. Coon's grandson. The crew took pictures of us as we walked along the road we had traveled fifty-eight years ago. But oh, how very, very different it was!

The British crew informed us that this documentary would be approximately one hour in length, and would appear on television in the year 2001. (As of this writing, it has been shown in England and in the United States. It was shown on *The Learning Channel* on December 7, anniversary of the attack on Pearl Harbor. The title is *Hell in the Pacific*.) After finishing the filming of the March, they went to Corregidor to film there. We then rejoined our tour group at Subic City at the Subic International Hotel that afternoon.

On Sunday, April 9, we had to rise at 3:30 a.m. and have our breakfast at 4:30 in order to be on our bus at 5:30 to leave to attend the Memorial Service at Mt. Samat on Bataan. This was not because we had to drive a long distance, but because when the park reached its capacity, the gates were closed. A large cross had been erected on top of Mt. Samat by the people of the Philippines to remember and honor their soldiers who fought and died in defense of their country.

It is a beautiful monument. It dominates the area for miles around. We got to sit on the stage with all the dignitaries, including the President of the Philippines and the American Ambassador.

When the long and impressive program was over, we left there and had lunch as we traveled on the bus to Mariveles, to the tip of Bataan where the March began. From there we moved along the winding road to Cabcaben where I was captured on April 9, 1942. Then we went to Lamao, where Barrington Beutell had placed a marker in memory of Gen. King's surrender of Bataan to the Japanese. Wreaths were placed there by Philippine and American ex-prisoners of war. I must admit to some tears during these ceremonies, tears of sorrow and tears of happiness at being a part of the remembrance.

The next day we checked out of our hotel and toured Alongpo on the way back to Manila. That evening we had dinner with a former Philippine soldier who was with the 31st Infantry on Bataan, at his very nice Chinese restaurant. This was quite a dinner, as it took us over two hours to be served all the courses.

Because of the lengthy meal, we were late getting to bed and had to rise early the next morning in order to catch the boat for our tour of Corregidor, which we called "The Rock." There we toured Bottomside and the famous Lorcha Dock where Gen. MacArthur departed for Australia (from where he vowed to return).

The highlight of our visit to Corregidor was our tour of the Malinta Tunnel. This was constructed sometime in the twenties, is eight hundred thirty-five feet long and twenty-four feet wide, with twenty-four lateral branches. In touring the tunnel we would come to one of the laterals and vibrations would begin just like bombs were falling. The lights would flicker and go out. When the "bombing" stopped we could smell burned powder just like I remembered in the bombing raids of the past. It all seemed very real. During the early years of WWII, it served as capitol of the Philippine Islands under President Quezon.

While on Corregidor we saw some of the gun batteries, but most were destroyed and lay in ruins. Also in ruins were the mile-long barracks, the Senior Officers Quarters, the parade ground and the Post Hospital. However, the Pacific War Memorial and Museum were a beautiful sight. We had lunch at the Corregidor Hotel and made a few more stops before we left, boarding the ferry for the Manila dock and returning to the Manila Hotel.

On our last day of touring, Barrington Beutell and I went, upon invitation, to the United States Embassy in Manila, one of the largest United States missions in the world. That morning Mr. Joseph P. Cooley, Assistant Veterans Administration Director, picked us up at our hotel and took us for a tour of the embassy. After I got home, I received a picture from Mr. Cooley with a picture he had taken of our group at the Philippine Memorial at O'Donnell.

The end of the tour had come. On the early afternoon of April 12, 2000, Barrington Beutell and I left Manila for Tokyo, where we spent the night. We had time for a little shopping and sightseeing before our plane, again a Boeing 777, left Tokyo for a non-stop flight to DFW. The earlier trip had taken fourteen and a half hours; the return trip was less, requiring eleven and a half hours. We caught the American Eagle for the short flight home, and arrived safely late that afternoon to find Edie Beutell and Mildred, with our daughter-in-law Georganne, waiting for us.

It was an experience I will never forget. I was so pleased with the treatment we received through the kindness of the Philippine people. In addition to our tour features, we were invited out to dinners, to memorial services and received recognition and extra tours. I also met new friends, one of whom is Federico, "Fred," son of Master Sergeant Jimmy Baldassarre.

It is difficult to explain the feeling I had at first when I returned to the Philippines. The memory of the place had been a nightmare in my life all these years. I did not realize the Philippine people would treat us like heroes. The day we had to surrender is a national holiday in the Philippines. The people have remembered it every year, and in the year 2000 I got to be a part of it.

THE LAST PICTURE

In the year 2002 I traveled again to the Philippine Islands to commemorate the 60th anniversary of the fall of Bataan.

This time Mildred went with me, accompanied by friends Art and Frances Campbell and their daughter, Shelda Upshaw. There were eighty of us, traveling in two buses. Twelve of us were survivors of the Bataan Death March. I was pleased to see Major and Mrs. Richard Gordon and Tillman Rutledge again, as well as others I had met on the previous trip. With us were wives, sons, daughters, nieces and nephews of those who had been on the March. There were also men who had been on Corregidor, and families who wanted to see for themselves where all the cruelty and death had happened and to pay their respects to the memory of their loved ones. Also with us were civilian internees who were at Santo Tomas, with their families, and some who were returning to places where they had lived as children but had fled with their families at the onset of hostilities.

We visited many of the same places we had seen two years before. We again crossed the bridge over the Penaranda River and saw the remains of the footings of the old bridge I had helped build; we drove over the steep and winding mountainous road that Sgt. Oliver and I had used to carry supplies while we were still fighting. We visited Bilibid prison where some American POWs were held during their captivity. We arrived there the day the prisoners' families came to visit, and attracted quite a bit of attention from the children who kept pointing to our hair, so different from their all-black hair. They smiled and waved to us.

We crossed over to Corregidor on a boat that scooted along over the water. There we saw the destruction of the military bases, the ruins still standing after all these years, with the jungle closing in over them.

But there was one outstanding new event. Those of us who believed we were physically able to do so, rose at 3 a.m., ate our breakfasts on the bus, and traveled to Capas, arriving at daybreak where the little train depot still stands, with the one rail still there, hidden in the sand where one has to search for it, to the place where 60 years ago we were taken from the boxcars and put on our last leg of the March to the first prison camp, O'Donnell. There, led by a group of Filipino Boy Scouts, and accompanied by the Mayor of Capas and other local dignitaries, photographers and newsmen, we set out on the walk; we began, young and old and middle-aged, determined to test our abilities to do what we had done 60 years before, walk the last few miles of the infamous Bataan Death March.

The road was no longer dusty and deserted; instead Filipino families lined the road in front of their houses to wave to us and cheer us on and to smile for photographs. We had water and juices and an air-conditioned bus following in case any of us needed to stop. Though now eighty-one years old, I made the walk without stopping. We had started at daybreak, while it was (relatively) cool, yet the heat became intense and Mildred had to get aboard the bus for a few minutes to cool off. But she left the bus and caught up with me, and we walked into the O'Donnell memorial hand in hand.

I will always remember these things we saw and did, the chaotic traffic, the friendliness of the people, our tour guides who took such good care of us. I wonder again how any of us survived the March. The Japanese need not have killed their prisoners; they did not have to deprive us of food and water to destroy us. The heat of the sun, coupled with the illnesses we were suffering, could have done that very effectively.

On the last day before we were to return home, Mildred and I sat at our hotel window overlooking Manila Bay and watched a sight unfamiliar to us inland Texans: seaplanes landing and taking off, big

217

ships towed by tiny tugboats; we watched as huge cranes loaded and unloaded their burdens on the wharves. And within our sight was Pier 7, the infamous Pier 7 which had played such a large part in my life, now silent, deserted, as though dead, as if all the horrors it had seen had taken the life from it. We said goodbye to it.

It would be our last visit to the Philippines with the *Battling Bastards of Bataan*, as they had decided there were too few survivors of the Death March to warrant a return trip.

On the last night of our visit, after the last of the feast had been eaten, the last of the wine had been drunk, the last speech had died away, after saying goodbye to our friends, old and new, the call was made for the Bataan Death March survivors to gather for the last picture. The last picture. And the last goodbye.

CONCLUSION

UNIT 731—BIOLOGICAL WARFARE

It was nearly forty years after the end of World War II, forty years after the Death March, the "hell ship" and years of imprisonment by the Japanese that these survivors, along with other American, British, Australian and Dutch prisoners, learned that there was a fourth hell facing them. It was one they had suspected, but did not know really existed.

During those years the men had discussed strange occurrences among themselves, with their families, and in interviews with the news media. At the time it was only a puzzle they could not solve. Why had feathers been rubbed under their noses? For what diseases had they been "inoculated" in all those multiple and repetitive shots? Why in the world had the Japanese doctors taken feces samples?

Why had the Japanese blown spray into their faces, and insisted that some prisoners use the tooth powder they had issued to them? Strange things had appeared in their packages from home and the Red Cross: colored feathers, cards with dots on certain numbers, dominoes cut in half and glued back together. They remembered the autopsies performed on dead prisoners who had been stored in wooden boxes all winter and who were ready for burial in the spring. And they all remembered with distaste the barracks being overrun with flea-laden rats, rodents that appeared overnight in massive numbers.[1] There were strange occurrences they wondered about, discussed. Did any of these things have an anything to do with the illnesses many of them were having? It was quite evident that the ex-prisoners held by the Japanese were dying at a faster rate than those held in German camps.[2] "What do you think?" they'd ask each other.

But no one had an answer until the existence of Unit 731 was made public. The work of Unit 731 became public knowledge, thanks to a few concerned and dedicated persons, both here and in Great Britain. After all these years—now sixty years since these men were taken prisoner—these dedicated individuals are still pursuing the truth, trying to bring the guilty to justice by making the truth known about this horror.

It was brought to our attention by the son of a Mukden prisoner, Greg Rodriguez. Greg, Jr., set out to find the reason for his Dad's strange recurring illness. Then, in the middle 1980s, several television documentaries told the story. One of these, *Chemical and Biological Warfare*, by TVS, a British company, was shown in England in August, 1985, and later in the U.S. on *20/20*.

Unit 731 began in the mind of General Shiro Ischii/Ishii (both spellings are used in various records). At a meeting of the League of Nations in Switzerland in 1925, twenty-nine nations met to sign a resolution prohibiting the use of the bacteriological method of warfare. Six nations failed to ratify this agreement; Japan was one of the six. Ischii evidently saw this as a means whereby Japan could conquer the world. If the rest of the world banned gas and germ warfare, then Japan could have that capability.[3]

Ischii was a bacteriologist as well as a soldier. In the 1930s, he set up a small laboratory in the Army Medical College in Tokyo. There he was asked to design a pump to purify water. In 1931, Japan overran Manchuria. In 1935, an incident played into Ischii's hands. Thousands of men and horses died of cholera. The army blamed a group of spies who were caught carrying glass bottles containing germs of dysentery, cholera and anthrax. The spies were accused of poisoning wells of drinking water. The army decided it needed protection, and within months Ischii was given huge sums of money to build a major germ warfare installation.[4]

It was in a village called Ping Fan, in Manchuria, about forty miles from Harbin, near the Siberian border. The shelter name for the germ warfare unit was "The Anti-Epidemic Water Supply Unit"—Unit 731.[5] It was said that here the unit could produce, in large vats, up to eight tons of typhus, anthrax, small pox, salmonella and glanders (a contagious, sometimes fatal disease of horses and other animals characterized by a nasal discharge and ulcers) per month.[6] This establishment was guarded with strictest security.

Hundreds of prisoners were sent to Ping Fan, including the so-called spies who had allegedly poisoned the wells, as well as some petty criminals and Chinese, Korean, Manchurian and Russian soldiers. The code name for the men who would die painfully and anonymously, sacrificed in human experiments, thousands of them, known by numbers, was *maruta* (or *marata*) meaning "logs of wood." In later testimony they were referred to merely as "logs."[7]

The establishment was large enough to house laboratories and living quarters for three thousand scientists, technicians and soldiers, in addition to the sixty to eighty *maruta* kept on hand at a time. As these "logs" died or were "sacrificed," others were shipped in to take their places. One member of the unit later told, that to the best of his knowledge, the number of *maruta* sacrificed was between 2,500 and 3,000.[8]

Also a member of the unit told of experiments with cyanide gas in small bombs. About 100 *maruta* were used and all died except one. After they died, the bodies were loaded onto trucks and taken to another place for autopsies.

Many experiments resulted in death: "Some were killed, injected with morphine in order to assess the progress of various diseases. Some were dissected while they were still alive."[9]

On one occasion the "logs of wood" fought back. This caused a riot; gas was injected into the cells until all were dead. Though this happened in only one building, the "logs" in another building received the same fate.[10]

Bombs and shells were built and filled with bacteria. When the bombs exploded they sent out the bacteria over prisoners who were staked out in an open field. The proof of this turned up years later in a surprising way. In 1984, a professor was browsing through the shelves of a second-hand book store in Tokyo and found a set of the actual records of a number of killings of prisoners, with mustard gas, in Unit 731![11]

On December 4, 1947, investigations were held concerning the subject of biological warfare. Reports were submitted to the Pentagon. These investigations were to clarify the report submitted by the Japanese personnel on this subject, to examine the human pathological material which had been transferred to Japan from biological installations and to understand the significance of this material.

Subjects of these interviews included: aerosols, anthrax, botulism, brucellosis, cholera, dysentery, fugu toxin (a substance resembling curare which was sometimes eaten in Japan "with suicidal intent"), gas gangrene, glanders, influenza, meningococcus (bacterium that causes cerebrospinal meningitis), plague, plant diseases, salmonella, songo (epidemic hemorrhagic fever, named after the Songo River in Manchuria where it was observed among Japanese soldiers in 1939), smallpox, tetanus, tick encephalitis, tsutsugamushi (an acute disease resembling louse borne typhus originating in Japan, transmitted by larval mites), tuberculosis, tularemia (infectious disease of rodents and man, transmitted by bites of insects), typhoid and typhus.[12]

Records on human cases included anthrax, botulism, brucellosis, carbon monoxide, cholera, dysentery, glanders, meningococcus, mustard gas, plague, poisoning, salmonella, songo, small pox, streptococcus, suicide, tetanus, tick encephalitis, tsutsugamushi, tuberculosis, typhoid, typhus and assorted vaccinations.[13]

Summary of this investigation stated, "Evidence gathered in this investigation has greatly supplemented and amplified previous aspects of this field. It represents data which have been obtained by Japanese scientists at the expenditure of many dollars and years of work. Information has been accrued with respect to human susceptibility to those diseases indicated by specific doses of bacteria. Such information could not have been obtained in our own laboratories because of scruples to human experimentation. These data were secured with a total outlay of 250,000 yen to date, a mere pittance by comparison with the actual cost of the studies."[14]

"Furthermore, the pathological material which has been collected constitutes the only material evidence of the nature of these experiments. It is hoped that individuals who voluntarily contributed this information will be spared embarassment (sic) because of it and that every effort will be taken to prevent this information from falling into other hands." This was signed by a medical doctor at Camp Detrick, Maryland.[15]

Descriptions of these experiments were documented and dated. The numbers of humans used were given, and the number who developed the disease, as well as the number of times each experiment was done.

Statements from some of these members of the "Devil's Brigade," as early investigators called them, when speaking to investigators, to members of the press and later to Japanese inquiries, include the following:

One Japanese doctor spoke of experiments done in Mukden in the laboratory of the Manchurian Railway in the 1930s, using guinea pigs, mice and rats. Another said, "One subject was injected . . . He developed diarrhea and tetanus on the 3rd day, and hanged himself on the 4th day . . ."[16]

Regarding songo: "In 1942, human experiments were started. 204 mites picked from field mice in that area were (contained) in 2 cc saline and injected . . . in one man with positive results." "Mites fed on sick people did not transmit the disease—2 cases." "Blood from febrile man was injected into horses . . . Blood from febrile horses was injected into other horses with positive results in one of two cases. Conversely, blood of febrile horses injected into man was positive in 2 of 8 experiments."[17]

Tularimia: "Experiments . . . were conducted with 10 subjects who were injected . . . developed fever lasting as long as 6 months. None died or were sacrificed."[18]

Typhoid: "One subject was exposed to a bomb burst containing buckshot mixed with 10 mg bicilli and 10 mg of clay. The buckshot had grooves which were impregnated with the bacteria-clay mixture. Bomb burst 1 meter from the rear of the subject. He developed symptoms of typhoid fever with positive laboratory signs." "Laboratory infections occurred in 2 Japanese invectigators (sic) who seemed to be much sicker than Manchurians although none died."[19]

Another experiment at the "Water Purification Unit" was the freezing of prisoners. They were led outdoors at temperatures below zero. Arms were bared and made to freeze with the use of an artificial current of air. This was done until their frozen arms, when struck with a stick, emitted a sound resembling that which a "board gives when struck." One account described men and women with rotting hands from which bones protruded. Another report of freezing was that of two Russian prisoners who were stripped naked and put into a cell and left there until they froze to death.[20]

A former Japanese captain published his memoirs and told how plague was spread by air, by dropping rats and voles (mice-like rodents) and gave details of flea "nurseries" for Ischii's rapid production of fleas.

"In October 4, 1940, in Chek Yang Province a plane from Unit 731 sprayed the civilian population with fleas, rice and wheat infected with bubonic plague. On October 29, 1940, plague broke out in Chek Yang province." The report continues, "Another province Nov. 28, 1940, yet another Nov. 4th, 1941."[21]

The reports go on: bubonic plague, anthrax, glanders.
In August 1942, paratyphoid and anthrax spread in central
China. Thousands died during these three years.[22]

But one went wrong. A unit of 731 with three divisions of soldiers who went into Central China withdrew after they had dis-
persed cholera and typhoid bacteria into the area. It had been so
secret that the Japanese troops became victims. Seventeen hundred
of them died, infected by germs Unit 731 had spread to kill the
enemy.[23]

Thus the sixty-four-million-dollar question: Why should Americans who survived the experience in the Philippines be taken all the
way to Mukden, Manchuria?

More evidence, this from prisoners in Mukden and people from
Unit 731:

"The first winter, out of 1,450 in Mukden, 430 dead, according to
British count." "Mukden—350 miles from 731 Hq. at Ping Fan,
clear evidence that Ping Fan went to Mukden." One member of
731 team said that many of the scientific team went to Mukden
(says about 3,000 prisoners): "To the best of my recollection, the
report which we prepared almost wholly related to malnutrition."
From a POW: "They came and went to the POW hospital; carried
out their operation and then disappeared." One member of 731,
talking on the telephone to a reporter in the 1980s: "I was in the
dysentery group and we studied whether this could be developed
for use in weapons ... Normally we gave the autopsies to ascertain
the symptoms. We had to observe the program and had to ascertain
the potency of the various viruses ...
Reporter: "Were any blood samples ever taken from the Mukden
prisoner-of-war camp?" 731: "Yes. We also actually carried out the
same experiments at the headquarters of Unit 731."
POW: "As men died their bodies were stored in a wooden
warehouse. As spring approached a team of Japanese arrived
with an autopsy table and began removing brains and vital
organs from the dead. (I was required to work with the Japanese
in doing this.)"
One member of the 731 team said if a scientist refused to join
Ishii willingly, he would receive red papers, meaning he was
conscripted into the unit. He tells of going to a place called

Songo near the Soviet Border (this is the place from which songo fever got its name). Their work involved obtaining mites from rats captured in the area where the disease was most prevalent. From these they made a solution for injecting into spies captured in Manchuria. "I was only accustomed to university laboratory and university-style research, and until I went to Ischii unit, I didn't even know such a thing as human experiment existed, or what the word *maruta* meant. I was very naive."[24]

One document was found in Japan's military archives that had the emperor's seal, indicating he knew of Unit 731.[25] It was also known that the emperor's brother visited Ping Fan, and it is also believed that the emperor himself visited Ping Fan at least once in 1939.[26]

Then the war ended and Soviet troops moved into Manchuria, and eventually into Mukden and to the prison camp where they turned the guns over to the prisoners, and the guards became the imprisoned. At Unit 731, they were very busy. The laboratory at Ping Fan Station at Harbin was destroyed prior to the flight of the scientists to South Korea. They killed the remaining human guinea pigs, saying, "It took 30 hours to lay them in ashes." Ischii had no time to use his weapons against the Russians, so he destroyed the evidence.[27]

First thing was to destroy the *maruta*. The incineration equipment was insufficient so some of the specimens were moved to the incineration plant at Harbin. The barracks were burned and the laboratory destroyed by explosives. All members of the 731 team were issued cyanide tablets and ordered them to use them if captured as their secrets had to be kept. Ischii and his men mingled with the retreating armies. In their escape they took some documents with them.[28]

On September 2, 1945, on the battleship *Missouri* in Tokyo Bay, the United States accepted the unconditional surrender of the Japanese by Gen. MacArthur.

While the Allies searched for Japanese who should be brought to trial, Ischii and his men waited. Unit 731 drew up a plan to trade the information. An English-speaking member, Lt. Col. Ryohi Nyito approached Col. Murray Sanders, MacArthur's man who was in charge of investigating germ warfare. At this time Col. Sanders did not know of Unit 731, even though there was some evidence that Chiang Kai-Shek, China's leader, had informed Churchill of its existence, and Churchill had shared this secret with American and Russian leaders. The 731 member, under the pretense of being Col. Sander's interpreter, approached him with the idea of a trade. He finally gave the colonel a manuscript of unbelievable material. This contained the chain of command of Unit 731, everything.[29]

Sanders took the document to Gen. MacArthur, and they made a deal. Biological warfare workers would not be prosecuted as war criminals in exchange for the information. The Russians asked the Americans to hand Ischii over to them for questioning, but the Americans would not. So, as other Japanese war criminals were brought to trial, members of Unit 731 went scot-free.[30]

In September, 1947, the State Department warned MacArthur about the deal. "It is recognized that this government may at a later date be seriously embarrassed."[31]

The Russians brought their Unit 731 members to trial and gave them up to 25 years. But in the two years of United States trials, not one mention was made of Unit 731.[32] Even today, as the few remaining POWs are trying to get an apology, or admission from the Japanese government, the U. S. is standing by its word. Now, after nearly sixty years, the only admissions or apologies have been to individuals.

One such individual is Greg Rodriquez, Jr., who first brought the existence of Unit 731 to our attention. He said that several Japanese individuals from 731 admitted to him that they had indeed gone to Mukden to test the blood of American prisoners. One, who apologized to him, admitted that he had been in charge of raising the rats that were sent to Mukden.

No other apology or compensation has been forthcoming, neither from the Japanese government, nor from the Unit 731 members who went on to make fortunes from their human experiments. The former American prisoners of war who were at Mukden believe that at least our government should say, 'Yes, we made a mistake.'

A letter, not dated, from Tokyo Broadcasting System, signed by the Chief Director, contains these paragraphs:

> "Since 1972 TBS news documentary group . . . has been conducting research and news gathering activities on the subject of 731st Unit. 731st Unit was an ultra-secret biological warfare unit of former Japanese Imperial Army during World War II."
>
> "The headquarters of 731st Unit was located at Ping Fan, Manchuria, and has been developing bacteriological weapons as well as conducting living body tests on nearly 3,000 Chinese and Russian POWs for medical and scientific researches until 1945 (sic) when Japan was defeated . . ."[33]

Once the fact had been established that Ischii used Chinese and others as laboratory test subjects, it seemed a fair assumption that he also might have used American and possibly British, prisoners. Until some twenty years ago the only hints were brief references buried in the 1949 Soviet Trial summary, one of which says, "As early as 1943 . . . a researcher belonging to the Detachment 731, was sent to prisoner of war camps to test the properties of blood and immunity to contagious diseases of American soldiers."[34]

A top-secret U.S. document "clearly indicates that American POWs were used as human guinea pigs Mukden areas."[35]

And what happened to the "Devil's Brigade," which for years had carried out the most horrible experiments on human beings? One of the pathologists was made Medical Director of Kinki University, Osaka, emeritus professor at Kyoto University.[36] A plague expert became director of Osaka County University's School of Medicine. The scientist who worked on ways of spreading disease on wheat became Secretary to the Japanese Penicillin Association.[37] Another pathologist became a professor at Kanizawa University. It is said he secretly took specimens of his experiments to the University. The recruiting officer became emeritus professor at Tokyo University and

President of the Japanese Medical Association.[38]

Another member, emeritus vice president at Kitisato Hospital and Research Unit in Tokyo, authorized several medical publications, some thought to be based on his experiments on human beings at Ping Fan.[39]

Yet another scientist who worked for Unit 731 conducting frostbite experiments, now a professor at Kobe Women's University, was awarded one of Japan's highest honors: The Order of the Rising Sun, in 1978.[40]

Scores of the men of Unit 731 went to work in a new company Dr. Nyito (Col. Sander's "interpreter") set up: the Green Cross Corporation. The Green Cross works mostly in blood research (plasma, albumin and gamma globulin), similar to the work done in Unit 731. It is one of the most successful drug companies in Japan. In 1985 its profits were forecast to be more than six thousand million yen.[41]

And Shiro Ischii? He suffered in his later years from chronic dysentery and internal inflammation, diseases he'd inflicted on others at Ping Fan. Like them, he died slowly, and painfully, of cancer of the throat.[42]

If you had been a prisoner of war in Mukden, subjected to experiments through the bites of fleas or feathers under the nose— for what purpose but the spread of disease?—suffered unidentified injections, not knowing what, if any—terrible disease had been inflicted on you that you may have brought home with you to be transferred to your innocent and unaware family—would you not wonder, "Does anybody care?"

ADDENDUM

Unit 731 may have affected more than *maruta* and prisoners of war. It may even now be capable of affecting us, years after the end of the war.

The Denver Post reported: "Less than sixty years ago, the U.S. mainland—specifically the American West—was attacked many times. But the Japanese 'bombing' of America in World War II has been over-looked by commentators and politicians who inaccurately paint the September 11, 2001 attack as the first homeland assault by a foreign foe since the War of 1812."[1]

In November, 1944, Japan released the first of several thousand hydrogen balloons. Each balloon contained a 15-kilometer anti-personnel bomb and two devices to start fires. Military analysts believe that at least one thousand of these bombs reached states from Alaska, then along the Pacific coast, even as far east as Michigan. American leaders, with the cooperation of the press, decided to keep this secret. Not only was the secrecy designed to prevent panic at home, but also to prevent the Japanese from knowing of the success of their unguided bombs. This secrecy has continued; it is said to still be difficult to obtain this information.

In September, 1942, a Japanese plane dropped phosphorous bombs in Oregon. These were intended to start forest fires. Those who knew about these bombs feared that the Japanese might deliver Unit 731's biological and chemical weapons. It is believed that the Japanese did not use chemical weapons because they were afraid of retaliation.[2]

Now, sixty years later, we have this fear renewed from another source.

—∿— Mildred Allen

FOOTNOTES

PREFACE

[1] President Manuel L. Quezon served as the first president of the Commonwealth of the Philippines. He was commissioned as a second lieutenant in the revolutionary army. He remained president until the outbreak of World War II.

[2] MacArthur, D., "Disaster and Glory in the Philippines," *The Reader's Digest Illustrated History of World War II: The World at Arms,* ed. Michael Wright, London/New York: Reader's Digest Association, Ltd., 1989, page 161.

[3] The Geneva Convention is an international treaty first signed in 1864 by several European countries. It has been revised twice, in 1906 and 1929. Thus it has been enlarged and expanded and signed by 47 countries. This treaty was brought about by the experiences of several wars, and basically sets forth humane treatment for the sick and wounded and prisoners of war. (*The Book of Knowledge,* Vols. 9 and 10, *The Children's Encyclopedia,* Editor-in-Chief, E.J. McGloughlin, New York: The Grolier Society, Inc., 1957, page 161.

[4] In the trial of Japanese war criminals, begun in Tokyo in 1946, Australian Judge, William Webb said, "... beginning to end, the customary and conventional rules of war were flagrantly disregarded: ruthless killing of prisoners by shooting, decapitation, drowning and other methods; death marches in which prisoners, including the sick, were forced to march long distances under conditions which not even well-conditioned troops could stand; many of those dropping out, being shot or bayonetted by the guards; forced labour in tropical heat without protection from the sun; complete lack of housing and medical supplies, in many cases resulting in thousands of deaths from disease; beatings and torture of all kinds to extract information, for confessions or for minor offences; killing without trial of recaptured prisoners after escape, or for attempt to escape; killing without trial of captured aviators and even cannibalism." From *Chemicals and Biological Warfare,* television broadcast, TVS Production, Television Center Vinters Park,

Maidstone, Kent, England, August 13, 1985. Script, pages 56-57.

HOW WORLD WAR II BEGAN

GERMANY

[1] "The Nazi Rise to Power, Early German Conquests, 1936-1939," *Reader's Digest Illustrated History of World War II*, The Reader's Digest Association, Inc., Pleasantville, New York, 1969, page 48.

[2] Shirer, William L., "Hitler's Seizure of Europe," *Reader's Digest Illustrated History of World War II*, The Reader's Digest Association, Inc., Pleasantville, New York, 1969, page 50.

[3] Ibid, page 50.

[4] Hitler, Adolf, "Mein Kampf," *Reader's Digest Illustrated History of World War II*, The Reader's Digest Association, Inc., Pleasantville, New York, 1969, page 89. Also "World War I," *The Book of Knowledge, Volume 18*, The Children's Encyclopedia, E.V. McLoughlin, Editor-in-Chief, The Grolier Society, Inc., New York, Jan. 1957, page 6465.

[5] Shirer, William L., "Hitler's Seizure of Europe," *Reader's Digest Illustrated History of World War II*, The Reader's Digest Association, Inc., Pleasantville, New York, 1969, page 50.

[6] Ibid, page 53.

[7] Ibid, page 52.

[8] Ibid, page 63.

[9] Ibid, page 60.

[10] Ibid, page 67.

JAPAN

[11] "The Story of Japan," *The Book of Knowledge, Volume 9*, The Children's Encyclopedia, E.V. McLoughlin, Editor-in-Chief, The Grolier Society, Inc., New York, January 1957, page 3184.

[12] Ibid, page 3185.

[13] Morison, Rear Adm., Samuel Eliot, USNR (Ret.), "How and Why Japan Prepared for World War," *Reader's Digest Illustrated History of World War II*, The Reader's Digest Association, Inc., Pleasantville, New York, 1969, page 100.

[14] Ibid, page 98.

[15] Ibid, page 100.

[16] Ibid.

[17] Ibid, page 103.

[18] Ibid, page 104.

[19] Ibid, page 106.

[20] Ibid, page 107.

See also "Japan," *Grolier Encyclopedia, Volume XI,* The Grolier Society, Inc., Publishers, New York, Toronto, August 1956, pages 233-242.

SNEAK ATTACK

[21] Snyder, Louis L., "Why the Sneak Attack Succeeded," *Reader's Digest Illustrated History of World War II,* The Reader's Digest Association, Inc., Pleasantville, New York, 1969, page 30.

[22] Ibid, page 31.

[23] Ibid.

[24] Ibid, page 32.

[25] Ibid.

GREAT BRITAIN

[26] Barber, Noel, "The Fall of Singapore," *Reader's Digest Illustrated History of World War II,* The Reader's Digest Association, Inc., Pleasantville, New York, 1969, page 42.

[27] Ibid, page 43.

[28] Ibid, page 44.

PEOPLE OF AMERICA

[29] Lyons, Eugene, "America on the Brink of War," *Reader's Digest Illustrated History of World War II,* The Reader's Digest Association, Inc., Pleasantville, New York, 1969, page 34.

[30] Ibid, page 35.

[31] Ibid, page 39.

For more about World War II, also see:
Elson, Robert T., *Prelude to War,* Time-Life Books, Inc., Morristown, N.J., 1976.

Japan At War, Time-Life Books, Inc., Chicago, Ill., 1980, pages 156-157.

The Historical Encyclopedia of World War II, Maral Baudot, Ed., Greenwich House, Crown Publishers, Inc., New York, 1977, pages ix-xxii.

The Oxford Companion to World War II, Oxford University Press, Oxford/New York, 1995, origins of the war, pages 840-846.

Pearl Harbor and the War in the Pacific, Tony Hall, ed., BCA/Salamander Books, London, England, 199, sources of conflict, pages 7-21.

The World Almanac Book of World War II, Brigadier Peter Young, ed., World Almanac Publications, Prentice Hall, Inc., Englewood Cliffs, N.J., 1981, pages 10-45.

Zich, Arthur, *The Rising Sun,* Time-Life Books, Inc., New York, 1977, pages 18-27.

CHAPTER 12

[1] It is now believed MKK stood for Mitsubishi Ku-Kan, or specifically, the MKK Machine and Tool Factory. Mitsubishi was one of three Japanese companies that exploited the largest number of American prisoners (Mitsubishi Motor Company, Mitsui and Nippon Steel). From Linda Goetz Holmes' *Unjust Enrichment: How Japan's Companies Build Postwar Fortunes Using American POWs,* Stackpole Press, Mechanicsburg, Pa., pages xxi, 22, 31, 84-94, 87, 130, 142-143.

Another reference is to the Manchuria Industrial Machine Company (MKK). From "Japanese Biological Warfare Experiments on American POWs during World War II," digest and translation from *The Weekly Post* Magazine (Tokyo), July 9, 1982, page 2.

For additional information about the MKK Machine and Tool Factory at Mukden, Manchuria, see Holmes, page 86-87.

CHAPTER 15

[1] Records show the Japanese at Mitsubishi's vast factory complex in Mukden, Manchuria, forced prisoners to sign pay sheets but few of the men were ever paid. See Holmes, page 31.

CHAPTER 16

[1] To learn more about how the Japanese' callous disregard for the rules of war doomed Allied prisoners on Japanese merchant ships, read Smith, Robert Barr, "Tragic Voyage of Junyo Maru," *World War II* Magazine,

(Leesburg, VA: Primedia Publications), Vol. 16, No. 7, March 2002, pp. 40-44.

For additional information about the numbers involved, see also: Knox, Donald, *Death March: The Survivors of Bataan,* Harcourt Brace Jovanovich, Inc., New York, 1983.

Conroy, Robert, *The Battle of Bataan: America's Greatest Defeat,* Toronto, Canada: The MacMillan Company, 1969.

Whitman, John W., *Bataan: Our Last Ditch (The Bataan Campaign, 1942)*, New York: Hippocrene Books, 1990, p. 605.

Dyess, Lt. Col. William, "Death March From Bataan," *Reader's Digest Illustrated History of World War II,* The Reader's Digest Association, Inc., Pleasantville, New York, 1969, pages 164-171.

More information on statistics is available in Maj. Richard Gordon's short history from the *Battling Bastards of Bataan* web site:

> http://home.pacbell.net/fbaldie/Battling_Bastards_of_Bataan.html, Jan. 12, 2002. He writes: "In addition to the P.I. Army the American forces consisted of 11,796 men and several regiments of the P.I. Scouts which were part of the U.S. Army. Of the 11,796 American soldiers on Bataan about 1,500 remained, wounded or sick, in hospitals. A few made it to Corregidor at the surrender. About 9,300 [American] men made it to Camp O'Donnell, about 600 - 650 Americans died on the March. Of the 66,000 Filipino troops about 2,500 remained in hospitals and about 1,700 escaped to Corregidor . . . During the first 40 days at O'Donnell 1,500 Americans died and at least 25,000 Filipinos." He believes that between 44,000 and 50,000 arrived at O'Donnell, leaving 12,000 to 18,000 unaccounted for. At the next camp, Cabanatuan, where there were prisoners from Bataan and Corregidor, 1,500 Americans and 25,000 Filipinos died, most of them from Bataan.

CHAPTER 17

[1] To learn more about prisoners of war from Australia and other countries, read Hank Nelson's *Prisoners of War: Australians Under Nippon*, ABC Enterprises for the Australian Broadcasting Corporation, 1985, reprinted 2001.

AFTERWORD

UNIT 731

[1] It is believed the fleas were used for spreading bubonic plague. Epidemics of plague broke out in a number of Chinese provinces

in 1940 and 1941. *Chemical and Biological Warfare*, television broad cast, TVS Production, Television Center Vinters Park, Maidstone, England, August 13, 1985. Peter Williams, Head of Factual Programmes. Script, page 32-34.

See also: Powell, John W., *Japan's Germ Warfare: The U.S. Cover-up of a War Crime*, Bulletin of Concerned Asian Scientists, Charlemont, Massa chusetts, 1989, page 3.

[2] A total of 36,943 American soldiers, sailors, marines, airmen and con struction workers became Japan's prisoners, along with nearly 14,000 American civilians, including men, women and children living or work ing in territory occupied by Imperial Japanese Forces. To compare the fates of American prisoners held in the two major theaters of war from 1941 to 1945, nearly 40 percent of U.S. military prisoners died in Japan ese captivity, while just over 1 percent of American POWs died in Nazi hands, according to a report from U.S. military records, entered into the Congressional Record, December, 1942. Nine out of ten prisoners who died in World War II perished while in Japanese custody. This information is from Holmes' *Unjust Enrichment*, page xvii.

[3] *Chemical and Biological Warfare*, page 7.

[4] Ibid, page 8.

[5] Ibid, page 9.

[6] Powell, John W., *Japan's Germ Warfare: The U.S. Cover-up of a War Crime*, Bulletin of Concerned Asian Scientists, Charlemont, Mass., 1979, page 10.

[7] *Chemical and Biological Warfare*, page 113.

[8] Ibid, page 12.

[9] Ibid, page 13.

[10] Ibid, page 15.

[11] Ibid, page 16-17.

[12] *Summary Report on B.W. (Biological Warfare)*, to Chief, Chemical Corps, Pentagon, Washington, D.C., from Chief, Basic Sciences, Camp Detrick, Maryland, December 12, 1947, pages 1-4.

[13] Ibid.

[14] Ibid.

[15] *Japan's Germ Warfare: The U.S. Cover-up of a War Crime*, page 10.

[16-19] *Chemical and Biological Warfare*, pages 13, 14, 19, 20, 29, 32, 33.

See also: *Summary Report on B.W.*, pages 1-4, and *Japan's Germ Warfare*, page 10.

[20] *Chemical and Biological Warfare*, page 22. See also "Documentary said to tell of Japanese Germ Warfare," London. The Paris News, Paris, Texas, August 13, 1985, and *Japan's Germ Warfare*, page 4.

[21] *Chemical*, pages 32-33.

[22] Ibid.

[23] Ibid.

[24] Ibid.

[25] Ibid, page 34.

[26] Ibid. page 49.

[27] Ibid, pages 41-42.

[28] Ibid. See also *Japan's Germ Warfare*, page 3.

[29] Ibid, page 53.

[30] Ibid, page 54.

[31] Ibid, page 55.

[32] Ibid, page 57.

[33] *Letter to Ex-POW Vision Quest*, Tokyo Broadcasting System, Inc. (TBS), Tokyo, Japan, Haruko Yoshinaga, Chief Director, November 19, 1976.

[34] *Japan's Germ Warfare*, pages 1, 8, 9. See also Epstein, Aaron, "MD.: U.S. hid Japan's experiments on POWs," Aaron Epstein, Herald Washington Bureau, *The Miami Herald*, Miami, Florida, December 7, 1985.

[35] State-War-Navy Coordinating Subcommittee (SWNCC) for the Far East, interrogation of certain Japanese by Russian prosecutors, September 29, 1947, as referred in "Japanese Biological Warfare Experiments on American POWs during WWII, "digest and translation from *The Weekly Post* Magazine (Tokyo), July 9, 1982.

[36] *Chemical*, page 24.

[37] Ibid, page 26. See also pages 1, 25, 27, 61-63.

[38] Ibid.

[39] Ibid, page 27.

[40] Ibid, page 22.

[41] Ibid, page 63.

[42] Ibid.

ADDENDUM

[1] *Japan Bombs the Mainland, The Denver Post,* Sunday, December 2, 2001, page 2.

[2] Ibid.

For a comprehensive analysis of the atrocities of Unit 731, read: Harris, Sheldon H., *Factories of Death: Japanese Biological Warfare, 1932-1945, and the American Cover-Up,* Routledge, London, England, 1994.

Related articles:

Germ Camp Survivors Want Pay, The Associated Press, Washington, The Albuquerque Tribune, Albuquerque, New Mexico, September 18, 1986.

Horror Bugs at Jap Camp, by Laraine Clay, Caernarfon Herald, North Wales, Britain, August 20, 1985.

Japan Breaks Silence on Germ Warfare, London Observer Service, Tokyo, The Albuquerque Tribune, Albuquerque, New Mexico, September 25, 1986.

Japanese Biological Warfare Experiments on American POWs During WWII, Digest and Translation from the Weekly Post Magazine, Tokyo, Japan, July 9, 1982.

U.S. "Sold Out" POWs--Officer, by Susan Schauer, Republic Washington Bureau, Ravaili Republic Newspaper, Hamilton, Montana, December 7, 1983.

Army of the United States
Honorable Discharge

This is to Certify That OLIVER C. ALLEN, 18 020 946 Staff Sergeant

7th Material Squadron Cutoon

ARMY OF THE UNITED STATES

is hereby Honorably Discharged from the military service of the United States of America.

This certificate is awarded as a testimonial of Honest and Faithful Service to this country.

SEPARATION CENTER

Given at FORT SAM HOUSTON, TEXAS

Date 12 June 1946

ENLISTED RECORD AND REPORT OF SEPARATION
HONORABLE DISCHARGE

MILITARY HISTORY

PAY DATA

INSURANCE NOTICE

xi

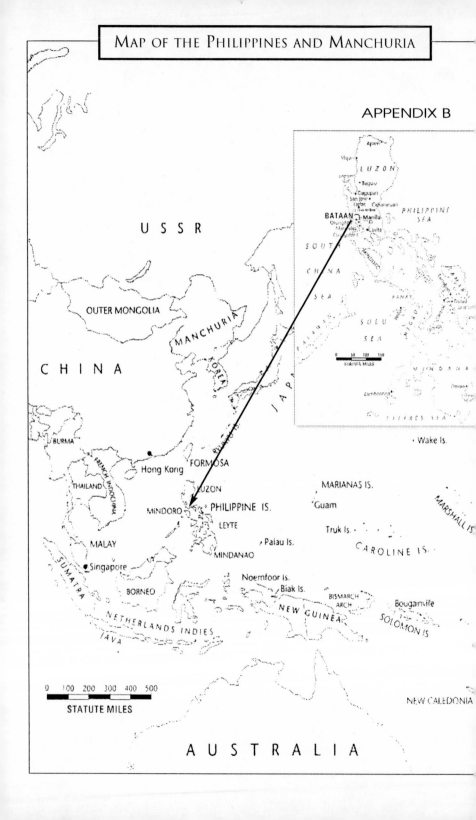

OUTLINE OF EVENTS

1. On Dec. 7, 1941, Japan attacked Pearl Harbor. The American Pacific Naval Fleet suffered heavy losses in lives and ships. The Fleet was incapacitated and could not, in that state, defend American interest in the Pacific Rim and in Asia.

2. Only eight hours later, on Dec. 8, 1941 (due to the difference in time zones), Japan launched an aerial attack on Philippines. Most of the American Air Force in the Philippines was destroyed while the planes were on the ground.

3. A few days later, Japanese forces, led by Lt. Gen. Masaharu Homma, landed on the Philippines. The Japanese landings were in Northern Luzon and in the Southern Mindanao Islands.

4. Gen. Douglas MacArthur, Commander of the Filipino-American forces, decided to meet the Japanese at their points of landing. This course of action deviated from the original War Plan, devised prior to WW II, which called for the American forces to withdraw into the Bataan Peninsula in case of attack.

5. Inexperienced troops failed to stop the Japanese at these points of landing. MacArthur had to revert back to the original plan, withdrawing the Filipino-American forces into the Bataan Peninsula. By the January 2, 1942, the Northern Luzon forces were in place for the defense of Bataan.

6. Their mission, in the baseball vernacular, was to "lay down a bunt." They were to stall the Japanese advancement by forcing them to use much of their troops and resources in the capturing of the Philippines for as long as possible. This would buy the necessary time needed to rebuild the American Pacific Fleet, which at the time had been crippled by the Pearl Harbor attack

and the bombing of the American Air Bases in the Philippines.

7. The Filipino-American Defense of Bataan was hampered by many factors:

   a) A shortage of food, ammunition, medicine and attendant materials.
   b) Most of the ammunition was old and corroded. The AA shells lacked proper fuses, as did many of the 155mm artillery shells.
   c) Tanks, trucks, and other vehicles were in short supply, as was the gasoline needed to power these items of warfare.
   d) Poorly-trained Filipino troops, most of whom had never fired a weapon, were thrown into frontline combat against highly-trained Japanese veterans. Americans from non-combatant outfits such as air corpsmen and, in some instances, even civilians, were formed into provisional infantry units.

8. The Defenders of Bataan continued to hold their ground, without reinforcements and without being re-supplied. Disease, malnutrition, fatigue and a lack of basic supplies took their toll.

9. On March 11, 1942, Gen. MacArthur was ordered to Australia, Gen. Wainwright took his place in Corregidor as Commander of the Philippine forces, and Gen. King took Wainwright's place as Commander of the Filipino-American forces in Bataan.

10. Around the latter part of March, Gen. King and his staff assessed the fighting capabilities of his forces, in view of an impending major assault planned by Gen. Homma. Gen. King and his staff determined the Filipino-American forces, in Bataan, could only fight at 30% of their efficiency due to malnutrition, disease, a lack of ammunition and basic supplies, and fatigue. On April 3, 1942, the Japanese launched their all-out final offensive to take Bataan.

11. On April 9, 1942, Gen. King surrendered his forces on Bataan, after the Japanese had broken through the Filipino-American last main line of resistance.

12. The Japanese assembled their captive Filipino-American soldiers in the various sectors in Bataan, but mainly at Mariveles, the southernmost tip of the Peninsula. Although American trucks were available to transport the prisoners, the Japanese decided to march the Defenders of Bataan to their destinations. This march came to be known as the "Death March."

13. The "Death March" was really a series of marches which lasted from five to nine days. The distance a captive had to march was determined by where on the trail the captive began the march.

14. The basic trail of the "Death March" was as follows: a 55-mile march from Mariveles, Bataan, to San Fernando, Pangpanga. At San Fernando, the prison-

ers were placed into train-cars, made for cargo, and railed to Capas, Tarlac, a distance of around 24 miles. Dozens died standing up in the railroad cars, as the cars were so cramped that there was no room for the dead to fall. They were, then, marched another six miles to their final destination, Camp O'Donnell.

15. Several thousand men died on the "Death March." Many died because they were not in any physical condition to undertake such a march. Once on the march, they were not given any food or water. Japanese soldiers killed many of them through various means. Also, POWs were repeatedly beaten them and treated inhumanely as they marched.

16. Approximately 1,600 Americans died in the first forty days in Camp O'Donnell. Almost 20,000 Filipinos died in their first four months of captivity in the same camp. The healthier prisoners took turns burying their comrades into mass graves, just as they, themselves, would be buried, days or weeks later.

17. Camp O'Donnell did not have the sanitation sub-structure or water supply necessary to hold such a large amount of men. Many died from diseases they had contracted on Bataan. Many caught new diseases while at the camp. There was little medicine available to the prisoners. Their inadequate diets also contributed to the high death rate. Diseases such as dysentery from a lack of safe drinking water, and beri-beri from malnutrition, were common to the POWs. The Japanese soldiers continued to murder and mistreat their captives.

18. Due to the high death rate in Camp O'Donnell, the Japanese transferred all Americans to Cabanatuan, north of Camp O'Donnell, on June 6, 1942, leaving behind five hundred as caretakers and for funeral details. They, in turn, were sent to Cabanatuan on July 5, 1942. The Filipino prisoners were paroled, beginning in July, 1942.

19. Cabanatuan was the camp in which the men from Corregidor were first united with the men from Bataan. No Americans* from Corregidor ever made the "Death March" or were imprisoned in Camp O'Donnell. Not having suffered the extreme depravations and conditions endured by the men from Bataan, the prisoners from Corregidor were, overall, much healthier. (*There were Philippine Scouts and some men from the Philippine Army, captured in Corregidor, who were interned in Camp O'Donnell.)

20. Cabanatuan, for most prisoners, ended up being a temporary camp. The Japanese had a policy (which was a direct violation of the Geneva Convention) that prisoners were to be used as a source of labor. They sent most of the prisoners from Cabanatuan to various other camps in the Philippines, China, Japan, and Korea, where they were used as slave labor. Some worked

in mines, others in farms, others in factories, and others unloaded ships in Port Areas for the remainder of the war. Each subsequent prison camp, after Cabanatuan, has a story of its own.

21. Left behind in Cabanatuan were approximately, 511 officers and the prisoners too sick to move (and most of those too sick to move never recovered and died in Cabanatuan). Towards the end of the war, most of the men who stayed behind were placed on ships and sent to other camps in Japan, Korea, and China. The Japanese did not mark these ships to note that there were prisoners on board. They were bombed and torpedoed by American planes and submarines. Most of these men died, by drowning at sea.

22. Most prisoners who left Cabanatuan in 1942 were sent to the other countries mentioned in ships appropriately called "Hell Ships." These "Hell Ships" sailed from Manila to their various destinations in Japan, Korea, or China. As mentioned earlier, the Japanese did not mark these ships as being prison ships, so they were targets for American planes and submarines. Thousands of Americans, who were passengers on these ships, met their deaths by drowning at sea.

23. The conditions on these ships are indescribable and far worse than the conditions endured in "Death March" and Camp O'Donnell.

24. For the remaining three years of their captivity, the Defenders of Bataan were spread throughout the various slave labor camps in Japan, Korea, China and the Philippines, until each camp was individually liberated in 1945. These prisoners endured the whims of their brutal captors, with similar conditions and miss-treatment as those experienced in the "Death March" and Camp O'Donnell and the uncertainty of when, if ever, their captivity would end.

25. Coming from the warm tropical climate of the Philippines, the men sent to Japan, Korea, and China had to adjust to the sub-freezing temperatures of Northern Asia, without the proper personal equipment and indoor heating to survive such cold temperatures. In Manchuria, China, the POWs, who died in the winter, were placed in an unheated shack for their bodies to freeze, because the ground was so frozen and hard that they could not be buried until the spring.

26. After they were released, these men were sent to various military hospitals for physical examinations. Many of their ailments, due to malnutrition, went undiagnosed. Many of the systemic fevers they had contracted went undiagnosed. More importantly, the psychological scars they suffered were never recognized. It was not until years after the Vietnam War, the US government recognized "Post Traumatic Stress Disorder" or PTSD, as a legitimate disorder. It is safe to say each of these men has carried these scars for the rest

of their lives and indirectly, so did their families.

27. After the war, little was made of the plight of these men. Until recently, few books were written about their ordeal. There were many reasons for this: by the time the Defenders of Bataan came home, the U.S. had already heard a multitude of war stories about the great battles in the Pacific and in Europe. The Defenders of Bataan had surrendered. (Most Americans failed to recognize that the Defenders of Bataan were surrendered as a force, by their Commanding General. They did not surrender as individuals).

28. After the War, Japan and the U.S. formed an alliance to ensure their mutual economic prosperity and to ensure their mutual security. It became an unwritten policy to play down Japanese War Crimes, satisfied with the meager results produced by the Tokyo and Manila War Crimes trials.

29. Unknown to most: POWs held by the Germans died at a rate of 1.1%. POWs held by the Japanese died at a rate of 37%. The death rate amongst the Defenders of Bataan was much higher, because of their weakened condition prior to their capture.

30. Germany has acknowledged their war crimes and has made restitution to the victims. Japan has denied everything. In their history books and in their school books, they have re-written history in an effort to falsely show they were the victims of the war, citing the atomic bombs in Hiroshima and Nagasaki as proof of their victimization.

31. After the war, and faced with the threat of the Soviet Union, the United States and its allies permitted Japan to escape the close scrutiny given to the Germans. Known Japanese war criminals went free to not only walk the streets of Japan, but the streets of the United States, as well.

Timeline provided by *The Battling Bastards of Bataan*.

ABOUT THE AUTHORS

Oliver 'Red' Allen was a young man who left college to join the Army Air Corps in 1941, hoping to fulfill his dream of flying. However, through early events in World War II, he wound up in the hands of the Japanese as a prisoner of war. He spent three and a half years as a prisoner on Bataan and in Manchuria. He survived to return home and later became a schoolteacher.

After thirty years of teaching, he was forced to retire because of ill health due primarily to his war experiences. He wanted his sons, Tim and Danny, to know the full story of his part in the war and of his captivity, so he began putting his experiences on tapes. This was done over a period of many months, as the telling of these events was tantamount to living them again. His wife later transcribed the tapes.

The horror of his experiences and the wonder of his survival are described in unforgettable detail in this book.

Mildred Allen had hoped for a career in journalism. She became editor of her college newspaper and served as a Past National Editor of *American Ex-Prisoners of War Bulletin*. She did not follow a journalism career, however. In 1946, she became an elementary school teacher at age nineteen. Toward the end of her career she taught dyslexic children.

Upon her retirement, after forty-three years in education, Mildred began creating puzzles in mathematics for a major crossword puzzle magazine. She also began the difficult task of transcribing her husband's tapes. Mrs. Allen says, "His descriptions were so vivid, it was as if he were still there. It was heart-wrenching."

She is the author of a short story, *The Red Shoes*, and three soon-to-be-published books: *The Aeries, Come Home My Children* and *Job and Me and Other Fools*. She is currently working on a fourth book.

The Allens have two sons, Tim and Danny, and four grandchildren.